Betty Crocker® CHRISTMAS

Betty Crocker®
CHRISTMAS

For more great recipes and ideas, go to
bettycrocker.com

PUBLISHED BY
Taste of Home Books
Reiman Media Group, LLC
5400 S. 60th St., Greendale WI 53129
www.tasteofhome.com

Printed in the U.S.A.

International Standard Book Number (10):
0-89821-898-5

International Standard Book Number (13):
978-0-89821-898-5

CREDITS
General Mills, Inc.
EDITORIAL DIRECTOR: Jeff Nowak
PUBLISHING MANAGER: Christine Gray
COOKBOOK EDITOR: Grace Wells
EDITORIAL ASSISTANTS: Lisa Olson, Kelly Gross
DIGITAL ASSETS MANAGER: Carrie Jacobson
RECIPE DEVELOPMENT AND TESTING:
Betty Crocker Kitchens
PHOTOGRAPHY: General Mills Photography Studio

Reiman Media Group, LLC
EDITOR: Heidi Reuter Lloyd
ASSOCIATE EDITOR: Victoria Soukup Jensen
SENIOR EDITOR/BOOKS: Mark Hagen
ASSOCIATE CREATIVE DIRECTOR: Edwin Robles, Jr.
ART DIRECTOR: Gretchen Trautman
CONTENT PRODUCTION MANAGER: Julie Wagner
LAYOUT DESIGNERS: Nancy Novak, Kathy Crawford
COPY EDITOR: Victoria Soukup Jensen

COVER PHOTOGRAPHY:
Reiman Media Group Photo Studio
PHOTOGRAPHER: Jim Wieland
FOOD STYLIST: Sue Draheim
SET STYLIST: Melissa Haberman

EDITOR-IN-CHIEF: Catherine Cassidy
VICE PRESIDENT, EXECUTIVE EDITOR, BOOKS:
Heidi Reuter Lloyd
NORTH AMERICAN CHIEF MARKETING OFFICER:
Lisa Karpinski
VICE PRESIDENT/BOOK MARKETING: Dan Fink
CREATIVE DIRECTOR/CREATIVE MARKETING:
James Palmen

The Reader's Digest Association, Inc.
PRESIDENT & CHIEF EXECUTIVE OFFICER:
Tom Williams
EXECUTIVE VICE PRESIDENT, RDA, AND
PRESIDENT, LIFESTYLE COMMUNITIES:
Suzanne M. Grimes

PICTURED ON FRONT COVER:
Raspberry-Laced Vanilla Cake, p. 282

PICTURED ON BACK COVER:
Herb-Scented Roast Turkey & Cornbread Stuffing, p. 122;
Green Beans with Lemon-Herb Butter, p. 102; Beef Tenderloin
with Red Wine Sauce, p. 124; White Candy Fantasy Clusters, p. 214.

p. 156

p. 307

table of contents

301 Ways to Capture the Magic of Christmas

Christmas brings its own magic, whether you celebrate it as one precious day with family or as an entire season of festive gatherings.

It's all about creating special moments that can be treasured for years to come—remembering the people, the sentiments, the conversations, the laughter and the wonderful foods that tie it all together.

There's the sit-down family dinner at Grandpa and Grandma's house, the bountiful appetizer and dessert buffet for your holiday open house, the spectacular dish you'll make for the neighborhood round-robin or potluck at work, and the new recipe that will wow your friends at the cookie exchange.

Betty Crocker Christmas has 301 mix-and-match menu options to make all of your holiday celebrations everything you want them to be.

Choose from elegant entrees, casual main dishes, seasonal side dishes and salads, amazing appetizers, refreshing beverages, mouth-watering bars and candies and a host of impressive desserts.

You'll also find a chapter of home-baked gifts from the kitchen and a big selection of classic and modern cookies that are sure to make your holiday party tray overflow with homemade goodness.

With *Betty Crocker Christmas*, you're ready for any and every holiday occasion.

p. 14

p. 22

holiday starters & beverages

This jolly assortment of savory finger foods and sparkling beverages will help get your party started.

fruit-cheese log

PREP TIME: 35 minutes • **START TO FINISH:** 1 hour 5 minutes • **MAKES:** 12 servings

3/4 cup finely chopped pecans
1 package (8 oz) cream cheese, softened
2 ounces Muenster cheese, shredded (1/2 cup)
1/3 cup shredded fresh Parmesan cheese
1/2 cup Cheddar cold-pack cheese food
(from 8-oz container), softened
1/2 cup chopped dried apricots
1/4 cup chopped dried figs
1/4 cup chopped dried cranberries
Crackers, if desired

① Line square pan, 8x8x2 inches, with 16-inch piece of waxed paper, leaving ends overhanging. Spread pecans evenly over waxed paper in bottom of pan; set aside.

② Beat cream cheese, Muenster cheese and Parmesan cheese in medium bowl with electric mixer on medium speed until well mixed. Spoon cheese mixture over pecans, using teaspoon; spread evenly. Spoon Cheddar cheese food over cream cheese layer, using teaspoon; spread evenly. Sprinkle with dried fruits; press in lightly.

③ Lift ends of waxed paper to remove cheese mixture from pan and place on smooth surface. Roll up cheese mixture, jelly-roll style. (If cheese is too soft to roll, return to pan and refrigerate about 20 minutes or until firm.) Wrap cheese log in waxed paper; place in resealable plastic food-storage bag. Refrigerate about 30 minutes or until firm. Serve with crackers.

High Altitude (3500-6500 ft): No change.

1 SERVING: Calories 220; Total Fat 17g (Saturated Fat 7g, Trans Fat nc); Cholesterol 35mg; Sodium 300mg; Total Carbohydrate 11g (Dietary Fiber 2g); Protein 6g. EXCHANGES: 1 Fruit, 1 High-Fat Meat. CARBOHYDRATE CHOICES: 1.

tips&ideas

Be sure to use waxed paper when rolling up this festive log. Other types of kitchen wraps will not work as well.

holiday shrimp wreath with cocktail dip

PREP TIME: 25 minutes • **START TO FINISH:** 25 minutes • **MAKES:** 10 servings

Green or clear plastic wrap
- 1 floral foam wreath form, 10 inches in diameter and about 2 inches thick
- 1 head curly endive, bibb or leaf lettuce
- 1-1/2 lb extra-large cooked tail-on shrimp (about 40 shrimp), thawed if frozen
- 2 tablespoons lemon juice
- 1 teaspoon seafood seasoning
- 1 cup cocktail sauce
- 1/2 cup finely chopped seeded peeled cucumber
- 1/2 teaspoon grated lemon peel

tips&ideas

Make the wreath and sauce up to 3 hours before serving to avoid the last-minute partytime crunch.

① Cut four 18-inch-long sheets of plastic wrap; fold in half lengthwise. Cover wreath with plastic wrap by pulling wrap through center and around wreath, overlapping plastic to cover wreath completely. Place on serving plate. Cover wreath with lettuce leaves.

② In large bowl, toss shrimp, lemon juice and seafood seasoning. Arrange shrimp on wreath, using the natural curve of the shrimp to cover the outside edge of the wreath.

③ In small bowl, mix remaining ingredients; spoon into serving bowl. Place bowl of sauce in middle of wreath for dipping. Cover and refrigerate until serving.

High Altitude (3500-6500 ft): No change.

1 SERVING: Calories 80; Total Fat 0.5g (Saturated Fat 0g, Trans Fat 0g); Cholesterol 90mg; Sodium 490mg; Total Carbohydrate 8g (Dietary Fiber 0g); Protein 10g. EXCHANGES: 1/2 Other Carbohydrate, 1-1/2 Very Lean Meat. CARBOHYDRATE CHOICES: 1/2.

warm cheddar and olive dip

PREP TIME: 10 minutes • START TO FINISH: 10 minutes • MAKES: 20 servings (2 tablespoons dip and 2 slices bread each)

1 container (8 oz) sharp Cheddar cold-pack cheese food
1 package (8 oz) cream cheese, cut into cubes
1/2 cup milk
1/4 teaspoon garlic powder
1/4 teaspoon pepper
1/2 cup salad sliced Spanish olives
1 loaf (10 oz) French baguette bread, cut into 40 slices

① In large microwavable bowl, place cold-pack cheese food, cream cheese and milk. Microwave uncovered on High 1 minute; stir. Continue microwaving 1 minute at a time, stirring after each minute, until smooth. Stir in remaining ingredients except bread.

② Spoon dip into 1- to 2-quart slow cooker to keep warm; do not cover. Serve with bread. Dip will hold on Low heat setting up to 2 hours.

High Altitude (3500-6500 ft): No change.

1 SERVING: Calories 130; Total Fat 8g (Saturated Fat 4.5g, Trans Fat 0g); Cholesterol 20mg; Sodium 290mg; Total Carbohydrate 9g (Dietary Fiber 0g); Protein 5g. EXCHANGES: 1/2 Starch, 1/2 High-Fat Meat, 1 Fat. CARBOHYDRATE CHOICES: 1/2.

stuffed eggs with smoked salmon and herb cheese

PREP TIME: 25 minutes • **START TO FINISH:** 25 minutes • **MAKES:** 12 servings

6 eggs
1/4 cup mayonnaise or salad dressing
1/4 cup garlic-and-herb spreadable cheese
4 oz sliced salmon lox

① In 2-quart saucepan, place eggs in single layer. Cover with cold water at least 1 inch above eggs. Cover and heat to boiling; remove from heat. Cover and let stand 20 minutes; drain. Immediately run cold water over eggs or place them in ice water until completely cooled.

② Peel eggs; cut in half lengthwise. Slip out yolks and place in small bowl. Mash yolks with fork. Stir in mayonnaise and cheese.

③ Reserve 2 slices of salmon for garnish. Coarsely chop remaining salmon; fold into yolk mixture. Fill egg whites with yolk mixture, heaping it lightly. Arrange on serving dish.

④ Cut reserved salmon crosswise into 1/2-inch-wide strips, trimming to about 1 inch long. Loosely roll up pieces of salmon into rosebud shape. Place 1 rosebud on each egg.

High Altitude (3500-6500 ft): In Step 1, add pinch of salt to water. After heating water, salt and eggs to boiling, boil 5 minutes; remove from heat. Cover and let stand 15 minutes. Drain; rinse with cold water.

1 SERVING: Calories 100; Total Fat 8g (Saturated Fat 2.5g, Trans Fat 0g); Cholesterol 115mg; Sodium 160mg; Total Carbohydrate 0g (Dietary Fiber 0g); Protein 5g. EXCHANGES: 1/2 Medium-Fat Meat, 1 Fat. CARBOHYDRATE CHOICES: 0.

tips&ideas

Tuck a sprig of parsley, thyme or another green herb under the salmon rosebuds for added color.

cheese and fruit kabobs with cranberry dip

PREP TIME: 40 minutes • START TO FINISH: 40 minutes • MAKES: 12 servings

KABOBS

12 (1/2-inch) cubes Gouda cheese (about 6 oz)
12 (1/2-inch) cubes fontina cheese (about 6 oz)
12 (1/2-inch) cubes Cheddar cheese (about 6 oz)
12 small strawberries or 6 large strawberries, cut in half
2 kiwifruit, peeled and cut into 12 pieces
12 fresh or canned pineapple cubes

DIP

2/3 cup strawberry cream cheese spread (from 8-oz container)
1/4 cup frozen (thawed) cranberry-orange relish (from 10-oz container)
1/4 cup frozen (thawed) whipped topping

① Thread cheese and fruit alternately on each of twelve 6-inch wooden skewers.

② In small bowl, beat cream cheese and cranberry relish with electric mixer on medium speed until smooth. Fold in whipped topping. Spoon into serving bowl. Serve kabobs with dip.

High Altitude (3500-6500 ft): No change.

1 SERVING: Calories 225; Total Fat 16g (Saturated Fat 10g, Trans Fat nc); Cholesterol 55mg; Sodium 340mg; Total Carbohydrate 8g (Dietary Fiber 1g); Protein 12g. EXCHANGES: 1/2 Fruit, 2 Medium-Fat Meat, 1 Fat. CARBOHYDRATE CHOICES: 1/2.

tips&ideas

You can prepare the dip a day ahead of time; cover and refrigerate. Cut the cheese and fruit the day ahead as well. Store them all separately in plastic bags in the refrigerator. Assemble the kabobs up to 2 hours before serving; cover and refrigerate.

shrimp with bourbon cocktail sauce

PREP TIME: 15 minutes • **START TO FINISH:** 15 minutes • **MAKES:** 24 servings

1/2 cup mayonnaise or salad dressing

1/4 cup seafood cocktail sauce

1/4 cup whipping (heavy) cream

1 tablespoon bourbon whiskey, if desired

1/8 teaspoon red pepper sauce

1 pound cooked peeled deveined large shrimp (about 24 to 30), thawed if frozen

① Mix all ingredients except shrimp in a small bowl.

② Serve sauce as dip for shrimp.

High Altitude (3500-6500 ft): No change.

1 SERVING: Calories 65; Total Fat 5g (Saturated Fat 1g, Trans Fat nc); Cholesterol 40mg; Sodium 100mg; Total Carbohydrate 1g (Dietary Fiber 0g); Protein 4g. EXCHANGES: 1 Fat. CARBOHYDRATE CHOICES: 0.

warm chicken spread

PREP TIME: 15 minutes • START TO FINISH: 45 minutes • MAKES: 28 servings (2 tablespoons spread and 2 bread slices each)

3 cans (9.75 to 10 oz each) chunk chicken, drained

1/2 cup mayonnaise or salad dressing

2 tablespoons Dijon mustard with horseradish (from 7.2-oz jar)

1/2 cup frozen stir-fry bell peppers and onions (from 1-lb bag), thawed and drained

3 tablespoons mayonnaise or salad dressing

3/4 cup Progresso® plain dry bread crumbs

1-1/2 loaves (12-oz size) French baguette bread, cut into 1/4-inch slices

1 Heat oven to 375°F. Spray 9-inch pie plate with cooking spray. In large bowl, mix chicken, 1/2 cup mayonnaise, the mustard and stir-fry vegetables. Spread in pie plate.

2 In small bowl, mix 3 tablespoons mayonnaise and the bread crumbs. Sprinkle evenly over top of chicken mixture.

3 Bake 20 to 30 minutes or until light golden brown and hot. Serve with bread.

High Altitude (3500-6500 ft): No change.

1 SERVING: Calories 120; Total Fat 6g (Saturated Fat 1g, Trans Fat 0g); Cholesterol 15mg; Sodium 290mg; Total Carbohydrate 12g (Dietary Fiber 0g); Protein 7g. EXCHANGES: 1 Starch, 1/2 High-Fat Meat. CARBOHYDRATE CHOICES: 1.

dilled salmon

PREP TIME: 25 minutes • **START TO FINISH:** 1 hour 45 minutes • **MAKES:** 16 servings

SALMON
- 2 lb fresh salmon, skin removed
- 1 teaspoon dried dill weed
- 1/2 teaspoon salt
- 1/4 teaspoon onion powder
- 1/4 teaspoon garlic powder
- 1/4 teaspoon pepper
- 3/4 cup water

DILL SAUCE
- 1-1/2 cups sour cream
- 3/4 cup chopped seeded cucumber
- 4 medium green onions, chopped (1/4 cup)
- 1 tablespoon dried dill weed
- 1/4 teaspoon salt
- 1/2 teaspoon grated lemon peel
- 1/2 teaspoon lemon juice

① Rinse salmon; pat dry. Cut in half if necessary to fit into 12-inch skillet. Place salmon in skillet. In small bowl, mix 1 teaspoon dill weed, 1/2 teaspoon salt, the onion powder, garlic powder and pepper; sprinkle over salmon. Carefully pour water around salmon until 1/4 to 1/2 inch deep.

② Cover and cook salmon over medium heat 10 to 12 minutes or until salmon flakes easily with fork; carefully drain.

③ Remove salmon from skillet with 2 large slotted spatulas; place on serving plate. Use paper towels to remove any excess cooking liquid from salmon and plate. Refrigerate about 1 hour or until chilled.

④ Meanwhile, in medium bowl, mix all sauce ingredients. Cover and refrigerate until serving. Serve sauce with salmon.

High Altitude (3500-6500 ft): In Step 2, cover and cook salmon over medium heat for 12 to 14 minutes.

1 SERVING: Calories 110; Total Fat 7g (Saturated Fat 3.5g, Trans Fat 0g); Cholesterol 45mg; Sodium 150mg; Total Carbohydrate 1g (Dietary Fiber 0g); Protein 11g. EXCHANGES: 1-1/2 Medium-Fat Meat. CARBOHYDRATE CHOICES: 0.

tips&ideas

Set out a platter of pumpernickel or rye cocktail-size bread slices or hearty crackers to serve with this elegant salmon appetizer.

cranberry-topped three-cheese spread

PREP TIME: 15 minutes • START TO FINISH: 2 hours 15 minutes • MAKES: 32 servings (2 tablespoons spread and 2 crackers each)

2 packages (8 oz each) cream cheese, softened
1 cup freshly grated Parmesan cheese
1/2 cup Swiss almond cold-pack cheese food (from 8-oz container)
1/4 teaspoon white pepper
1/4 teaspoon garlic powder
1/8 teaspoon salt
1/3 cup whole berry cranberry sauce
Sliced almonds, if desired
Assorted crackers

(1) In medium bowl, beat all ingredients except cranberry sauce, almonds and crackers with electric mixer on medium-low speed until mixture is smooth.

(2) Line 2-cup mold with plastic wrap. Spoon cheese mixture into mold. Cover and refrigerate until firm, at least 2 hours but no longer than 2 days.

(3) When ready to serve, turn mold upside down onto serving plate and remove plastic wrap. Spoon cranberry sauce over mold; sprinkle with almonds. Serve with crackers.

High Altitude (3500-6500 ft): No change.

1 SERVING: Calories 100; Total Fat 7g (Saturated Fat 4.5g, Trans Fat 0g); Cholesterol 20mg; Sodium 170mg; Total Carbohydrate 4g (Dietary Fiber 0g); Protein 3g. EXCHANGES: 1/2 Medium-Fat Meat, 1 Fat. CARBOHYDRATE CHOICES: 0.

holiday spiced snack mix

PREP TIME: 50 minutes • START TO FINISH: 1 hour 35 minutes • MAKES: 26 servings (1/2 cup each)

1/2 cup butter or margarine
1/2 cup packed brown sugar
2 teaspoons pumpkin pie spice
1 teaspoon grated orange peel
1 teaspoon vanilla
1/4 teaspoon pepper
6 cups Corn Chex® cereal
3 cups sourdough pretzel nuggets
2 cups unblanched or blanched whole almonds
1 package (6 oz) sweetened dried cranberries
1 bag (12 oz) white chocolate chunks

(1) Heat oven to 300°F. In 1-quart saucepan, melt butter over medium heat; remove from heat. Stir in brown sugar, pumpkin pie spice, orange peel, vanilla and pepper until well mixed.

(2) In 15x11-inch roasting pan, mix cereal, pretzels and almonds. Pour butter mixture over cereal; toss until evenly coated.

(3) Bake 45 to 60 minutes, stirring every 15 minutes, until golden brown. Cool completely, about 45 minutes. Stir in cranberries and chocolate chunks. Store in tightly covered container.

High Altitude (3500-6500 ft): Heat oven to 325°F.

1 SERVING: Calories 260; Total Fat 14g (Saturated Fat 5g, Trans Fat 0g); Cholesterol 10mg; Sodium 180mg; Total Carbohydrate 29g (Dietary Fiber 2g); Protein 4g. EXCHANGES: 1 Starch, 1 Other Carbohydrate, 2-1/2 Fat. CARBOHYDRATE CHOICES: 2.

nutty cheese spread with fruit chutney

PREP TIME: 20 minutes • **START TO FINISH:** 1 hour 30 minutes • **MAKES:** 16 servings

3/4 cup diced dried fruit and raisin mixture
   (from 7-oz package)
1/4 cup sweetened dried cranberries
1/2 cup apple cider
  1 tablespoon cider vinegar
1/4 teaspoon ground ginger
1/4 teaspoon ground cinnamon
1/4 cup chopped walnuts
  1 package (8 oz) cream cheese, softened
Crackers, if desired

① Mix all ingredients except walnuts, cream cheese and crackers in 2-quart saucepan. Cook over medium heat about 5 minutes, stirring frequently, until fruit is plump and mixture is thick. Cover and refrigerate about 1 hour or until completely cooled.

② Meanwhile, heat oven to 350°. Spread walnuts on cookie sheet. Bake 5 to 7 minutes, stirring twice, until light golden brown; cool.

③ Mix walnuts and cream cheese in medium bowl. Spread cream cheese mixture in 1/2-inch thick layer on serving plate. Top with chutney. Serve with crackers.

High Altitude (3500-6500 ft): No change.

1 SERVING: Calories 90; Total Fat 6g (Saturated Fat 3g, Trans Fat nc); Cholesterol 15mg; Sodium 45mg; Total Carbohydrate 7g (Dietary Fiber 1g); Protein 2g. EXCHANGES: nc. CARBOHYDRATE CHOICES: 1/2.

tips&ideas

Make extra chutney, package it in a pretty jar and give it as a hostess gift. It is delicious served with ham or turkey.

hot crab crostini

PREP TIME: 20 minutes • **START TO FINISH:** 30 minutes • **MAKES:** 24 appetizers

1/2 French baguette, cut into 1/4-inch slices
    (24 slices)
  1 tablespoon olive or vegetable oil
  1 can (6 oz) crabmeat, well drained and flaked
  1 jar (2 oz) diced pimientos, well drained
  2 ounces shredded Swiss cheese (1/2 cup)
1/2 cup grated Parmesan cheese
1/4 cup chive and onion cream cheese spread
    (from 8-oz container)
1/4 teaspoon red pepper sauce
  1 tablespoon chopped fresh chives

① Heat oven to 400°. Place bread slices on large ungreased cookie sheet. Brush tops lightly with oil. Bake 3 to 5 minutes or until crisp and very light brown.

② Meanwhile, mix remaining ingredients except chives in medium bowl. Spread about 1 rounded table-spoonful crabmeat mixture on each bread slice.

③ Bake about 5 minutes or until filling is hot and cheese is melted. Sprinkle with chives.

High Altitude (3500-6500 ft): No change.

1 APPETIZER: Calories 125; Total Fat 4g (Saturated Fat 2g, Trans Fat nc); Cholesterol 10mg; Sodium 260mg; Total Carbohydrate 16g (Dietary Fiber 1g); Protein 6g. EXCHANGES: 1 Starch. CARBOHYDRATE CHOICES: 1.

tips&ideas _____

If a shop that sells imported cheeses is available to you, try a different firm and flavorful cheese such as Manchego or Asiago in place of the Swiss cheese.

smoked salmon with dill spread

PREP TIME: 15 minutes • **START TO FINISH:** 15 minutes • **MAKES:** 12 servings

1 tablespoon lemon juice
1/2 cup soft light cream cheese
 (from 8-oz container)
1 tablespoon chopped fresh dill weed
1/2 teaspoon garlic powder
12 slices cocktail rye bread or pumpernickel
 bread
3 oz salmon lox, cut into 12 pieces
1 tablespoon finely chopped red onion
Fresh dill weed sprigs, if desired

① In small bowl, gradually stir lemon juice into cream cheese until smooth. Stir in chopped dill weed and garlic powder.

② Spread 2 teaspoons cheese mixture on each bread slice. Place 1 piece of salmon on each appetizer. Top with onion and a dill sprig.

High Altitude (3500-6500 ft): No change.

1 SERVING: Calories 45; Total Fat 2g (Saturated Fat 1g, Trans Fat 0g); Cholesterol 10mg; Sodium 70mg; Total Carbohydrate 4g (Dietary Fiber 0g); Protein 3g. EXCHANGES: 1 Vegetable. CARBOHYDRATE CHOICES: 0.

shrimp cocktail platter

2 lb (26 to 30 count) cooked peeled deveined
   large shrimp with tails, thawed if frozen
1 cup purchased cocktail sauce
1 tablespoon lime juice
1 teaspoon chipotle or regular chile powder
Watercress or fresh parsley sprigs
Lemon slices

① Rinse shrimp; pat dry. Line a 4-cup bowl
with enough plastic wrap so that it hangs over
edge of bowl. Arrange a layer of shrimp in a
spiral pattern in bottom of bowl. Add additional
layers, filling all spaces and pressing down, until
bowl is full.

② Fold the plastic wrap over shrimp. Place two
1-pound cans on top of shrimp and refrigerate
for 1 hour.

③ Meanwhile, in small bowl combine cocktail
sauce, lime juice and chile powder; mix well.
Cover and refrigerate until serving.

④ Unwrap bowl. Pull plastic wrap away from
top of bowl. To unmold, place a large platter
upside down over bowl, then turn platter and
bowl over; remove plastic wrap. Garnish the
shrimp spiral with watercress and lemon slices.
Serve with sauce.

High Altitude (3500-6500 ft): No change.

1 SERVING: Calories 45; Total Fat 0g (Saturated Fat 0g,
Trans Fat 0g); Cholesterol 65mg; Sodium 190mg; Total
Carbohydrate 3g (Dietary Fiber 0g); Protein 7g. EXCHANGES:
1 Very Lean Meat CARBOHYDRATE CHOICES: 0.

tips&ideas

*Shrimp doesn't need a lot of dressing up to be beautiful, plus using cooked,
peeled shrimp pares down the prep time.*

pesto-cheese cups

PREP TIME: 20 minutes • **START TO FINISH:** 45 minutes • **MAKES:** 30 servings

1 package (8 oz) cream cheese, softened
1 egg
1/2 cup shredded Swiss cheese (2 oz)
1/4 cup basil pesto
2 medium green onions, chopped (2 tablespoons)
2 packages (2.1 oz each) frozen mini phyllo (filo) dough shells (15 shells each)
1/3 cup shredded Swiss cheese (1-1/2 oz)

① Heat oven to 375°F. Line cookie sheet with foil or cooking parchment paper. In medium bowl, beat cream cheese and egg with wire whisk. Stir in 1/2 cup cheese, the pesto and onions.

② Place phyllo shells on cookie sheet. Fill each shell with slightly less than 1 tablespoon of the cheese mixture. Sprinkle each with 1/2 teaspoon of the 1/3 cup cheese.

③ Bake 20 to 25 minutes or until cups begin to turn golden brown and are puffed. Serve warm.

High Altitude (3500-6500 ft): No change.

1 SERVING: Calories 60; Total Fat 5g (Saturated Fat 2.5g, Trans Fat 0g); Cholesterol 20mg; Sodium 65mg; Total Carbohydrate 3g (Dietary Fiber 0g); Protein 2g. EXCHANGES: 1 Fat. CARBOHYDRATE CHOICES: 0.

tips&ideas

You'll find mini phyllo (filo) dough shells in the frozen pastry section of most large supermarkets.

creamy roasted garlic and onion meatballs

PREP TIME: 20 minutes • **START TO FINISH:** 40 minutes • **MAKES:** 26 meatballs

2 tablespoons butter or margarine
1 large onion, cut in half, then cut into 1/4-inch wedges
2 tablespoons chopped roasted or regular garlic (from 4-oz jar)
2 tablespoons Gold Medal® all-purpose flour
1/4 teaspoon pepper
2 cups half-and-half
1 package (16 oz) frozen meatballs
Chopped fresh parsley, if desired

① In 4-quart saucepan, melt butter over medium heat. Cook onion and garlic in butter 10 to 12 minutes, stirring frequently, until golden brown.

② Sprinkle flour and pepper over onion mixture. Cook 1 minute, stirring constantly. Slowly add half-and-half, stirring constantly. Stir in meatballs.

③ Cook 15 to 20 minutes, stirring occasionally, until sauce is thickened and meatballs are hot. To serve, place in 1-1/2 to 2 quart slow cooker on Low heat setting. Meatballs will hold up to 2 hours in slow cooker. Garnish with chopped fresh parsley.

High Altitude (3500-6500 ft): In Step 2, cook about 2 to 3 minutes, stirring constantly.

1 MEATBALL: Calories 60; Total Fat 3.5g (Saturated Fat 1.5g, Trans Fat 0g); Cholesterol 20mg; Sodium 110mg; Total Carbohydrate 3g (Dietary Fiber 0g); Protein 4g. EXCHANGES: 1/2 Medium-Fat Meat, 1/2 Fat. CARBOHYDRATE CHOICES: 0.

tips&ideas

The sauce and meatballs can both be prepared the day before. Just before serving, heat them and place in the slow cooker to keep warm.

cosmo slush

PREP TIME: 10 minutes • START TO FINISH: 8 hours 10 minutes • MAKES: 14 servings (1/2 cup each)

6 oz frozen (thawed) limeade concentrate (from 12-oz. can)

3 tablespoons powdered sugar

2 cups citrus-flavored vodka or orange juice

1 cup orange-flavored liqueur or orange juice

4 cups 100% cranberry juice blend

① In blender, place limeade concentrate and powdered sugar. Cover; blend on high speed until well mixed. Add vodka and orange liqueur. Cover; blend until well mixed.

② In 13x9-inch (3-quart) glass baking dish, stir limeade mixture and cranberry juice until well mixed. Cover; freeze at least 8 hours or until slushy.

③ To serve, stir mixture; spoon 1/2 cup slush into each glass.

High Altitude (3500-6500 ft): No change.

1 SERVING: Calories 100; Total Fat 0g (Saturated Fat 0g, Trans Fat 0g); Cholesterol 0mg; Sodium 0mg; Total Carbohydrate 24g (Dietary Fiber 0g); Protein 0g. EXCHANGES: 1 Fruit, 1/2 Other Carbohydrate. CARBOHYDRATE CHOICES: 1-1/2.

tips&ideas

For the most flavor and brighter color, make this slush with 100% cranberry juice, not cranberry juice cocktail.

pepper jack cheese ball

PREP TIME: 15 minutes • **START TO FINISH:** 15 minutes • **MAKES:** 18 servings (2 tablespoons cheese ball and 4 crackers each)

1-1/2 cups shredded pepper Jack cheese (6 oz)
1 cup shredded sharp Cheddar cheese (4 oz)
2 packages (3 oz each) cream cheese, softened
1 tablespoon lime juice
1/2 teaspoon onion powder
1/4 cup sliced ripe olives
1/4 cup chopped fresh cilantro
3/4 cup nacho-flavored tortilla chips, crushed
Assorted crackers or tortilla chips

(1) In food processor, place cheeses, lime juice and onion powder. Cover; process until well mixed. Spoon into medium bowl. Stir in olives and cilantro.

(2) Place crushed tortilla chips on waxed paper. Spoon cheese mixture onto chips. Roll to coat cheese ball with chips. Serve with crackers.

High Altitude (3500-6500 ft): No change.

1 SERVING: Calories 190; Total Fat 13g (Saturated Fat 6g, Trans Fat 1.5g); Cholesterol 25mg; Sodium 310mg; Total Carbohydrate 12g (Dietary Fiber 0g); Protein 6g.
EXCHANGES: 1 Starch, 1/2 High-Fat Meat, 1-1/2 Fat.
CARBOHYDRATE CHOICES: 1.

meatballs with roasted red pepper sauce

PREP TIME: 15 minutes • **START TO FINISH:** 7 hours 15 minutes • **MAKES:** 16 servings (3 meatballs each)

1-1/2 pounds frozen meatballs (from two 1-pound packages), thawed
1 jar (7.25 ounces) roasted red bell peppers, drained
1/4 cup grated Parmesan cheese
1/4 cup Italian dressing
1 jar (26 ounces) marinara sauce

(1) Place meatballs in 3- to 4-quart slow cooker. Place bell peppers in blender; cover and blend until smooth. Add cheese and Italian dressing; cover and blend until mixed. Add marinara sauce; pulse until just blended. Pour sauce over meatballs.

(2) Cover and cook on Low heat setting 6 to 7 hours.

(3) Stir before serving. Meatballs will hold on Low heat setting up to 2 hours; stir occasionally.

VARIATION: For a super meatball sub, layer the meatballs and slices of mozzarella cheese on a crusty French baguette.

High Altitude (3500-6500 ft): No change.

1 SERVING: Calories 190; Total Fat 10g (Saturated Fat 3g, Trans Fat 0g); Cholesterol 45mg; Sodium 560mg; Total Carbohydrate 15g (Dietary Fiber 1g); Protein 10g. EXCHANGES: 1 Other Carbohydrate, 1-1/2 High-Fat Meat. CARBOHYDRATE CHOICES: 1.

tips&ideas

In a snap, this tasty appetizer becomes a party meal when you serve the meatballs over your favorite pasta. Sprinkle freshly grated Parmesan cheese and chopped red or green bell peppers over the meatballs just before serving.

southwest chicken nachos

PREP TIME: 15 minutes • **START TO FINISH:** 4 hours 45 minutes • **MAKES:** 21 servings (1/4 cup topping and 5 chips each)

1 package (16 ounces) mild Mexican pasteurized prepared cheese product with jalapeño peppers, cut into cubes

3/4 cup Old El Paso® Thick 'n Chunky salsa

1 can (15 ounces) black beans, rinsed and drained

1 package (9 ounces) frozen cooked Southwest-seasoned chicken breast strips, thawed and cubed

1 container (8 ounces) Southwest ranch sour cream dip

1 medium green bell pepper, chopped (1 cup)

1 medium red bell pepper, chopped (1 cup)

12 ounces large tortilla chips

① Place cheese, salsa, beans and chicken in 3- to 4-quart slow cooker.

② Cover and cook on Low heat setting 3 to 4 hours, stirring halfway through cooking, until cheese is melted and mixture is hot.

③ Stir in sour cream dip and bell peppers. Increase heat setting to High. Cover and cook about 30 minutes or until mixture is hot. Serve over tortilla chips. Topping will hold on Low heat setting up to 2 hours; stir occasionally.

High Altitude (3500-6500 ft): In Step 3, cover and cook on High about 35 minutes.

1 SERVING: Calories 230; Total Fat 12g (Saturated Fat 5g, Trans Fat 0g); Cholesterol 30mg; Sodium 600mg; Total Carbohydrate 20g (Dietary Fiber 2g); Protein 11g. EXCHANGES: 1 Starch, 1 Vegetable, 1 Medium-Fat Meat. CARBOHYDRATE CHOICES: 1.

tips&ideas

To reduce the amount of chopping, thaw 2 cups from a bag of frozen stir-fry bell pepper blend and stir into the nacho topping instead of using the bell peppers.

layered shrimp spread

PREP TIME: 15 minutes • **START TO FINISH:** 15 minutes • **MAKES:** 16 servings (2 tablespoons spread and 3 crackers each)

1 container (8 oz) pineapple cream cheese spread
1/2 cup peach or apricot preserves
2 tablespoons seafood cocktail sauce
1 bag (4 oz) frozen cooked salad shrimp, thawed, drained
2 medium green onions, thinly sliced (2 tablespoons)
1/4 cup coconut chips
Assorted crackers

1. On 10- to 12-inch serving plate, spread cream cheese to within 1 inch of edge of plate. In small bowl, mix preserves and cocktail sauce. Spread over cream cheese.

2. Top evenly with shrimp. Sprinkle with onions and coconut. Serve with crackers.

High Altitude (3500-6500 ft): No change.

1 SERVING: Calories 150; Total Fat 8g (Saturated Fat 4g, Trans Fat 1g); Cholesterol 25mg; Sodium 240mg; Total Carbohydrate 15g (Dietary Fiber 0g); Protein 4g. EXCHANGES: 1/2 Starch, 1/2 Other Carbohydrate, 1/2 Very Lean Meat, 1-1/2 Fat. CARBOHYDRATE CHOICES: 1.

tips&ideas

Coconut chips are larger than flaked or shredded coconut. They usually can be found in the baking aisle. If they aren't available, flaked coconut could be substituted.

mini crab points

PREP TIME: 15 minutes • **START TO FINISH:** 15 minutes • **MAKES:** 16 servings

1/4 cup mayonnaise or salad dressing
1 small clove garlic, finely chopped
1 can (6 oz) crabmeat, well drained, flaked
1/4 cup finely chopped celery
2 tablespoons diced red bell pepper
2 medium green onions, thinly sliced
 (2 tablespoons)
1/4 teaspoon seafood seasoning
 (from 6-oz container)
4 slices whole wheat bread, toasted
Chopped fresh parsley

① In medium bowl, mix mayonnaise and garlic. Stir in crabmeat, celery, bell pepper, onions and seafood seasoning.

② Top toasted bread with crab mixture. Cut diagonally into quarters. Sprinkle with parsley.

High Altitude (3500-6500 ft): No change.

1 SERVING: Calories 50; Total Fat 3g (Saturated Fat 0.5g, Trans Fat 0g); Cholesterol 10mg; Sodium 100mg; Total Carbohydrate 4g (Dietary Fiber 0g); Protein 3g. EXCHANGES: 1/2 Starch, 1/2 Fat. CARBOHYDRATE CHOICES: 0.

curried cheese ball with fruit

PREP TIME: 20 minutes • START TO FINISH: 20 minutes • MAKES: 24 servings (1 tablespoon cheese and 3 fruit slices each)

1 package (8 oz) cream cheese, softened
1/2 cup shredded Cheddar cheese (2 oz)
1/4 cup sweetened dried cranberries
1/4 cup golden raisins
1/4 cup finely chopped red onion
2 tablespoons apple juice
1 tablespoon curry powder
1/2 cup chopped cocktail peanuts
3 apples, cut into 12 slices each
3 pears, cut into 12 slices each

① In large bowl, beat all ingredients except peanuts, apples and pears with electric mixer on medium speed 2 to 3 minutes until well mixed and fluffy.

② Spoon cheese mixture onto plastic wrap; shape into a ball. Coat cheese ball with peanuts. Cover and refrigerate until serving. Serve with apple and pear slices.

High Altitude (3500-6500 ft): No change.

1 SERVING: Calories 90; Total Fat 5g (Saturated Fat 2.5g, Trans Fat 0g); Cholesterol 15mg; Sodium 70mg; Total Carbohydrate 10g (Dietary Fiber 2g); Protein 2g. EXCHANGES: 1/2 Fruit, 1 Fat. CARBOHYDRATE CHOICES: 1/2.

tips&ideas

You can make the cheese ball 2 days ahead, but wait to coat it with the nuts until the day of the party.

potato bites

PREP TIME: 40 minutes • START TO FINISH: 55 minutes • MAKES: 45 appetizers

1 package (20 oz) refrigerated mashed potatoes
  (about 2 cups)
1 cup Green Giant® frozen sweet peas
  (from 1-lb bag)
1/3 cup chopped red onion
1 teaspoon ground coriander
1/2 teaspoon ground cumin
1/4 teaspoon salt
1/8 teaspoon ground red pepper (cayenne)
1 cup Progresso® plain bread crumbs
2 eggs
2 tablespoons milk
Cooking spray
Tomato chutney or Old El Paso® Thick 'n Chunky salsa, if desired

① Heat oven to 400°F. Line cookie sheet with foil or cooking parchment paper; spray foil or paper with cooking spray. In medium bowl, mix potatoes, peas, onion, coriander, cumin, salt and red pepper.

② Place bread crumbs in shallow bowl. In another shallow bowl, beat eggs and milk with fork or wire whisk. Shape potato mixture by tablespoonfuls into about 1-inch balls. Roll balls in bread crumbs to coat, then dip into egg mixture and coat again with bread crumbs. Place on cookie sheet. Spray tops of balls with cooking spray.

③ Bake 10 to 14 minutes or until light golden brown and hot. Serve warm with chutney.

High Altitude (3500-6500 ft): Bake 17 to 21 minutes.

1 APPETIZER: Calories 30; Total Fat 1g (Saturated Fat 0g, Trans Fat 0g); Cholesterol 10mg; Sodium 65mg; Total Carbohydrate 4g (Dietary Fiber 0g); Protein 1g. EXCHANGES: 1 Vegetable. CARBOHYDRATE CHOICES: 0.

tips&ideas

To quickly make potato balls that are all the same size, use a small ice-cream scoop.

beef and swiss roll-ups

PREP TIME: 45 minutes • START TO FINISH: 45 minutes • MAKES: 8 servings (3 pieces each)

1 teaspoon vegetable oil

1 medium green or red bell pepper, cut into thin strips

1 small onion, cut into thin strips

2 oz cream cheese, softened

2 tablespoons mayonnaise or salad dressing

2 tablespoons thick-style steak sauce

3 Old El Paso® flour tortillas for burritos (from 11.5-oz package)

1/4 lb thinly sliced deli roast beef

1/2 cup shredded Swiss cheese (2 oz)

① In 10-inch skillet, heat oil over medium heat. Cook bell pepper and onion in oil 8 to 10 minutes, stirring occasionally, until vegetables are tender. Remove from heat; refrigerate vegetables about 10 minutes or until cool.

② Meanwhile, in small bowl, mix cream cheese, mayonnaise and steak sauce until smooth.

③ On microwavable plate, stack tortillas. Cover with microwavable plastic wrap, folding back one edge 1/4 inch to vent steam. Microwave on High 30 seconds.

④ Spread cream cheese mixture over each tortilla to within 1/4 inch of edge. Place equal amounts of roast beef and vegetables on each tortilla. Sprinkle with cheese. Roll up each tortilla tightly. Cut each roll into 8 pieces; secure with cocktail toothpick.

High Altitude (3500-6500 ft): No change.

1 SERVING: Calories 180; Total Fat 11g (Saturated Fat 4.5g, Trans Fat 0g); Cholesterol 30mg; Sodium 240mg; Total Carbohydrate 11g (Dietary Fiber 0g); Protein 8g. EXCHANGES: 1/2 Starch, 1 Lean Meat, 1-1/2 Fat. CARBOHYDRATE CHOICES: 1.

tips&ideas

Look for roast beef with garlic or Italian seasoning at the deli to add additional flavor to the roll-ups.

bloody mary dip

PREP TIME: 10 minutes • **START TO FINISH:** 3 hours 10 minutes • **MAKES:** 12 servings (2 tablespoons dip and 2 shrimp each)

1 jar (14 oz) tomato pasta sauce (any variety)
1/3 cup sliced pimiento-stuffed green olives
1/4 cup vodka
2 tablespoons tomato paste
1 teaspoon celery seed
1 teaspoon red pepper sauce
24 cooked peeled deveined large shrimp, thawed if frozen

1 Mix all ingredients except shrimp in 1 to 1-1/2 quart slow cooker.

2 Cover and cook on Low heat setting 2 to 3 hours.

3 Serve with shrimp for dipping. Dip will hold on Low heat setting up to 2 hours; stir occasionally.

VARIATION: In addition to shrimp, try diving into this dip with celery sticks or dill pickle spears.

High Altitude (3500-6500 ft): No change.

1 SERVING: Calories 60; Total Fat 2g (Saturated Fat 0g, Trans Fat 0g); Cholesterol 25mg; Sodium 300mg; Total Carbohydrate 8g (Dietary Fiber 0g); Protein 3g. EXCHANGES: 1 Vegetable, 1/2 Very Lean Meat, 1/2 Fat. CARBOHYDRATE CHOICES: 1/2.

apricot baked brie

PREP TIME: 20 minutes • START TO FINISH: 45 minutes • MAKES: 12 servings

1/3 cup apricot preserves

1/4 cup chopped pecans

2 tablespoons finely chopped red onion

1 sheet puff pastry (from 17.3-oz package), thawed

1 round (8 oz) Brie cheese, cut horizontally in half

1 tablespoon whipping (heavy) cream or half-and-half

① Heat oven to 400°F. Line cookie sheet with foil or cooking parchment paper; lightly spray foil or paper with cooking spray. In small bowl, mix preserves, pecans and onion; set aside.

② On lightly floured surface, roll pastry into 10x14-inch rectangle. Using the round of cheese as a pattern, cut a pastry circle 3 to 4 inches larger than the cheese. Set aside excess pastry.

③ Spread half of the preserves mixture in center of pastry circle, leaving 3-inch edge. Place 1 cheese round (in rind) on preserves. Spoon remaining preserves over cheese. Top with remaining cheese round.

④ Gently fold edges of pastry up and over cheese to cover, folding and pinching edges to seal. Place seam side down on cookie sheet. Cut out decorative pieces from excess pastry. Brush pastry with whipping cream; place pastry cutouts on top.

⑤ Bake 20 to 25 minutes or until golden brown. Serve warm.

High Altitude (3500-6500 ft): No change.

1 SERVING: Calories 170; Total Fat 11g (Saturated Fat 4.5g, Trans Fat 0.5g); Cholesterol 30mg; Sodium 105mg; Total Carbohydrate 15g (Dietary Fiber 0g); Protein 4g. EXCHANGES: 1 Starch, 2 Fat. CARBOHYDRATE CHOICES: 1.

tips&ideas

Sourdough bread slices, assorted crispy crackers or apple and pear slices go well with this dressed-up cheese appetizer.

bacon-tomato dip

PREP TIME: 15 minutes • **START TO FINISH:** 15 minutes • **MAKES:** 12 servings (2 tablespoons dip and 3 vegetable pieces each)

1 container (8 oz) reduced-fat sour cream
1/4 cup reduced-fat mayonnaise or salad dressing
2 tablespoons cooked real bacon pieces
(from 2.8-oz package)
1 medium tomato, seeded, diced (3/4 cup)
2 medium green onions, sliced (2 tablespoons)
Assorted fresh vegetables (bell pepper strips, broccoli, cauliflower florets, cucumber slices, radishes)

① In medium bowl, mix sour cream and mayonnaise. Stir in bacon, tomato and onions.
② Serve with vegetables for dipping.

High Altitude (3500-6500 ft): No change.

1 SERVING: Calories 60; Total Fat 4.5g (Saturated Fat 2g, Trans Fat 0g); Cholesterol 10mg; Sodium 75mg; Total Carbohydrate 4g (Dietary Fiber 1g); Protein 2g. EXCHANGES: 1 Vegetable, 1 Fat. CARBOHYDRATE CHOICES: 0.

tips&ideas

Packages of cooked real bacon are found near the salad dressings in the grocery store. If you prefer, you can cook and crumble 2 slices of bacon yourself.

sangria

PREP TIME: 10 minutes • START TO FINISH: 10 minutes • MAKES: 8 servings

2/3 cup lemon juice
1/3 cup orange juice
1/4 cup sugar
1 lemon, cut into thin slices
1 orange, cut into thin slices
1 bottle (750 milliliters) dry red wine or nonalcoholic red wine

① In half-gallon glass pitcher, mix juices and sugar until sugar is dissolved. Add lemon and orange slices to pitcher.

② Stir wine into juice mixture. Add ice if desired.

High Altitude (3500-6500 ft): No change.

1 SERVING: Calories 100; Total Fat 0g (Saturated Fat 0g, Trans Fat 0g); Cholesterol 0mg; Sodium 10mg; Total Carbohydrate 10g (Dietary Fiber 0g); Protein 0g. EXCHANGES: 1/2 Other Carbohydrate, 1 Fat. CARBOHYDRATE CHOICES: 1/2.

raspberry-mint-marshmallow creme dip

PREP TIME: 25 minutes • START TO FINISH: 2 hours 25 minutes • MAKES: 15 servings (2 tablespoons dip and 6 fruit pieces each)

4 oz cream cheese (from 8-oz package), softened
1 cup marshmallow creme
1 container (6 oz) Yoplait® Original 99% Fat Free lemon burst yogurt
1/2 cup fresh raspberries
2 teaspoons chopped fresh mint leaves
15 fresh strawberries, stems removed, cut lengthwise in half
3 kiwifruit, each cut into 10 wedges
30 pieces (2-inch) fresh pineapple

① In medium bowl, beat cream cheese, marshmallow creme, yogurt and raspberries with electric mixer on high speed until smooth. Stir in mint. Cover; refrigerate at least 2 hours but no longer than 12 hours.

② Serve dip with strawberries, kiwifruit and pineapple.

High Altitude (3500-6500 ft): No change.

1 SERVING: Calories 80; Total Fat 3g (Saturated Fat 2g, Trans Fat 0g); Cholesterol 10mg; Sodium 35mg; Total Carbohydrate 14g (Dietary Fiber 1g); Protein 1g. EXCHANGES: 1 Fruit, 1/2 Fat. CARBOHYDRATE CHOICES: 1.

sesame toast-vegetable bites

PREP TIME: 40 minutes • **START TO FINISH:** 40 minutes • **MAKES:** 24 appetizers

1 can (8 oz) refrigerated crescent dinner rolls (8 rolls)
1 egg, beaten
1 teaspoon sesame seed
4 oz cream cheese (from 8-oz package), softened
1/2 teaspoon grated lemon peel
1/4 teaspoon dried dill weed
12 fresh sugar snap peas, cut crosswise in half
1/2 medium red bell pepper, cut into 24 (1-1/2-inch) strips
24 small broccoli or cauliflower florets
1 medium carrot, cut lengthwise in half, then cut crosswise into 12 slices (24 pieces total)

① Heat oven to 375°F. Unroll dough into 12x8-inch rectangle; press perforations to seal. Brush dough with egg; sprinkle with sesame seed. Cut dough lengthwise into 4 strips. Cut each strip crosswise into 6 pieces. On ungreased cookie sheet, place pieces 2 inches apart.

② Bake 6 to 8 minutes or until golden brown. Remove from cookie sheet to cooling rack. Cool completely, about 10 minutes.

③ Meanwhile, in small bowl, mix cream cheese, lemon peel and dill weed until smooth.

④ Spread cream cheese mixture over cooled toasts. Arrange 1 piece of each vegetable on each toast.

High Altitude (3500-6500 ft): No change.

1 APPETIZER: Calories 60; Total Fat 4g (Saturated Fat 2g, Trans Fat 0.5g); Cholesterol 15mg; Sodium 95mg; Total Carbohydrate 5g (Dietary Fiber 0g); Protein 2g. EXCHANGES: 1/2 Starch, 1/2 Fat. CARBOHYDRATE CHOICES: 0.

tips & ideas

Use reduced-fat crescent rolls and cream cheese (Neufchâtel) to trim the fat to 3 grams and the calories to 55 per serving.

seven-layer bean dip

PREP TIME: 20 minutes • START TO FINISH: 20 minutes • MAKES: 16 servings (1/2 cup each)

1 can (16 oz) Old El Paso® refried beans

1 package (1 oz) Old El Paso® taco seasoning mix

1 package (8 oz) cream cheese, softened

1 can (4.5 oz) Old El Paso® chopped green chiles

1 cup Old El Paso® Thick 'n Chunky salsa

2 cups shredded lettuce

2 cups shredded Cheddar cheese or Mexican cheese blend (8 oz)

1 can (2-1/4 oz) sliced ripe olives, drained

1 medium tomato, diced (3/4 cup)

Tortilla chips, if desired

① In medium bowl, mix refried beans and taco seasoning mix. Spread mixture on large platter.

② In another medium bowl, stir together cream cheese and chiles. Carefully spread over bean mixture.

③ Top with salsa, lettuce, cheese, olives and tomato. Refrigerate until serving time. Serve with tortilla chips.

High Altitude (3500-6500 ft): No change.

1 SERVING: Calories 150; Total Fat 10g (Saturated Fat 6g, Trans Fat 0g); Cholesterol 30mg; Sodium 750mg; Total Carbohydrate 9g (Dietary Fiber 2g); Protein 6g. EXCHANGES: 1/2 Other Carbohydrate, 1 High-Fat Meat, 1/2 Fat. CARBOHYDRATE CHOICES: 1/2.

amaretto cheese-filled apricots

PREP TIME: 20 minutes • **START TO FINISH:** 1 hour 20 minutes • **MAKES:** 30 apricots

4 oz cream cheese (half of 8-oz package), softened

1/3 cup slivered almonds, toasted, chopped (see tip below)

1/4 cup chopped dried cherries or sweetened dried cranberries

2 tablespoons amaretto liqueur

30 soft whole dried apricots

① In small bowl, mix cream cheese, 1/4 cup of the almonds, the cherries and amaretto with spoon. Spoon into small resealable food-storage plastic bag. Cut 1/2 inch off 1 corner of bag.

② With fingers, open apricots along one side so they resemble partially open clamshells. Pipe about 1 teaspoon cheese mixture into each apricot.

③ Finely chop remaining almonds. Dip cheese edge of apricots into almonds. Refrigerate 1 hour before serving to chill.

High Altitude (3500-6500 ft): No change.

1 APRICOT: Calories 45; Total Fat 2g (Saturated Fat 1g, Trans Fat 0g); Cholesterol 0mg; Sodium 10mg; Total Carbohydrate 6g (Dietary Fiber 0g); Protein 0g. EXCHANGES: 1/2 Fruit, 1/2 Fat. CARBOHYDRATE CHOICES: 1/2.

tips&ideas

To toast nuts, bake uncovered in ungreased shallow pan in 350°F oven 6 to 10 minutes, stirring occasionally, until light brown.

crab fondue

2 cups shredded Gruyère or Swiss cheese (8 oz)

2 packages (8 oz each) cream cheese, softened

1/4 cup frozen stir-fry bell peppers and onions (from 1-lb bag)

1/2 cup dry white wine or milk

1/8 teaspoon ground red pepper (cayenne)

3 cans (6 oz each) crabmeat, drained and cartilage removed

1 loaf (14 to 16 oz) French bread, cut into 1-inch cubes

① In 2-quart saucepan or chafing dish, heat all ingredients except crabmeat and bread over medium heat, stirring constantly, until cheese is melted. Stir in crabmeat. Pour into fondue pot or chafing dish to keep warm; dip will hold for 2 hours.

② Spear bread cubes with fondue forks; dip into fondue. (If fondue becomes too thick, stir in a small amount of dry white wine or milk.)

High Altitude (3500-6500 ft): No change.

1 SERVING: Calories 150; Total Fat 9g (Saturated Fat 5g, Trans Fat 0g); Cholesterol 45mg; Sodium 220mg; Total Carbohydrate 8g (Dietary Fiber 0g); Protein 9g. EXCHANGES: 1/2 Starch, 1 High-Fat Meat. CARBOHYDRATE CHOICES: 1/2.

tips&ideas

This sensational seafood dip is also great served with raw zucchini sticks, red bell pepper strips or blanched pea pods.

brie with cranberry chutney

PREP TIME: 10 minutes • **START TO FINISH:** 45 minutes • **MAKES:** 10 servings (2 tablespoons each)

1 cup fresh or dried cranberries
2/3 cup sugar
1/3 cup cider vinegar
2 tablespoons water
2 teaspoons finely chopped gingerroot
1/4 teaspoon ground cinnamon
1/8 teaspoon ground cloves
Vegetable oil
1 round Brie cheese (8 oz)
Slivered almonds, toasted, if desired
Crackers, if desired

① Mix cranberries, sugar, vinegar, water, gingerroot, cinnamon and cloves in 1-quart saucepan. Heat to boiling; reduce heat to low. Cook uncovered about 20 minutes, stirring frequently, until thickened. Cool slightly. (Chutney will thicken as it stands.)

② Heat oven to 350°F. Lightly brush ovenproof plate with vegetable oil. Place unpeeled cheese on center of plate. Bake uncovered 8 to 10 minutes or until cheese is soft and is starting to melt.

③ Spoon half of the chutney over cheese. Sprinkle with almonds. Serve with crackers. Spoon remaining chutney onto cheese as needed, or save for future use.

VARIATION: Spoon the cranberry chutney over a block of cream cheese and serve with crackers for another delicious and easy appetizer idea.

High Altitude (3500-6500 ft): No change.

1 SERVING: Calories 135; Total Fat 6g (Saturated Fat 3g, Trans Fat nc); Cholesterol 15mg; Sodium 190mg; Total Carbohydrate 15g (Dietary Fiber 0g); Protein 5g. EXCHANGES: 1 Fruit, 1 Medium-Fat Meat. CARBOHYDRATE CHOICES: nc.

tips&ideas

Brie rind is designed to be eaten. It complements the cheese. However you can cut it off if you prefer.

crab bites

PREP TIME: 15 minutes • START TO FINISH: 40 minutes • MAKES: 45 appetizers

3/4 cup mayonnaise or salad dressing
3/4 cup grated Parmesan cheese
1/2 teaspoon finely chopped garlic
8 medium green onions, finely chopped
(1/2 cup)
1 can (14 oz) artichoke hearts, drained, diced
1 pouch (6 oz) ready-to-eat crabmeat, flaked
3 packages (2.1 oz each) frozen baked mini
phyllo (filo) dough shells (15 shells each),
thawed

① Heat oven to 375°F. Line cookie sheet with foil or cooking parchment paper.

② In large bowl, mix all ingredients except phyllo shells with spoon about 2 minutes or until well blended.

③ Place phyllo shells on cookie sheet. Fill each shell with about 1 tablespoon crab mixture. Bake 20 to 25 minutes or until shells are puffed and golden brown. Serve warm.

High Altitude (3500-6500 ft): No change.

1 APPETIZER: Calories 50; Total Fat 3.5g (Saturated Fat 0.5g, Trans Fat 0g); Cholesterol 5mg; Sodium 85mg; Total Carbohydrate 3g (Dietary Fiber 0g); Protein 2g. EXCHANGES: 1/2 Very Lean Meat, 1/2 Fat. CARBOHYDRATE CHOICES: 0.

zippy dill vegetable dip

PREP TIME: 20 minutes • **START TO FINISH:** 20 minutes • **MAKES:** 8 servings (2 tablespoons dip and 8 vegetable pieces each)

1/2 package (0.7-oz size) dill dip mix
    (about 4 teaspoons)
1 container (8 oz) sour cream
2 tablespoons finely sliced chives
1 tablespoon lemon juice
1 cup ready-to-eat baby-cut carrots
2 cups broccoli florets
1/2 pint (1 cup) cherry or grape tomatoes
1 medium cucumber, cut into 1/4-inch slices
    (2 cups)

(1) In medium bowl, mix dip mix (dry), sour cream, chives and lemon juice.

(2) On serving platter, arrange carrots, broccoli, tomatoes and cucumber slices. Serve with dip.

High Altitude (3500-6500 ft): No change.

1 SERVING: Calories 80; Total Fat 5g (Saturated Fat 2.5g, Trans Fat 0g); Cholesterol 10mg; Sodium 220mg; Total Carbohydrate 6g (Dietary Fiber 2g); Protein 2g. EXCHANGES: 1 Vegetable, 1 Fat. CARBOHYDRATE CHOICES: 1/2.

tips&ideas

Add fresh pea pods, orange and yellow bell pepper strips or jicama sticks to the vegetable assortment to create variety and crunch.

spiced dessert coffee

PREP TIME: 5 minutes • START TO FINISH: 15 minutes • MAKES: 8 servings (3/4 cup each)

6 cups water
3/4 cup strong ground coffee (such as French roast)
1-1/2 teaspoons ground cinnamon
8 whole cloves
1/4 cup packed brown sugar
1/2 cup whipped cream topping in aerosol can, if desired

① Pour water into 10-cup coffeemaker. In filter basket, mix remaining ingredients except whipped cream. Brew coffee.

② Pour coffee into mugs. Top each mug with whipped cream.

High Altitude (3500-6500 ft): No change.

1 SERVING: Calories 30; Total Fat 0g (Saturated Fat 0g, Trans Fat 0g); Cholesterol 0mg; Sodium 5mg; Total Carbohydrate 7g (Dietary Fiber 0g); Protein 0g. EXCHANGES: 1/2 Other Carbohydrate. CARBOHYDRATE CHOICES: 1/2.

garlic-herb cheese spread

PREP TIME: 15 minutes • START TO FINISH: 15 minutes • MAKES: 35 servings (1 tablespoon spread and 3 crackers each)

2 packages (8 oz each) cream cheese, softened
3 tablespoons half-and-half or milk
1 teaspoon Italian seasoning
1/8 teaspoon salt
1 clove garlic, finely chopped
About 12 oz round buttery crackers

① In large bowl, beat all ingredients except crackers with electric mixer on medium speed for 2 to 3 minutes or until light and fluffy.

② Place cheese mixture in serving bowl. Cover and refrigerate until serving. Serve with crackers.

High Altitude (3500-6500 ft): No change.

1 SERVING: Calories 100; Total Fat 7g (Saturated Fat 3.5g, Trans Fat 1g); Cholesterol 15mg; Sodium 130mg; Total Carbohydrate 6g (Dietary Fiber 0g); Protein 2g. EXCHANGES: 1/2 Starch, 1 Fat. CARBOHYDRATE CHOICES: 1/2.

artichoke triangles

PREP TIME: 50 minutes • **START TO FINISH:** 1 hour 25 minutes • **MAKES:** 24 servings

1 can (14 to 16 oz) artichoke hearts, well drained and chopped
1/2 cup mayonnaise or salad dressing
1/4 cup shredded Swiss cheese (1 oz)
1/4 cup freshly grated Parmesan cheese
1 clove garlic, finely chopped
1/8 teaspoon freshly cracked pepper
1 package (17.3 oz) frozen puff pastry, thawed
2 tablespoons half-and-half

① Heat oven to 400°F. Line large cookie sheet with foil or cooking parchment paper; lightly spray foil or paper with cooking spray. In medium bowl, mix all ingredients except pastry and half-and-half.

② On lightly floured surface, roll 1 sheet of pastry into 12x9-inch rectangle, trimming edges if necessary. Cut into twelve 3-inch squares.

③ Place 1 tablespoon artichoke mixture on each square. Lightly brush edges with half-and-half. Fold pastry over filling to make triangles. Crimp edges with fork to seal. Place on cookie sheet. Repeat with remaining pastry and artichoke mixture. Brush tops of triangles with half-and-half. Refrigerate 20 minutes.

④ Bake 20 to 25 minutes or until golden brown. Serve warm.

High Altitude (3500-6500 ft): Bake 22 to 27 minutes.

1 APPETIZER: Calories 170; Total Fat 12g (Saturated Fat 4g, Trans Fat 1g); Cholesterol 30mg; Sodium 150mg; Total Carbohydrate 11g (Dietary Fiber 1g); Protein 3g. EXCHANGES: 1 Starch, 2 Fat. CARBOHYDRATE CHOICES: 1.

zesty beef and bean dip

PREP TIME: 15 minutes • **START TO FINISH:** 30 minutes • **MAKES:** 32 servings (2 tablespoons dip and 6 tortilla chips each)

1/2 pound lean (at least 80%) ground beef
1 small onion, chopped (1/4 cup)
1 can (16 oz) Old El Paso® refried beans
1 can (14.5 oz) diced tomatoes with zesty mild green chilies, undrained
1 cup shredded taco-flavored Cheddar cheese (4 oz)
8 oz round red and green tortilla chips

① Spray 12-inch skillet with cooking spray; heat over medium heat. Cook beef and onion in skillet 8 to 10 minutes, stirring occasionally, until beef is brown; drain well.

② Stir in refried beans and tomatoes. Cook 3 to 4 minutes, stirring occasionally, until hot. Stir in 3/4 cup of the cheese.

③ Spoon dip into serving dish or 1-1/2 to 2 quart slow cooker on Low heat setting. Dip will hold up to 2 hours in slow cooker. Top with remaining 1/4 cup of cheese. Serve with tortilla chips.

High Altitude (3500-6500 ft): No change.

1 SERVING: Calories 80; Total Fat 4g (Saturated Fat 1.5g, Trans Fat 0g); Cholesterol 10mg; Sodium 130mg; Total Carbohydrate 8g (Dietary Fiber 1g); Protein 4g. EXCHANGES: 1/2 Starch, 1/2 High-Fat Meat. CARBOHYDRATE CHOICES: 1/2.

salmon-pimiento appetizers

PREP TIME: 15 minutes • **START TO FINISH:** 15 minutes • **MAKES:** 16 appetizers

1 package (4.5 oz) smoked salmon (hot-smoked),
  skin removed, flaked
1/3 cup pimiento cheese spread (from 5-oz jar)
2 teaspoons mayonnaise or salad dressing
2 medium green onions, thinly sliced
  (2 tablespoons)
1/8 teaspoon pepper
16 slices cocktail pumpernickel bread
16 thin slices seedless cucumber
2 tablespoons tiny dill weed sprigs

① In medium bowl, mix salmon, cheese spread,
mayonnaise, onions and pepper. Spread evenly
on bread slices.

② Cut cucumber slices in half almost to edge
and twist; place on salmon mixture. Garnish
with dill weed sprigs.

High Altitude (3500-6500 ft): No change.

1 APPETIZER: Calories 45; Total Fat 2g (Saturated Fat
1g, Trans Fat 0g); Cholesterol 5mg; Sodium 150mg; Total
Carbohydrate 4g (Dietary Fiber 0g); Protein 3g. EXCHANGES:
1/2 Starch, 1/2 Fat. CARBOHYDRATE CHOICES: 0.

tips&ideas

*Salmon can be hot-smoked or cold-smoked. Cold-smoked salmon (lox) is
usually sliced very thinly and doesn't flake.*

frosty mocha

PREP TIME: 5 minutes • START TO FINISH: 5 minutes • MAKES: 4 servings

1 cup water
2 tablespoons instant coffee granules
1/2 cup chocolate-flavor syrup
2 cups vanilla fat-free no-sugar-added ice cream
2 cups ice cubes

1 In blender, place water, coffee granules and chocolate syrup. Cover; blend on high speed until well blended.

2 Add ice cream. Cover; blend on high speed until smooth. Add ice cubes. Cover; blend on high speed until ice is crushed. Pour into 4 serving glasses.

High Altitude (3500-6500 ft): No change.

1 SERVING: Calories 160; Total Fat 3g (Saturated Fat 2g, Trans Fat 0g); Cholesterol 15mg; Sodium 85mg; Total Carbohydrate 31g (Dietary Fiber 0g); Protein 4g. EXCHANGES: 1-1/2 Other Carbohydrate, 1/2 Skim Milk, 1/2 Fat. CARBOHYDRATE CHOICES: 2.

creamy buffalo-style cocktail wieners

PREP TIME: 10 minutes • START TO FINISH: 5 hours 10 minutes • MAKES: 50 servings (about 3 wieners each)

3 pounds cocktail wieners
1 can (10-3/4 ounces) condensed reduced-sodium and reduced-fat cream of chicken soup
1/2 cup buffalo wing sauce (from 12-ounce bottle)
1/2 cup regular or nonalcoholic beer

1 Mix all ingredients in 3- to 4-quart slow cooker.

2 Cover and cook on Low heat setting about 4 to 5 hours.

3 Wieners will hold on Low heat setting up to 2 hours; stir occasionally.

High Altitude (3500-6500 ft): No change.

1 SERVING: Calories 90; Total Fat 8g (Saturated Fat 3g, Trans Fat 0g); Cholesterol 15mg; Sodium 370mg; Total Carbohydrate 3g (Dietary Fiber 0g); Protein 3g. EXCHANGES: 1/2 High-Fat Meat, 1 Fat. CARBOHYDRATE CHOICES: 0.

smoky cranberry chicken wings

PREP TIME: 15 minutes • **START TO FINISH:** 3 hours 5 minutes • **MAKES:** 16 servings

2 lb chicken wings
1 can (16 oz) jellied cranberry sauce
1/2 cup mesquite smoke marinade or hickory smoke barbecue sauce
1/3 cup chopped onion

① Cut each chicken wing at joints to make 3 pieces; discard tip. Cut off and discard excess skin.

② In large bowl, mix remaining ingredients. Add chicken; stir to coat well. Cover and refrigerate 2 to 3 hours, stirring occasionally.

③ Heat oven to 375°F. Line 15x10x1-inch pan with foil or cooking parchment paper; lightly spray foil or paper with cooking spray. Remove chicken from marinade; reserve marinade. Place chicken in pan.

④ Bake 50 to 60 minutes or until well browned and no longer pink in center. Meanwhile, in 1-quart saucepan, heat marinade to boiling over medium-high heat. Reduce heat to medium; cook 3 to 4 minutes longer, stirring occasionally, until slightly thickened. Brush chicken with sauce halfway through baking.

High Altitude (3500-6500 ft): No change.

1 SERVING: Calories 150; Total Fat 6g (Saturated Fat 1.5g, Trans Fat 0g); Cholesterol 35mg; Sodium 115mg; Total Carbohydrate 14g (Dietary Fiber 0g); Protein 11g. EXCHANGES: 1 Other Carbohydrate, 1-1/2 Lean Meat, 1/2 Fat. CARBOHYDRATE CHOICES: 1.

tips&ideas

Using regular barbecue sauce for these wings is also delicious. They will just be a little sweeter and not as smoky flavored.

p. 59

p. 67

festive breads & coffee cakes

Holiday gatherings will be warm and cozy when you serve fresh-from-the-oven coffee cakes or breads.

almond-poppy seed muffins

PREP TIME: 15 minutes • **START TO FINISH:** 30 minutes • **MAKES:** 12 muffins

1/2 cup sugar
1/3 cup vegetable oil
1 egg
1/2 teaspoon almond extract
1/2 cup sour cream
1/4 cup milk
1-1/3 cups Gold Medal® all-purpose flour
1/2 teaspoon baking powder
1/2 teaspoon salt
1/4 teaspoon baking soda
2 tablespoons poppy seed
1 tablespoon sugar
2 tablespoons sliced almonds

① Heat oven to 375°F. Line 12 regular-size muffin cups with paper baking cups (or spray cups with cooking spray or grease them with shortening).

② In large bowl, stir together 1/2 cup sugar, the oil, egg and almond extract. Beat in sour cream and milk with spoon until blended. Stir in flour, baking powder, salt, baking soda and poppy seed until well blended. Divide batter evenly among muffin cups. Sprinkle batter with 1 tablespoon sugar and the almonds.

③ Bake 14 to 17 minutes or until toothpick inserted in center comes out clean. Remove from pan to cooling rack. Serve warm or cooled.

High Altitude (3500-6500 ft): Bake 16 to 19 minutes.

1 MUFFIN: Calories 180; Total Fat 10g (Saturated Fat 2.5g, Trans Fat 0g); Cholesterol 25mg; Sodium 160mg; Total Carbohydrate 21g (Dietary Fiber 0g); Protein 3g. EXCHANGES: 1 Starch, 1/2 Other Carbohydrate, 1-1/2 Fat. CARBOHYDRATE CHOICES: 1-1/2.

tips&ideas

Make these muffins extra-special by using decorative cupcake liners. Go to www.fancyflours.com to check out a variety of options.

walnut-gorgonzola baguettes

PREP TIME: 25 minutes • **START TO FINISH:** 5 hours • **MAKES:** 2 loaves (12 slices each)

2-1/2 to 3 cups Gold Medal® Better for Bread™ flour
1 package regular active dry yeast
    (2-1/4 teaspoons)
1 cup very warm water (120°F to 130°F)
1 teaspoon salt
1/3 cup chopped walnuts
1/3 cup crumbled Gorgonzola cheese

① In large bowl, mix 1-1/2 cups of the flour and the yeast. Add warm water. Beat with electric mixer on low speed 1 minute, scraping bowl frequently. Cover tightly with plastic wrap and let stand about 1 hour or until bubbly.

② Stir in salt and enough remaining flour to form a soft dough. On lightly floured surface, knead dough 5 to 10 minutes or until dough is smooth and springy (dough will be soft). Grease large bowl with shortening or spray with cooking spray. Place dough in bowl, turning dough to grease all sides. Sprinkle walnuts and cheese over dough. Cover bowl loosely with plastic wrap and let rise in warm place 1 to 1-1/4 hours or until double. Dough is ready if indentation remains when touched.

③ Grease large cookie sheet with shortening or spray with cooking spray. On lightly floured surface, knead dough until nuts and cheese are worked into dough. Sprinkle top of dough with flour. Divide dough in half. Gently shape each half into a narrow loaf, about 12 inches long. Place about 4 inches apart on cookie sheet. Using spray bottle with fine mist, spray loaves with cool water. Let rise uncovered in warm place about 1 hour or until double in size.

④ Place 8-inch or 9-inch square pan on bottom rack in oven; add hot water to pan until about 1/2 inch from top of pan. Heat oven to 425°F.

⑤ Carefully cut 1/4-inch-deep slashes diagonally across loaves at 2-inch intervals with sharp serrated knife. Spray tops of loaves with cool water. Place loaves in oven and spray again.

⑥ Bake 15 to 20 minutes or until loaves are deep golden with crisp crust and sound hollow when tapped. Remove from cookie sheet to wire rack; cool completely, about 1 hour.

High Altitude (3500-6500 ft): Bake 25 to 30 minutes.

1 SLICE: Calories 70; Total Fat 2g (Saturated Fat 0.5g, Trans Fat 0g); Cholesterol 0mg; Sodium 105mg; Total Carbohydrate 11g (Dietary Fiber 0g); Protein 2g. EXCHANGES: 1 Starch. CARBOHYDRATE CHOICES: 1.

lemon-chive popovers

PREP TIME: 15 minutes • START TO FINISH: 55 minutes • MAKES: 6 popovers

2 eggs
1 cup Gold Medal® all-purpose flour
1 cup milk
2 tablespoons chopped fresh chives
1 teaspoon grated lemon peel
1/2 teaspoon salt

① Heat oven to 450°F. Generously grease 6-cup popover pan with shortening. Heat pan in oven 5 minutes.

② Meanwhile, in medium bowl, beat eggs slightly with wire whisk or fork. Stir in remaining ingredients just until smooth (do not overmix). Fill cups about half full.

③ Bake 20 minutes. Reduce oven temperature to 350°F. Bake 15 to 20 minutes longer or until deep golden brown. Immediately remove from cups. Serve hot.

High Altitude (3500-6500 ft): Use 1 cup plus 1 tablespoon flour. Bake at 400°F for 20 minutes; reduce oven temperature to 325°F and bake 15 to 20 minutes longer.

1 POPOVER: Calories 120; Total Fat 3g (Saturated Fat 1g, Trans Fat 0g); Cholesterol 75mg; Sodium 240mg; Total Carbohydrate 18g (Dietary Fiber 0g); Protein 6g. EXCHANGES: 1 Starch, 1 Fat. CARBOHYDRATE CHOICES: 1.

cranberry cornbread

PREP TIME: 15 minutes • START TO FINISH: 45 minutes • MAKES: 9 servings

1-1/4 cups Gold Medal® all-purpose flour
3/4 cup cornmeal
1/3 cup sugar
2 teaspoons baking powder
1/2 teaspoon salt
2 eggs
3/4 cup milk
1/4 cup vegetable oil
1 cup chopped fresh or frozen cranberries
2 tablespoons sugar

1 Heat oven to 400°F. Grease bottom and sides of 8-inch square pan with shortening or cooking spray.

2 In large bowl, stir flour, cornmeal, 1/3 cup sugar, the baking powder and salt until mixed. Add eggs, milk and oil; beat with spoon until mixed.

3 In small bowl, gently toss cranberries and 2 tablespoons sugar until coated. Fold into batter. Spread in pan.

4 Bake 25 to 30 minutes or until toothpick inserted in center comes out clean. Serve warm.

High Altitude (3500-6500 ft): No change.

1 SERVING: Calories 230; Total Fat 8g (Saturated Fat 1.5g, Trans Fat 0g); Cholesterol 50mg; Sodium 260mg; Total Carbohydrate 35g (Dietary Fiber 2g); Protein 5g. EXCHANGES: 1 Starch, 1 Other Carbohydrate, 2 Fat. CARBOHYDRATE CHOICES: 2.

tips&ideas

If you have fresh cranberries left over, place them on a cookie sheet and freeze. Once frozen, put them in a freezer bag and store in the freezer.

better-than-the-mall cinnamon rolls

PREP TIME: 25 minutes • START TO FINISH: 2 hours 30 minutes • MAKES: 12 large cinnamon rolls

ROLLS
1 cup warm milk (105°F to 115°F)
2 eggs
1/3 cup butter or margarine, melted
4-1/2 cups Gold Medal® all-purpose flour
1 teaspoon salt
1/2 cup granulated sugar
2 packages quick active dry yeast

FILLING
1 cup packed brown sugar
2 tablespoons ground cinnamon
1/3 cup butter or margarine, softened

FROSTING
1 package (3 oz) cream cheese, softened
1/4 cup butter or margarine, softened
1-1/2 cups powdered sugar
1/2 teaspoon vanilla

(1) Measure carefully, placing all roll ingredients in bread machine pan in the order recommended by the manufacturer.

(2) Select Dough/Manual cycle. Do not use Delay cycle.

(3) Gently remove dough from pan, using lightly floured hands; place on lightly floured surface. Cover dough and let rest 10 minutes. Meanwhile, in small bowl, mix brown sugar and cinnamon.

(4) Grease bottom and sides of 13x9-inch pan with shortening or spray with cooking spray. Roll dough into 20x16-inch rectangle. Spread 1/3 cup butter over dough; sprinkle evenly with brown sugar-cinnamon mixture. Roll up dough, beginning at 20-inch side; pinch edge of dough into roll to seal. Cut into 12 slices. Place in pan. Cover and let rise in warm place 35 to 45 minutes or until dough has almost doubled in size.

(5) Heat oven to 375°F. Bake 20 to 25 minutes or until golden brown. Meanwhile, in medium bowl, beat all frosting ingredients with electric mixer on medium speed until smooth and spreadable. Let rolls stand 5 minutes before frosting. Spread frosting on warm rolls.

High Altitude (3500-6500 ft): Bake 25 to 30 minutes.

1 ROLL: Calories 510; Total Fat 18g (Saturated Fat 9g, Trans Fat 1g); Cholesterol 80mg; Sodium 340mg; Total Carbohydrate 80g (Dietary Fiber 2g); Protein 8g. EXCHANGES: 2 Starch, 3-1/2 Other Carbohydrate, 3-1/2 Fat. CARBOHYDRATE CHOICES: 5.

pull-apart caramel loaf

PREP TIME: 10 minutes • START TO FINISH: 2 hours 50 minutes • MAKES: 6 servings

6 frozen cinnamon rolls (from 36.5-oz bag)
1/2 cup packed brown sugar
1/4 cup butter or margarine
2 tablespoons light corn syrup
2 tablespoons whipping cream

① Heat oven to 175°F. Place rolls on cutting board. Let stand for 10 minutes or until partially thawed.

② Meanwhile, in 1-quart saucepan, heat brown sugar and butter over medium heat, stirring constantly, until butter is melted. Stir in corn syrup and whipping cream. Pour brown sugar mixture into 9x5-inch loaf pan, covering bottom completely.

③ Cut each cinnamon roll in half crosswise. Arrange roll halves randomly over brown sugar mixture in pan. Cover loosely with plastic wrap sprayed with cooking spray. Place pan in oven and turn off heat. Let rise 1 hour 10 minutes to 1 hour 30 minutes or until loaf has at least doubled in size and top of loaf is 1 inch from top of pan. Remove from oven.

④ Heat oven to 350°F. Remove plastic wrap. Bake loaf 25 to 30 minutes or until golden brown. Place heatproof tray or serving plate upside down over pan; immediately turn tray and pan over. Let pan remain 1 minute so caramel can drizzle over loaf; remove pan. Serve warm.

High Altitude (3500-6500 ft): Bake 28 to 32 minutes.

1 SERVING: Calories 380; Total Fat 17g (Saturated Fat 8g, Trans Fat 2g); Cholesterol 40mg; Sodium 210mg; Total Carbohydrate 53g (Dietary Fiber 1g); Protein 4g. EXCHANGES: 1 Starch, 2-1/2 Other Carbohydrate, 3 Fat. CARBOHYDRATE CHOICES: 3-1/2.

tips&ideas

Corn syrup is available in both a light and dark variety. Light corn syrup, which has a sweet but mild flavor, has been clarified to remove color and cloudiness.

fresh raspberry coffee cake

PREP TIME: 20 minutes • **START TO FINISH:** 1 hour 10 minutes • **MAKES:** 9 servings

COFFEE CAKE

- 1/2 cup butter or margarine, melted
- 3/4 cup milk
- 1 teaspoon vanilla
- 1 egg
- 2 cups Gold Medal® all-purpose flour
- 1/2 cup granulated sugar
- 2 teaspoons baking powder
- 1/2 teaspoon salt
- 1 cup fresh raspberries

GLAZE

- 1/2 cup powdered sugar
- 1 tablespoon butter or margarine, softened
- 2 to 3 teaspoons water
- 1/4 teaspoon almond extract

① Heat oven to 400°F. Spray 9- or 8-inch square pan with baking spray with flour.

② In medium bowl, beat 1/2 cup butter, the milk, vanilla and egg with spoon. Stir in flour, granulated sugar, baking powder and salt just until flour is moistened. Fold in raspberries. Spread in pan.

③ Bake 25 to 30 minutes or until top is golden brown and toothpick inserted in center comes out clean. Cool 20 minutes.

④ In small bowl, mix glaze ingredients until smooth and thin enough to drizzle. Drizzle glaze over warm coffee cake.

High Altitude (3500-6500 ft): Do not use 8-inch pan.

1 SERVING: Calories 300; Total Fat 13g (Saturated Fat 8g, Trans Fat 0g); Cholesterol 55mg; Sodium 340mg; Total Carbohydrate 42g (Dietary Fiber 1g); Protein 5g. EXCHANGES: 1-1/2 Starch, 1 Other Carbohydrate, 2-1/2 Fat. CARBOHYDRATE CHOICES: 3.

tips&ideas

This coffee cake is best served warm, but you can microwave a piece for 10 to 15 seconds on High to bring back that fresh-from-the-oven taste.

chai-spiced bread

PREP TIME: 15 minutes • START TO FINISH: 3 hours 55 minutes • MAKES: 1 loaf (16 slices)

BREAD
3/4 cup granulated sugar
1/2 cup butter or margarine, softened
1/2 cup prepared tea or water
1/3 cup milk
2 teaspoons vanilla
2 eggs
2 cups Gold Medal® all-purpose flour
2 teaspoons baking powder
3/4 teaspoon ground cardamom
1/2 teaspoon salt
1/4 teaspoon ground cinnamon
1/8 teaspoon ground cloves

GLAZE
1 cup powdered sugar
1/4 teaspoon vanilla
3 to 5 teaspoons milk
Additional ground cinnamon

① Heat oven to 400°F. Grease bottom only of 8x4- or 9x5-inch loaf pan with shortening or cooking spray.

② In large bowl, beat granulated sugar and butter with electric mixer on medium speed until fluffy. On low speed, beat in tea, 1/3 cup milk, 2 teaspoons vanilla and the eggs until ingredients are well combined (will appear curdled). Stir in remaining bread ingredients just until moistened. Spread in pan.

③ Bake 50 to 60 minutes or until toothpick inserted in center comes out clean (do not underbake). Cool in pan on cooling rack for about 10 minutes. Loosen sides of loaf from pan; remove from pan to cooling rack. Cool for about 30 minutes.

④ In small bowl, stir powdered sugar, 1/4 teaspoon vanilla and 3 teaspoons of the milk, adding more milk by teaspoonfuls, until spreadable. Spread glaze over bread. Sprinkle with additional cinnamon. Cool completely, about 2 hours, before slicing. Wrap tightly and store at room temperature up to 4 days, or refrigerate up to 10 days.

High Altitude (3500-6500 ft): Decrease baking powder to 1-1/2 teaspoons. Bake 1 hour to 1 hour 10 minutes.

1 SLICE: Calories 190; Total Fat 7g (Saturated Fat 4g, Trans Fat 0g); Cholesterol 40mg; Sodium 190mg; Total Carbohydrate 30g (Dietary Fiber 0g); Protein 3g. EXCHANGES: 1 Starch, 1 Other Carbohydrate, 1 Fat. CARBOHYDRATE CHOICES: 2.

herb pull-apart bread

PREP TIME: 10 minutes • **START TO FINISH:** 4 hours 45 minutes • **MAKES:** 12 servings

3 tablespoons butter or margarine
1 teaspoon dried basil leaves
1 teaspoon parsley flakes
1/2 teaspoon dried thyme leaves
2 cloves garlic, finely chopped
24 balls frozen white dinner roll dough
    (from 3-lb package)

① Spray 12-cup fluted tube cake pan (do not use 10-cup) with cooking spray. In 1-quart saucepan, heat all ingredients except roll dough over low heat, stirring occasionally, until butter is melted.

② Place half of the frozen dough balls in pan. Generously brush butter mixture over dough in pan. Layer remaining dough balls in pan. Brush with remaining butter mixture. Cover and let stand in warm place about 4 hours or until double in size.

③ Heat oven to 350°F. Bake 22 to 27 minutes or until bread sounds hollow when tapped and top is deep golden brown. Cool 5 minutes; turn upside down onto serving plate.

High Altitude (3500-6500 ft): No change.

1 SERVING: Calories 220; Total Fat 11g (Saturated Fat 3.5g, Trans Fat 3g); Cholesterol 10mg; Sodium 690mg; Total Carbohydrate 27g (Dietary Fiber 0g); Protein 4g. EXCHANGES: 2 Starch, 1-1/2 Fat. CARBOHYDRATE CHOICES: 2.

orange scone wedges with cream cheese filling

PREP TIME: 25 minutes • **START TO FINISH:** 40 minutes • **MAKES:** 12 scones

FILLING
- 6 oz cream cheese, softened
- 1/4 cup granulated sugar
- 1 tablespoon grated orange peel

SCONES
- 1-3/4 cups Gold Medal® all-purpose flour
- 3 tablespoons granulated sugar
- 2 teaspoons baking powder
- 1/4 teaspoon salt
- 6 tablespoons firm butter or margarine
- 1 tablespoon grated orange peel
- 1/4 cup whipping cream
- 1 egg
- 1 egg, beaten
- 2 tablespoons coarse white sugar

① Heat oven to 400°F. In small bowl, beat all filling ingredients with electric mixer on medium speed until smooth; set aside.

② In large bowl, mix flour, 3 tablespoons sugar, the baking powder and salt. Cut in butter, using pastry blender (or pulling 2 table knives through ingredients in opposite directions) until mixture looks like fine crumbs. Stir in 1 tablespoon orange peel, whipping cream and 1 egg.

③ Place dough on lightly floured surface; gently roll in flour to coat. Knead lightly 10 times. Divide dough in half. Pat or roll each half into 9-inch round, about 1/4 inch thick. Spread filling over half of each round.

④ Fold each dough round in half over filling. With sharp knife, cut each half-round into 6 wedges. On ungreased cookie sheet, place wedges 1 inch apart. Brush tops with beaten egg; sprinkle with coarse sugar.

⑤ Bake 10 to 15 minutes or until light golden brown. Immediately remove from cookie sheet to cooling rack. Serve warm.

High Altitude (3500-6500 ft): Decrease baking powder to 1-1/2 teaspoons; increase whipping cream to slightly less than 1/2 cup. Bake 12 to 15 minutes.

1 SCONE: Calories 230; Total Fat 13g (Saturated Fat 8g, Trans Fat 0.5g); Cholesterol 70mg; Sodium 230mg; Total Carbohydrate 24g (Dietary Fiber 0g); Protein 4g. EXCHANGES: 1 Starch, 1/2 Other Carbohydrate, 2-1/2 Fat. CARBOHYDRATE CHOICES: 1-1/2.

tips & ideas

Coarse sugar is also called decorating sugar and has larger granules than regular sugar. It adds sparkle to baked goods such as these scones.

fresh herb-topped rolls

PREP TIME: 15 minutes • **START TO FINISH:** 1 hour 30 minutes • **MAKES:** 12 rolls

1 tablespoon cornmeal
1 loaf (1 lb) frozen honey-wheat or white bread dough, thawed as directed on package
36 fresh Italian (flat-leaf) parsley leaves
1 egg
1 tablespoon water

① Heat oven to 375°F. Grease cookie sheet with shortening or cooking spray; sprinkle with cornmeal. Divide thawed dough into 12 equal portions.

② Shape each portion of dough into a ball. Place rolls on cookie sheet. Spray sheet of plastic wrap with cooking spray; place sprayed side down over rolls. Cover with towel. Let rise in warm place 45 to 60 minutes or until doubled in size.

③ Meanwhile, place rinsed parsley leaves on paper towels; pat dry. With kitchen scissors, cut stems from leaves.

④ In custard cup, beat egg and water with fork. Brush mixture over top of each roll. Dip parsley leaves into egg mixture; place 3 leaves on top of each roll. Brush remaining egg mixture over parsley-topped rolls.

⑤ Bake 15 to 20 minutes or until golden brown. Immediately remove from cookie sheet. Serve warm.

High Altitude (3500-6500 ft): No change.

1 ROLL: Calories 110; Total Fat 1.5g (Saturated Fat 0g, Trans Fat 0g); Cholesterol 20mg; Sodium 260mg; Total Carbohydrate 20g (Dietary Fiber 0g); Protein 4g. EXCHANGES: 1-1/2 Starch. CARBOHYDRATE CHOICES: 1.

tips&ideas

Any fresh flat-leaf herb, such as dill weed, sage or marjoram, can be substituted for the Italian parsley.

bacon-cheddar muffins

PREP TIME: 20 minutes • **START TO FINISH:** 40 minutes • **MAKES:** 12 muffins

8 oz maple smoked bacon,
  cut into 1-inch pieces
1 egg
2 cups Original Bisquick® mix
3/4 cup shredded Cheddar cheese (3 oz)
3/4 cup milk
2 tablespoons butter or margarine, melted
1/4 teaspoon chili powder

① Heat oven to 400°F. Place paper baking cup in each of 12 regular-size muffin cups; spray paper cups with cooking spray.

② In 10-inch skillet, cook bacon over medium-high heat, stirring frequently, until crisp. Remove from skillet; drain on paper towel.

③ Meanwhile, in medium bowl, beat egg slightly. Stir in remaining ingredients and bacon just until moistened. Spoon the batter evenly into cups.

④ Bake 16 to 19 minutes or until golden brown. Immediately remove from pan to cooling rack. Serve warm.

High Altitude (3500-6500 ft): No change.

1 MUFFIN: Calories 170; Total Fat 10g (Saturated Fat 4.5g, Trans Fat 0.5g); Cholesterol 35mg; Sodium 470mg; Total Carbohydrate 13g (Dietary Fiber 0g); Protein 6g. EXCHANGES: 1 Starch, 1/2 High-Fat Meat, 1 Fat. CARBOHYDRATE CHOICES: 1.

tips&ideas

You can jazz up these muffins by using a savory Cheddar-Monterey Jack cheese blend with jalapeño peppers instead of plain Cheddar cheese. You will find this shredded cheese blend in the dairy section of your supermarket.

zesty cheddar bread

PREP TIME: 10 minutes • **START TO FINISH:** 1 hour 20 minutes • **MAKES:** 1 loaf (12 slices)

1 cup buttermilk
1/3 cup butter or margarine, melted
1 tablespoon sugar
2 tablespoons finely chopped chipotle chilies in adobo sauce (from 7-oz can)
2 eggs
2 cups Gold Medal® all-purpose flour
1 cup shredded Cheddar cheese (4 oz)
2 teaspoons baking powder
1 teaspoon baking soda
1/2 teaspoon salt

① Heat oven to 400°F. Grease bottom only of 8x4-inch or 9x5-inch loaf pan with shortening or spray bottom with cooking spray.

② In large bowl, stir buttermilk, butter, sugar, chilies and eggs until well mixed. Stir in remaining ingredients just until moistened. Spread in pan.

③ Bake 8-inch pan 45 to 55 minutes, 9-inch pan 40 to 50 minutes, or until toothpick inserted in center comes out clean (do not underbake). Cool 15 minutes in pan on wire rack. Loosen sides of loaf from pan; remove from pan to wire rack. Serve warm if desired.

High Altitude (3500-6500 ft): Heat oven to 375°F. Use 1-1/2 teaspoons baking powder and 1/2 teaspoon baking soda. Bake 8-inch pan 45 to 50 minutes, 9-inch pan 40 to 45 minutes.

1 SLICE: Calories 180; Total Fat 10g (Saturated Fat 6g, Trans Fat 0g); Cholesterol 60mg; Sodium 430mg; Total Carbohydrate 18g (Dietary Fiber 0g); Protein 6g. EXCHANGES: 1 Starch, 1/2 High-Fat Meat, 1 Fat. CARBOHYDRATE CHOICES: 1.

ciabatta

PREP TIME: 25 minutes · START TO FINISH: 18 hours 20 minutes · Makes 2 loaves (12 slices each)

STARTER

1/4 teaspoon regular active dry yeast
1/2 cup water
1 cup Gold Medal® Better for Bread™ flour

BREAD

3/4 cup water
2 teaspoons olive or vegetable oil
2-1/4 cups Gold Medal® Better for Bread™ flour
3/4 teaspoon regular active dry yeast
1-1/2 teaspoons salt
Cornmeal

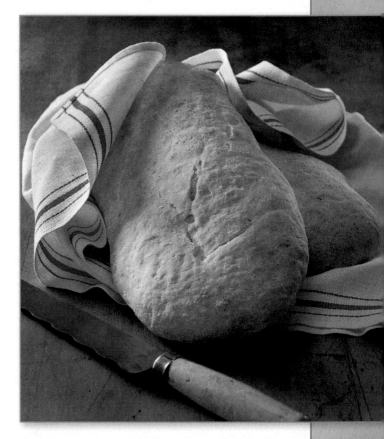

① In small bowl, stir all starter ingredients until well blended. Cover with plastic wrap and let stand at room temperature 12 to 24 hours.

② In large bowl, mix starter and all bread ingredients except cornmeal with heavy-duty electric mixer using dough hook on medium speed 4 minutes or in food processor fitted with metal blade for 1 minute. Dough will be very sticky.

③ Grease medium bowl with shortening or spray with cooking spray. Place dough in bowl, turning dough to grease all sides. Cover bowl loosely with plastic wrap and let rise at room temperature about 1-1/2 hours or until double. Dough is ready if indentation remains when touched. Gently stir down dough with rubber spatula. Cover with plastic wrap and let rise about 1 hour longer.

④ On generously floured surface, divide dough in half. Gently press each half with floured fingers into 10x4-inch rectangle. Sprinkle cornmeal over large cookie sheet; place loaves 3 inches apart on cornmeal. Using spray bottle with fine mist, spray tops of loaves with cool water. Cover loosely with plastic wrap and let rise 1-1/2 to 2 hours or until almost double.

⑤ Heat oven to 425°F. Using spray bottle with fine mist, spray tops of loaves with cool water. Bake 18 to 22 minutes or until loaves sound hollow when tapped. Remove from cookie sheet to wire rack; cool completely, about 1 hour.

High Altitude (3500-6500 ft): No change.

1 SLICE: Calories 70; Total Fat 0.5g (Saturated Fat 0g, Trans Fat 0g); Cholesterol 0mg; Sodium 150mg; Total Carbohydrate 14g (Dietary Fiber 0g); Protein 2g. EXCHANGES: 1 Starch. CARBOHYDRATE CHOICES: 1.

pecan-topped cornbread with honey butter

PREP TIME: 20 minutes • START TO FINISH: 1 hour 5 minutes • MAKES: 12 servings

CORNBREAD

1 cup cornmeal
1 cup Gold Medal® all-purpose flour
1/3 cup sugar
1/4 cup butter or margarine, melted
2 teaspoons baking powder
1/4 teaspoon salt
3 eggs
1 can (14.75 oz) Green Giant® cream-style corn
1/4 cup chopped pecans

HONEY BUTTER

1/2 cup butter, softened (do not use margarine)
1/4 cup honey
Dash salt

① Heat oven to 375°F. Spray 9- or 8-inch round cake pan with baking spray with flour. In medium bowl, stir all cornbread ingredients except pecans until well blended. Pour into pan. Sprinkle pecans evenly over top.

② Bake 35 to 45 minutes or until toothpick inserted in center comes out clean.

③ Meanwhile, in small bowl, beat 1/2 cup butter with spoon until creamy. Slowly beat in honey and salt until well blended.

④ Serve warm cornbread with honey butter.

High Altitude (3500-6500 ft): Bake 40 to 50 minutes.

1 SERVING: Calories 300; Total Fat 15g (Saturated Fat 8g, Trans Fat 0g); Cholesterol 85mg; Sodium 320mg; Total Carbohydrate 35g (Dietary Fiber 1g); Protein 5g. EXCHANGES: 1 Starch, 1-1/2 Other Carbohydrate, 3 Fat. CARBOHYDRATE CHOICES: 2.

tips&ideas

Keep your cornmeal fresh by storing it in the refrigerator or freezer.

french breakfast puffs

PREP TIME: 10 minutes • **START TO FINISH:** 35 minutes • **MAKES:** 12 puffs

1-1/2 cups Gold Medal® all-purpose flour
1-1/2 teaspoons baking powder
1/2 teaspoon salt
1/4 teaspoon ground nutmeg
1/3 cup shortening
1/2 cup sugar
1 egg
1/2 cup milk
1/2 cup sugar
1 teaspoon ground cinnamon
1/2 cup butter or margarine

1 Heat oven to 350°F. Grease 12 medium muffin cups with shortening or spray with cooking spray.

2 In small bowl, mix flour, baking powder, salt and nutmeg. In large bowl, stir shortening, 1/2 cup sugar and the egg until mixed. Stir in flour mixture alternately with milk. Divide batter evenly among muffin cups.

3 Bake 20 to 25 minutes or until tops are light golden brown and bottoms are golden brown.

4 Meanwhile, in shallow dish, mix 1/2 cup sugar and the cinnamon. Place melted butter in another shallow dish. Immediately roll hot muffins in melted butter, then carefully in sugar-cinnamon mixture. Serve warm.

High Altitude (3500-6500 ft): No changes.

1 PUFF: Calories 260; Total Fat 14g (Saturated Fat 7g, Trans Fat 1.5g); Cholesterol 40mg; Sodium 220mg; Total Carbohydrate 29g (Dietary Fiber 0g); Protein 2g. EXCHANGES: 1 Starch, 1 Other Carbohydrate, 2-1/2 Fat. CARBOHYDRATE CHOICES: 2.

tips&ideas

Do you want something smaller & more dainty? Prepare recipe as directed, except divide the dough among 24 greased mini muffin cups. Bake 11 to 13 minutes.

overnight lemon country coffee cake

PREP TIME: 15 minutes • **START TO FINISH:** 9 hours 10 minutes • **MAKES:** 15 servings

1/2 cup butter or margarine, softened
1 cup granulated sugar
2 eggs
2 containers (6 oz each) Yoplait® Original lemon burst yogurt
2 teaspoons grated lemon peel
2-1/3 cups Gold Medal® all-purpose flour
1-1/2 teaspoons baking powder
1/2 teaspoon salt
1/4 teaspoon baking soda
3/4 cup packed brown sugar
3/4 cup chopped pecans
1/2 teaspoon ground nutmeg

① Spray bottom only of 13x9-inch pan with cooking spray. Beat butter and granulated sugar with electric mixer on low speed until light and fluffy. Add eggs, one at a time, beating well after each addition. Add yogurt, lemon peel, flour, baking powder, salt and baking soda; beat on low speed until smooth. Spread batter in pan. Cover and refrigerate at least 8 hours but no longer than 16 hours.

② In small resealable plastic bag, mix brown sugar, pecans and nutmeg. Refrigerate.

③ When ready to bake, let coffee cake stand at room temperature while heating oven to 350°F. Uncover coffee cake; sprinkle with brown sugar mixture.

④ Bake 30 to 40 minutes or until toothpick inserted in center comes out clean. Cool 15 minutes. Serve warm.

VARIATION: Make an orange version of this coffee cake with orange yogurt and grated orange peel.

High Altitude (3500-6500 ft): Use 2-1/2 cups of flour.

1 SERVING: Calories 300; Total Fat 11g (Saturated Fat 4g, Trans Fat 0g); Cholesterol 45mg; Sodium 220mg; Total Carbohydrate 44g (Dietary Fiber 1g); Protein 4g. EXCHANGES: 2 Starch, 2 Fat. CARBOHYDRATE CHOICES: 3.

citrus-macadamia nut bread

PREP TIME: 15 minutes • **START TO FINISH:** 2 hours 25 minutes • **MAKES:** 1 loaf (16 slices)

2-1/2 cups Gold Medal® all-purpose flour
1 cup granulated sugar
1 cup orange juice
1/2 cup vegetable oil
1 tablespoon grated lemon peel
1 tablespoon grated lime peel
2 teaspoons baking powder
1/2 teaspoon salt
2 eggs, beaten
1/2 cup coarsely chopped macadamia nuts
Powdered sugar, if desired

1 Heat oven to 350°F. Grease bottom only of 9x5-inch loaf pan with shortening or cooking spray. In large bowl, mix all ingredients except nuts and powdered sugar with spoon until moistened. Stir in nuts. Pour into pan.

2 Bake 50 to 60 minutes or until toothpick inserted in center comes out clean.

3 Cool bread in pan 10 minutes. Loosen sides of bread from pan; remove from pan to cooling rack. Cool completely, about 1 hour. Sprinkle with powdered sugar before slicing.

High Altitude (3500-6500 ft): Heat oven to 375°F. Increase flour to 2-3/4 cups. Decrease baking powder to 1-1/2 teaspoons. Bake 55 to 60 minutes.

1 SLICE: Calories 220; Total Fat 10g (Saturated Fat 1.5g, Trans Fat 0g); Cholesterol 25mg; Sodium 150mg; Total Carbohydrate 30g (Dietary Fiber 0g); Protein 3g.
EXCHANGES: 1 Starch, 1 Other Carbohydrate, 2 Fat.
CARBOHYDRATE CHOICES: 2.

tips & ideas

This loaf can be baked in advance and frozen. For easier slicing, cut the loaf when it is only partially thawed. Wrap loaf in plastic wrap, and finish thawing at room temperature.

pear brunch cake

PREP TIME: 10 minutes • **START TO FINISH:** 50 minutes • **MAKES:** 8 servings

1 can (15 oz) pear halves, drained
1-3/4 cups Bisquick Heart Smart® mix
1/3 cup sugar
2/3 cup fat-free (skim) milk
1/4 cup margarine or butter, melted
1/2 teaspoon ground cinnamon
2/3 cup Yoplait® Fat Free plain yogurt
(from 2-lb container)

1 Heat oven to 400°F. Grease bottom and side of 9-inch round cake pan with shortening; lightly flour. Cut pear halves into thin slices.

2 In medium bowl, stir together Bisquick® mix, sugar, milk and margarine. Pour into pan. Arrange pear slices in circular pattern on batter; sprinkle with cinnamon.

3 Bake about 40 minutes or until golden brown and toothpick inserted in center comes out clean. Top each serving with yogurt.

VARIATION: If you're a nutmeg lover, sprinkle about 1/4 teaspoon ground nutmeg over the batter with the ground cinnamon.

High Altitude (3500-6500 ft): Bake about 45 minutes.

1 SERVING: Calories 230; Total Fat 7g (Saturated Fat 1g, Trans Fat 2g); Cholesterol 0mg; Sodium 320mg; Total Carbohydrate 37g (Dietary Fiber 1g); Protein 4g. EXCHANGES: 1 Starch, 1-1/2 Other Carbohydrate, 1-1/2 Fat. CARBOHYDRATE CHOICES: 2-1/2.

cherry-pecan ring

PREP TIME: 15 minutes • START TO FINISH: 50 minutes • MAKES: 10 servings

COFFEE CAKE

1/3 cup butter or margarine, melted
1/3 cup packed brown sugar
1 jar (6 oz) maraschino cherries (about 25 cherries), drained, stems removed
1/3 cup pecan halves
2 cups Original Bisquick® mix
2 tablespoons granulated sugar
2/3 cup milk
2 tablespoons butter or margarine, softened
1 egg

GLAZE

1 cup powdered sugar
4 teaspoons water
1/2 teaspoon vanilla

① Heat oven to 400°F. Spray 8- or 12-cup fluted tube cake pan with cooking spray. Pour 1/3 cup melted butter into pan; turn pan to coat with butter. Sprinkle brown sugar over butter. Arrange cherries and pecans on sugar mixture.

② In medium bowl, stir Bisquick mix, granulated sugar, milk, 2 tablespoons softened butter and egg until combined; beat vigorously 30 seconds. Spoon batter evenly over cherries and pecans.

③ Bake 20 to 25 minutes or until toothpick inserted in center comes out clean. Immediately place heatproof plate upside down on pan; carefully turn plate and pan over to remove coffee cake. Cool 10 minutes.

④ Meanwhile, in small bowl, mix glaze ingredients until smooth and thin enough to drizzle, adding additional water, 1 teaspoon at a time, until desired consistency. Drizzle glaze over warm coffee cake.

High Altitude (3500-6500 ft): No change.

1 SERVING: Calories 320; Total Fat 15g (Saturated Fat 7g, Trans Fat 1.5g); Cholesterol 45mg; Sodium 370mg; Total Carbohydrate 43g (Dietary Fiber 1g); Protein 3g. EXCHANGES: 1 Starch, 2 Other Carbohydrate, 3 Fat. CARBOHYDRATE CHOICES: 3.

tips&ideas

For a different flavor, use almonds instead of the pecans and replace half of the vanilla in the glaze with almond flavoring.

p. 91

p. 82

yuletide salads & sides

Rounding out your meal with something spectacular is easy with the impressive selections featured here.

mixed greens with cranberry vinaigrette

PREP TIME: 20 minutes • START TO FINISH: 20 minutes • MAKES: 12 servings (1-1/3 cups each)

CRANBERRY VINAIGRETTE

- 1/3 cup vegetable oil
- 1/4 cup frozen (thawed) cranberry juice concentrate
- 1 teaspoon Dijon mustard
- 1/4 teaspoon salt
- 1/2 cup sweetened dried cranberries

SALAD

- 2 bags (5 oz each) mixed spring greens
- 1 small bunch watercress, torn into pieces
- 2 tart red apples, thinly sliced, slices cut in half
- 1 avocado, pitted, peeled and sliced

① In small bowl, beat all vinaigrette ingredients except cranberries with wire whisk until smooth. Stir in cranberries.

② In serving bowl, toss all salad ingredients with vinaigrette just before serving.

High Altitude (3500-6500 ft): No change.

1 SERVING: Calories 130; Total Fat 8g (Saturated Fat 1g, Trans Fat 0g); Cholesterol 0mg; Sodium 70mg; Total Carbohydrate 12g (Dietary Fiber 2g); Protein 0g. EXCHANGES: 1/2 Other Carbohydrate, 1 Vegetable, 1-1/2 FAT. CARBOHYDRATE CHOICES: 1.

mashed sweet potatoes with bacon

PREP TIME: 25 minutes • **START TO FINISH:** 1 hour 45 minutes • **MAKES:** 10 servings (1/2 cup each)

3 lb dark-orange sweet potatoes (about 4 potatoes)
8 slices bacon
1 large onion, chopped (3/4 cup)
1/4 cup half-and-half, warmed
1 teaspoon chopped fresh thyme leaves
1/2 teaspoon salt
1/4 teaspoon pepper
Fresh thyme sprigs, if desired

① Heat oven to 350°F. Pierce sweet potatoes all over with fork; place on cookie sheet with sides. Bake about 1 hour 15 minutes or until tender when pierced with fork. Let stand 15 minutes or until cool enough to handle.

② Meanwhile, in 10-inch skillet, cook bacon over medium-high heat 4 minutes, turning occasionally, until brown. Remove bacon from skillet; place on paper towels to drain. Reserve 1 tablespoon drippings in skillet; discard remaining drippings. Add onion to skillet; cook over medium heat 5 to 8 minutes, stirring occasionally, until softened.

③ Peel sweet potatoes; place in large bowl. Mash until no lumps remain. Add warm half-and-half, thyme, salt and pepper; mash until very smooth.

④ Add onion to sweet potatoes. Crumble bacon; reserve 2 tablespoons for garnish. Add remaining bacon to potatoes; stir until blended. Garnish with reserved bacon and thyme sprigs.

High Altitude (3500-6500 ft): No change.

1 SERVING: Calories 130; Total Fat 3.5g (Saturated Fat 1.5g, Trans Fat 0g); Cholesterol 10mg; Sodium 300mg; Total Carbohydrate 19g (Dietary Fiber 3g); Protein 4g. EXCHANGES: 1 Starch, 1/2 Other Carbohydrate, 1/2 Fat. CARBOHYDRATE CHOICES: 1.

tips & ideas

Sweet potatoes sold commercially in the U.S. come in two varieties: one has light yellow skin and pale yellow flesh; the other is a darker-skinned variety with dark orange flesh. Darker potatoes are often confused with yams of Africa and Central and South America.

parmesan broccoli

PREP TIME: 25 minutes • START TO FINISH: 25 minutes • MAKES: 6 servings (1/2 cup each)

2 tablespoons butter or margarine
1/2 cup thinly sliced red onion
4 cups fresh broccoli florets
2 tablespoons water
1/2 teaspoon peppered seasoned salt
1/4 teaspoon Italian seasoning
1/4 cup shredded Parmesan cheese

1 In 12-inch nonstick skillet, melt butter over medium heat. Cook onion in butter 2 minutes, stirring occasionally.

2 Add broccoli and water. Cover; cook 6 to 8 minutes, stirring occasionally, until broccoli is crisp-tender and water has evaporated.

3 Sprinkle with peppered seasoned salt and Italian seasoning; toss to mix. Sprinkle with cheese.

High Altitude (3500-6500 ft): No change.

1 SERVING: Calories 70; Total Fat 5g (Saturated Fat 2.5g, Trans Fat 0g); Cholesterol 15mg; Sodium 230mg; Total Carbohydrate 4g (Dietary Fiber 2g); Protein 3g. EXCHANGES: 1 Vegetable, 1 Fat. CARBOHYDRATE CHOICES: 0.

tips&ideas

Choose broccoli that is firm and looks fresh. Keep it tightly wrapped in the refrigerator for up to 3 days after purchasing.

orange-almond salad in lettuce cups

PREP TIME: 10 minutes • **START TO FINISH:** 10 minutes • **MAKES:** 4 servings

1/4 cup orange juice
2 tablespoons honey
1/2 teaspoon Dijon mustard
12 Bibb lettuce leaves
2 medium oranges, peeled, divided into segments, membrane removed and cut into thirds
1/4 cup chopped smoked almonds

① In small bowl, mix orange juice, honey and mustard with fork.

② On each of 4 salad plates, arrange 3 lettuce leaves. Fill lettuce leaves with orange pieces and almonds. Drizzle with orange juice mixture.

High Altitude (3500-6500 ft): No change.

1 SERVING: Calories 130; Total Fat 4.5g (Saturated Fat 0g, Trans Fat 0g); Cholesterol 0mg; Sodium 45mg; Total Carbohydrate 20g (Dietary Fiber 3g); Protein 3g. EXCHANGES: 1 Fruit, 1/2 Other Carbohydrate, 1/2 Fat. CARBOHYDRATE CHOICES: 1.

vegetable confetti

PREP TIME: 10 minutes • START TO FINISH: 10 minutes • MAKES: 4 servings

2 medium carrots, shredded (1-1/2 cups)
1 medium bell pepper, chopped (1 cup)
1 small zucchini, shredded (1 cup)
1/4 cup fat-free Italian dressing
1/4 teaspoon pepper

① In medium glass or plastic bowl, mix all ingredients.
② Refrigerate any remaining salad no longer than 48 hours.

High Altitude (3500-6500 ft): No change.

1 SERVING: Calories 35; Total Fat 0g (Saturated Fat 0g, Trans Fat 0g); Cholesterol 0mg; Sodium 180mg; Total Carbohydrate 9g (Dietary Fiber 2g); Protein 1g. EXCHANGES: 1 Vegetable. CARBOHYDRATE CHOICES: 1/2.

tips&ideas

All bell peppers are a top-notch source of vitamins A and C, but the red and yellow varieties have the most nutrients—more than twice the vitamin C as green!

herb-roasted root vegetables

PREP TIME: 15 minutes • START TO FINISH: 1 hour 10 minutes • MAKES: 6 servings (1/2 cup each)

2 medium turnips, peeled, cut into 1-inch pieces (3 cups)

2 medium parsnips, peeled, cut into 1/2-inch pieces (1-1/2 cups)

1 medium red onion, cut into 1-inch wedges (1 cup)

1 cup ready-to-eat baby-cut carrots

Cooking spray

2 teaspoons Italian seasoning

1/2 teaspoon coarse salt

① Heat oven to 425°F. Spray 15x10x1-inch pan with cooking spray. Arrange vegetables in single layer in pan. Spray with cooking spray (2 or 3 seconds). Sprinkle with Italian seasoning and salt.

② Bake uncovered 45 to 55 minutes, stirring once, until vegetables are tender.

High Altitude (3500-6500 ft): No change.

1 SERVING: Calories 70; Total Fat 0.5g (Saturated Fat 0g, Trans Fat 0g); Cholesterol 0mg; Sodium 260mg; Total Carbohydrate 14g (Dietary Fiber 4g); Protein 1g. EXCHANGES: 1/2 Starch, 1 Vegetable. CARBOHYDRATE CHOICES: 1.

tips&ideas

Roasting brings out the natural sweetness of vegetables. As some of the moisture is evaporated in the high heat, the sugar is concentrated, so it tastes sweeter. Healthwise, roasting is a great way to cook because no fat is added to the dish.

winter fruit waldorf salad

PREP TIME: 25 minutes • START TO FINISH: 25 minutes • MAKES: 16 servings (1 cup each)

2 medium unpeeled red apples, diced
2 medium unpeeled pears, diced
1/2 cup thinly sliced celery
1/2 cup golden raisins
1/2 cup chopped dates
1/4 cup mayonnaise or salad dressing
1/4 cup Yoplait® Original 99% Fat Free orange crème yogurt (from 6-oz container)
2 tablespoons frozen orange juice concentrate
8 cups shredded lettuce
Walnut halves, if desired

① In large bowl, mix apples, pears, celery, raisins and dates.

② In small bowl, mix mayonnaise, yogurt and juice concentrate until well blended. Add to fruit; toss to coat. (Salad can be refrigerated up to 1 hour.) Serve on lettuce. Garnish with walnut halves.

High Altitude (3500-6500 ft): No change.

1 SERVING: Calories 90; Total Fat 3g (Saturated Fat 0g, Trans Fat 0g); Cholesterol 0mg; Sodium 30mg; Total Carbohydrate 16g (Dietary Fiber 2g); Protein 0g. EXCHANGES: 1 Fruit, 1/2 Fat. CARBOHYDRATE CHOICES: 1.

tips&ideas

This refreshing salad is perfect for a holiday meal. Serve it in your prettiest glass bowl, and garnish with orange peel curls. You could substitute or add regular raisins or dried cranberries, if you like.

sausage and cranberry baked stuffing

PREP TIME: 10 minutes • START TO FINISH: 8 hours 55 minutes • MAKES: 12 servings

8 cups lightly packed 3/4-inch cubes French bread
1 lb bulk spicy pork sausage
2 stalks celery (with leaves), chopped (1-1/2 cups)
1 medium onion, chopped (1/2 cup)
1/2 teaspoon dried sage leaves
1/2 cup dried cranberries
1 cup chicken broth
1 cup milk
2 eggs, beaten

tips & ideas

This dish is the perfect side for an unstuffed bird or a turkey breast. Add green beans and a fruit salad for an easy holiday meal.

① Heat oven to 350°F. Spray 13x9-inch glass baking dish with cooking spray. Place bread cubes in baking dish.

② In 10-inch skillet, cook sausage, celery and onion over medium heat, stirring occasionally, until sausage is no longer pink and vegetables are tender; drain.

③ Add sausage mixture, sage and cranberries to baking dish; mix lightly with bread cubes. In medium bowl, beat broth, milk and eggs with fork or wire whisk until well mixed; pour over bread and stir gently to soak all bread cubes in milk mixture. Cover and refrigerate at least 8 hours but no longer than 12 hours.

④ Bake uncovered 35 to 40 minutes or until knife inserted in center comes out clean and top is golden brown.

High Altitude (3500-6500 ft): Use 1-1/2 cups chicken broth. Cover and bake 15 minutes, then uncover and bake 25 to 30 minutes longer.

1 SERVING: Calories 180; Total Fat 8g (Saturated Fat 2.5g, Trans Fat 0g); Cholesterol 50mg; Sodium 480mg; Total Carbohydrate 18g (Dietary Fiber 1g); Protein 8g. EXCHANGES: 1 Starch, 1/2 Vegetable, 1/2 High-Fat Meat, 1 Fat. CARBOHYDRATE CHOICES: 1.

green beans with garlic butter and walnuts

PREP TIME: 20 minutes • START TO FINISH: 20 minutes • MAKES: 8 servings (1/2 cup each)

1 bag (14 oz) Green Giant SELECT® frozen whole
   green beans
2 tablespoons butter or margarine
1 small red bell pepper, cut into very thin strips
1 clove garlic, finely chopped
1/4 cup chopped walnuts or walnut pieces
1/2 teaspoon seasoned salt

① Cook green beans to desired doneness as directed on bag. Drain; cover to keep warm.

② Meanwhile, in 12-inch nonstick skillet, melt butter over medium-high heat. Cook bell pepper and garlic in butter 2 to 4 minutes, stirring constantly, until bell pepper is crisp-tender. Stir in walnuts; cook until hot.

③ Add green beans; sprinkle with seasoned salt. Cook and stir just until thoroughly heated. Spoon into serving dish.

High Altitude (3500-6500 ft): No change.

1 SERVING: Calories 70; Total Fat 5g (Saturated Fat 1.5g, Trans Fat 0g); Cholesterol 10mg; Sodium 110mg; Total Carbohydrate 4g (Dietary Fiber 2g); Protein 1g. EXCHANGES: 1 Vegetable, 1 Fat. CARBOHYDRATE CHOICES: 0.

cherry-cream cheese layered gelatin salad

PREP TIME: 15 minutes • START TO FINISH: 3 hours • MAKES: 8 servings

2 boxes (4-serving size each) cherry-flavored gelatin
1-1/2 cups boiling water
2 cups frozen unsweetened sweet cherries
2 cans (8 oz each) crushed pineapple in juice, undrained
1/2 cup honey-nut cream cheese (from 8-oz container)
Leaf lettuce leaves, if desired

① In large bowl, dissolve gelatin in boiling water, stirring constantly. Stir in frozen cherries until thawed. Stir in pineapple.

② Into ungreased 8-inch square (2-quart) glass baking dish or another serving dish, pour about half of the gelatin mixture. Refrigerate 30 to 45 minutes or until set.

③ Drop cream cheese by small spoonfuls over set gelatin mixture; carefully spread to cover. Pour remaining gelatin mixture over top. Refrigerate at least 2 hours until set. Cut into squares. Serve on lettuce leaves.

High Altitude (3500-6500 ft): No change.

1 SERVING: Calories 190; Total Fat 4.5g (Saturated Fat 3g, Trans Fat 0g); Cholesterol 15mg; Sodium 200mg; Total Carbohydrate 35g (Dietary Fiber 1g); Protein 3g. EXCHANGES: 1 Starch, 1 Other Carbohydrate, 1 Fat. CARBOHYDRATE CHOICES: 2.

tips&ideas

If the room-temperature gelatin for the top layer starts to set up, just microwave it for 10 to 20 seconds. You can make this salad up to 24 hours ahead of time and store in the refrigerator.

green beans with pickled onions

PREP TIME: 25 minutes • START TO FINISH: 25 minutes • MAKES: 4 servings

3 cups fresh green beans, strings removed
1/4 cup cider vinegar
1 tablespoon sugar
1/4 teaspoon salt
1/8 teaspoon pepper
1/2 medium red onion, very thinly sliced
2 teaspoons olive or vegetable oil

① In 2-quart saucepan, heat 1/2 cup water to boiling over high heat. Add green beans; cover and return to boiling. Reduce heat; simmer covered 10 to 12 minutes or until tender. Drain; cool in colander under cold running water.

② Meanwhile, in shallow bowl, stir vinegar, sugar, salt and pepper until sugar is dissolved. Add onion; toss to coat. Let stand 10 minutes, tossing occasionally. Drain, reserving 1 tablespoon vinegar mixture.

③ In medium serving bowl, place beans; top with onion. Drizzle with reserved vinegar mixture and the oil; toss to coat.

High Altitude (3500-6500 ft): No change.

1 SERVING: Calories 70; Total Fat 2.5g (Saturated Fat 0g, Trans Fat 0g); Cholesterol 0mg; Sodium 150mg; Total Carbohydrate 10g (Dietary Fiber 3g); Protein 1g. EXCHANGES: 1/2 Other Carbohydrate, 1 Vegetable, 1/2 Fat. CARBOHYDRATE CHOICES: 1/2.

honeyed carrots

PREP TIME: 25 minutes • START TO FINISH: 25 minutes • MAKES: 4 servings (1/2 cup each)

6 medium carrots (3/4 lb), cut into julienne (matchstick-cut) strips
4 medium green onions, sliced (1/4 cup)
1/3 cup honey
1 tablespoon butter
1 tablespoon lemon juice
1/2 teaspoon salt

① In 10-inch skillet, heat 1 inch water (salted if desired) to boiling. Add carrots. Heat to boiling. Reduce heat; cover and simmer about 5 minutes or until tender. Drain; remove from skillet and set aside.

② In same skillet, cook remaining ingredients over low heat, stirring frequently, until bubbly. Stir in carrots. Cook uncovered 2 to 3 minutes, stirring occasionally, until carrots are glazed.

High Altitude (3500-6500 ft): No change.

1 SERVING: Calories 160; Total Fat 3g (Saturated Fat 2g, Trans Fat 0g); Cholesterol 10mg; Sodium 380mg; Total Carbohydrate 32g (Dietary Fiber 3g); Protein 1g. EXCHANGES: 1-1/2 Other Carbohydrate, 1 Vegetable, 1/2 Fat. CARBOHYDRATE CHOICES: 2.

tips & ideas

If you do not have lemon juice readily available, feel free to substitute orange juice for a different flavor.

brie mashed potatoes

PREP TIME: 30 minutes • START TO FINISH: 1 hour 15 minutes • MAKES: 12 servings (3/4 cup each)

12 medium baking potatoes (about 5 lb), peeled, cut into large pieces
1 cup milk
1/4 cup butter or margarine
1 teaspoon salt
1/2 teaspoon freshly ground pepper
1 package (8 oz) Brie cheese, rind removed, cubed
2 teaspoons chopped fresh thyme leaves

① In 4-quart saucepan or 5-quart Dutch oven, place potatoes; add enough water just to cover potatoes. Heat to boiling. Reduce heat; cover and simmer 20 to 30 minutes or until potatoes are tender when pierced with a fork. Drain.

② Heat oven to 350°F. Spray 2- to 3-quart casserole with cooking spray. In 1-quart saucepan, heat milk, butter, salt and pepper over medium heat, stirring occasionally, until butter is melted. Measure out 1/4 cup milk mixture; set aside.

③ To potatoes, gradually add remaining milk mixture, cubed cheese and thyme, mashing with potato masher or electric mixer on medium speed until light and fluffy. Spoon potatoes into casserole. (Potatoes can be covered and refrigerated up to 24 hours at this point.)

④ Pour reserved 1/4 cup milk mixture over potatoes. Bake uncovered 40 to 45 minutes or until potatoes are hot. Stir potatoes before serving.

High Altitude (3500-6500 ft): Increase milk to 1-1/4 cups.

1 SERVING: Calories 260; Total Fat 10g (Saturated Fat 6g, Trans Fat 0g); Cholesterol 30mg; Sodium 360mg; Total Carbohydrate 35g (Dietary Fiber 4g); Protein 8g. EXCHANGES: 2 Starch, 1/2 High-Fat Meat, 1 Fat. CARBOHYDRATE CHOICES: 2.

tips & ideas

Brie adds a smooth texture and a rich flavor to these creamy mashed potatoes. You can substitute fresh parsley if you do not have fresh thyme on hand.

citrus salad with poppy seed-honey dressing

PREP TIME: 10 minutes • START TO FINISH: 10 minutes • MAKES: 4 servings (1/2 cup each)

2 tablespoons honey
1 teaspoon grated lemon peel
4 teaspoons lemon juice
1/2 teaspoon poppy seed
3 clementines or tangerines, peeled, divided into segments
1 red grapefruit, peeled, divided into segments
1 kiwifruit, peeled, sliced and slices cut in half

① In small bowl, mix honey, lemon peel, lemon juice and poppy seed.

② Remove membrane from clementine and grapefruit segments if desired. Cut each section into bite-size pieces.

③ In small serving bowl, mix clementines, grapefruit, kiwifruit and honey mixture.

High Altitude (3500-6500 ft): No change.

1 SERVING: Calories 100; Total Fat 0g (Saturated Fat 0g, Trans Fat 0g); Cholesterol 0mg; Sodium 0mg; Total Carbohydrate 23g (Dietary Fiber 2g); Protein 1g. EXCHANGES: 1 Fruit, 1/2 Other Carbohydrate. CARBOHYDRATE CHOICES: 1-1/2.

tips&ideas

To prepare citrus fruits, cut a slice off the top and bottom of the fruit. With a paring knife, slice off peel from top to bottom, removing membrane. To section, slide the paring knife between membrane and flesh to center of fruit; repeat on other side of section. Remove flesh.

roasted vegetables

PREP TIME: 15 minutes • **START TO FINISH:** 45 minutes • **MAKES:** 10 servings

3 tablespoons olive or vegetable oil
1/2 teaspoon salt
1/8 teaspoon pepper
1 clove garlic, finely chopped
1 cup baby-cut carrots
6 small red potatoes, cut into fourths
2 small onions, cut into 1/2-inch wedges
1 small red bell pepper, cut into 1-inch pieces
1 medium zucchini, cut lengthwise in half, then cut crosswise into 1-inch slices
1 cup grape tomatoes or cherry tomatoes

① Heat oven to 450°F.

② In small bowl, stir oil, salt, pepper and garlic until well mixed. In 15x10x1-inch pan, toss carrots, potatoes, onions, bell pepper and zucchini with oil mixture until coated.

③ Bake uncovered 20 to 25 minutes, carefully stirring mixture once after 15 minutes.

④ Stir in tomatoes. Bake about 5 minutes longer or until vegetables are tender and starting to brown.

High Altitude (3500-6500 ft): No change.

1 SERVING: Calories 100; Total Fat 4-1/2g (Saturated Fat 1/2g, Trans Fat 0g); Cholesterol 0mg; Sodium 130mg; Total Carbohydrate 16g (Dietary Fiber 3g); Protein 2g. EXCHANGES: 1/2 Starch, 1 Vegetable, 1 Fat. CARBOHYDRATE CHOICES: 1.

tips&ideas

For your safety, remove the pan of vegetables from the oven when it's time to stir. Then place the pan on a heatproof surface, and close the oven door to retain heat.

broccoli with sweet red pepper and garlic

PREP TIME: 20 minutes • **START TO FINISH:** 20 minutes • **MAKES:** 4 servings (1/2 cup each)

1 tablespoon olive or vegetable oil
2 cloves garlic, finely chopped
2 cups broccoli florets
1 large red bell pepper, coarsely chopped (1 cup)
1 small onion, coarsely chopped (1/2 cup)
3 tablespoons water
1/4 teaspoon salt
2 tablespoons shredded Parmesan cheese

1 In 12-inch nonstick skillet, heat oil over medium-high heat.

2 Stir garlic into hot oil. Immediately add broccoli, bell pepper, onion and water. Cook 4 to 6 minutes, stirring constantly, until broccoli is crisp-tender and onion is beginning to brown. Stir in salt.

3 Place in serving dish; top with cheese.

High Altitude (3500-6500 ft): No change.

1 SERVING: Calories 80; Total Fat 4.5g (Saturated Fat 1g, Trans Fat 0g); Cholesterol 0mg; Sodium 220mg; Total Carbohydrate 7g (Dietary Fiber 3g); Protein 3g. EXCHANGES: 1 Vegetable, 1 Fat. CARBOHYDRATE CHOICES: 1/2.

christmas salad with balsamic vinaigrette

PREP TIME: 20 minutes • **START TO FINISH:** 20 minutes • **MAKES:** 6 servings

BALSAMIC VINAIGRETTE
- 1/3 cup olive or vegetable oil
- 1/4 cup balsamic vinegar
- 2 tablespoons sugar
- 1 clove garlic, finely chopped
- 1 teaspoon Dijon mustard

SALAD
- 1 bag (10 ounces) mixed baby greens or Italian-blend salad greens
- 1 avocado, pitted, peeled and sliced
- 1/3 cup pistachio nuts
- 1/4 cup dried cranberries

① In small bowl, beat all Balsamic Vinaigrette ingredients with wire whisk until smooth.

② In serving bowl, toss vinaigrette and all salad ingredients just before serving.

VARIATION 1: 2 cups quartered strawberries, 1 package (4 ounces) goat cheese crumbles, 1/3 cup slivered almonds, toasted.

VARIATION 2: 1 medium green apple, chopped (1 cup), 4 ounces Gorgonzola or blue cheese, crumbled (1/2 cup), 1/3 cup walnuts, toasted.

VARIATION 3: 2 cups sliced fresh mushrooms, 1-1/2 cups grape tomatoes, cut in half, 1/3 cup finely sliced purple onion.

High Altitude (3500-6500 ft): No change.

1 SERVING: Calories 235; Total Fat 20g (Saturated Fat 3g, Trans Fat nc); Cholesterol 0mg; Sodium 35mg; Total Carbohydrate 14g (Dietary Fiber 3g); Protein 3g. EXCHANGES: 3 Vegetable, 3-1/2 Fat. CARBOHYDRATE CHOICES: nc.

tips & ideas

To toast nuts, heat oven to 350°F. Spread nuts in ungreased shallow pan. Bake for about 10 minutes, stirring occasionally, until golden brown and fragrant. Watch nuts carefully because they will brown quickly. Or cook nuts in ungreased heavy skillet over medium-low heat for 5 to 7 minutes, stirring frequently until browning begins, then stirring constantly until they are golden brown and fragrant.

italian cauliflower

PREP TIME: 10 minutes • START TO FINISH: 10 minutes • MAKES: 6 servings (1/2 cup each)

4 cups fresh cauliflowerets
2 tablespoons water
2 teaspoons olive or vegetable oil
2 tablespoons Progresso® Italian style dry bread crumbs
1 teaspoon dried basil leaves
1 tablespoon chopped fresh parsley

① In medium microwavable bowl, cover and microwave cauliflower and water on High about 6 minutes, stirring once after 3 minutes, until tender; drain.

② Meanwhile, in 7-inch skillet, heat oil over medium heat. Stir in bread crumbs and basil. Cook 1 to 2 minutes, stirring frequently, until bread crumbs are toasted. Stir in parsley. Sprinkle over cauliflower.

High Altitude (3500-6500 ft): No change.

1 SERVING: Calories 40; Total Fat 2g (Saturated Fat 0g, Trans Fat 0g); Cholesterol 0mg; Sodium 40mg; Total Carbohydrate 5g (Dietary Fiber 2g); Protein 2g. EXCHANGES: 1 Vegetable, 1/2 Fat. CARBOHYDRATE CHOICES: 0.

sage roasted potatoes

PREP TIME: 15 minutes • START TO FINISH: 1 hour 10 minutes • MAKES: 8 servings (6 slices each)

3 tablespoons olive or vegetable oil
1 teaspoon dried sage leaves
1/2 teaspoon seasoned salt
1/2 teaspoon garlic pepper blend
1/2 teaspoon paprika
6 medium unpeeled Yukon gold potatoes, each cut into 8 lengthwise slices

① Heat oven to 425°F. Spray 15x10x1-inch pan with cooking spray. In large bowl, mix all ingredients except potatoes. Add potatoes; toss to coat. Spread in pan.

② Roast uncovered 30 to 40 minutes, turning and stirring after about 20 minutes, until potatoes are tender.

High Altitude (3500-6500 ft): No change.

1 SERVING: Calories 130; Total Fat 5g (Saturated Fat 0.5g, Trans Fat 0g); Cholesterol 0mg; Sodium 95mg; Total Carbohydrate 20g (Dietary Fiber 2g); Protein 2g. EXCHANGES: 1 Starch, 1 Fat. CARBOHYDRATE CHOICES: 1.

acorn squash with dates

PREP TIME: 5 minutes • **START TO FINISH:** 25 minutes • **MAKES:** 4 servings

1 acorn squash (1-1/2 to 2 lb)
2 tablespoons chopped dates or raisins
1 tablespoon packed brown sugar
1-1/2 teaspoons no-trans-fat vegetable oil spread

(1) Pierce squash with knife in several places to allow steam to escape. Place on microwavable paper towel in microwave oven. Microwave uncovered about 5 minutes or until squash feels warm to the touch. Cut in half; remove seeds.

(2) In shallow microwavable dish, place squash halves, cut sides down. Cover with microwavable plastic wrap, folding back one edge or corner about 1/4 inch to vent steam. Microwave on High 5 to 8 minutes, rotating dish every 2 minutes, until tender. Let stand 5 minutes.

(3) In small bowl, mix remaining ingredients. Turn squash cut sides up. Spoon date mixture into centers of squash. Microwave uncovered on High about 1 minute or until sugar is melted. Cut each squash half into 2 serving pieces.

High Altitude (3500-6500 ft): No change.

1 SERVING: Calories 45; Total Fat 1.5g (Saturated Fat 0g, Trans Fat 0g); Cholesterol 0mg; Sodium 20mg; Total Carbohydrate 7g (Dietary Fiber 0g); Protein 0g. EXCHANGES: 1 Vegetable. CARBOHYDRATE CHOICES: 1/2.

peas and corn with thyme-butter

PREP TIME: 20 minutes • START TO FINISH: 20 minutes • MAKES: 6 servings (1/2 cup each)

3 slices bacon, cut into 1/2-inch pieces
2 cups Green Giant SELECT® frozen baby sweet peas
2 cups Green Giant® Niblets® frozen extra-sweet whole kernel corn (from 1-lb bag)
2 tablespoons water
1/4 teaspoon salt
1/4 to 1/2 teaspoon dried thyme leaves
2 tablespoons butter or margarine

1 In 12-inch nonstick skillet, cook bacon over medium heat, stirring frequently, until crisp. Remove bacon from skillet; drain on paper towel. Reserve 1 tablespoon drippings in skillet; discard any remaining drippings.

2 Add peas, corn and water to skillet. Cover and cook over medium heat 6 to 8 minutes, stirring occasionally, until vegetables are tender and water has evaporated.

3 Stir in salt, thyme and butter until vegetables are coated. Spoon into serving bowl. Sprinkle with bacon.

High Altitude (3500-6500 ft): No change.

1 SERVING: Calories 160; Total Fat 8g (Saturated Fat 3.5g, Trans Fat 0g); Cholesterol 15mg; Sodium 220mg; Total Carbohydrate 16g (Dietary Fiber 3g); Protein 5g. EXCHANGES: 1 Starch, 1-1/2 Fat. CARBOHYDRATE CHOICES: 1.

twice-baked sweet potatoes

PREP TIME: 25 minutes • START TO FINISH: 1 hour 15 minutes • MAKES: 6 servings

6 small dark-orange sweet potatoes
    (5 to 6 oz each)
2 tablespoons Gold Medal® all-purpose flour
2 tablespoons packed brown sugar
2 tablespoons butter or margarine, softened
1/4 cup chopped pecans
2 tablespoons butter or margarine, softened
2 tablespoons half-and-half
1 teaspoon pumpkin pie spice
1/4 teaspoon salt

① Pierce each potato twice with point of sharp knife to vent steam. Place in single layer in microwave oven. Microwave on High 5 minutes. If potatoes are not cooked through, turn potatoes over and continue microwaving for 1 minute at a time until softened. Remove any fully cooked potatoes from microwave while cooking remaining potatoes. Cool potatoes about 10 minutes.

② Meanwhile, in small bowl, mix flour, brown sugar, 2 tablespoons butter and the pecans; set aside.

③ Heat oven to 350°F. Cut off top 1/3 of each potato. Using spoon, scoop flesh into large bowl, being careful not to tear potato skins; discard potato tops. Add 2 tablespoons butter, half-and-half, pumpkin pie spice and salt to potatoes. Mash potato mixture with potato masher or beat with electric mixer on medium speed until creamy. Spoon potato mixture back into skins. Place filled potatoes in 13x9-inch pan. (Potatoes can be covered and refrigerated at this point up to 8 hours.)

④ Sprinkle pecan mixture over tops of potatoes. Bake uncovered 30 to 35 minutes or until topping is brown and potatoes are hot. (If filled potatoes were refrigerated, remove from refrigerator 30 minutes before serving; top and bake as directed.)

High Altitude (3500-6500 ft): No change.

1 SERVING: Calories 250; Total Fat 12g (Saturated Fat 4.5g, Trans Fat 0g); Cholesterol 20mg; Sodium 160mg; Total Carbohydrate 34g (Dietary Fiber 4g); Protein 3g.
EXCHANGES: 1 Starch, 1 Other Carbohydrate, 2-1/2 Fat.
CARBOHYDRATE CHOICES: 2.

tips&ideas

Prepare 2-1/4 pounds large sweet potatoes as directed, but bake mashed mixture topped with pecan mixture in a 2-quart casserole instead of filling the potato skins.

balsamic green beans and fennel

PREP TIME: 20 minutes • **START TO FINISH:** 20 minutes • **MAKES:** 4 servings (about 3/4 cup each)

2 teaspoons olive or canola oil
1 medium bulb fennel, cut into thin wedges
1 small onion, cut into thin wedges
2 cups Green Giant® SELECT® frozen whole green beans
1/4 cup water
2 teaspoons packed brown sugar
1/4 teaspoon salt
1/4 teaspoon freshly ground black pepper
1 tablespoon balsamic vinegar

① In 12-inch nonstick skillet, heat oil over medium heat. Add fennel and onion; cook 7 to 8 minutes, stirring frequently, until fennel is light golden brown.

② Add beans and water; heat to boiling. Stir; reduce heat to low. Cover; simmer 6 to 8 minutes or until beans are crisp-tender.

③ Stir in remaining ingredients; cook and stir 15 to 30 seconds longer or until vegetables are coated.

High Altitude (3500-6500 ft): No change.

1 SERVING: Calories 80; Total Fat 2.5g (Saturated Fat 0g, Trans Fat 0g); Cholesterol 0mg; Sodium 180mg; Total Carbohydrate 13g (Dietary Fiber 4g); Protein 2g. EXCHANGES: 1/2 Other Carbohydrate, 1 Vegetable, 1/2 Fat. CARBOHYDRATE CHOICES: 1.

tips&ideas

Fennel is cultivated in the Mediterranean and in the United States. Both the bulb and the stems can be eaten raw or cooked. The flavor is a little bit like anise but sweeter and more delicate. The feathery greenery can be used as a garnish or snipped like dill weed and used for a last-minute flavor enhancer.

twice-baked potato casserole

PREP TIME: 15 minutes • **START TO FINISH:** 55 minutes • **MAKES:** 14 servings (1/2 cup each)

6 medium baking potatoes (2-1/2 to 3 lb),
  peeled, cut into fourths
1/2 cup milk, heated
1 teaspoon salt
1/8 teaspoon pepper
1/2 cup sour cream
3 tablespoons chopped fresh chives
1-1/2 cups finely shredded Cheddar cheese (6 oz)

① In 4-quart saucepan, place potato pieces and add enough water to cover. Heat to boiling; reduce heat to medium-low. Cook uncovered 15 to 20 minutes or until tender. Drain and return to saucepan.

② Heat potatoes over low heat about 1 minute to dry potatoes, shaking pan often to keep potatoes from sticking and burning. (This will help make mashed potatoes fluffy.)

③ Heat oven to 350°F. Spray 8-inch square (2-quart) glass baking dish with cooking spray. Add milk, salt and pepper to potatoes. Mash with potato masher until no lumps remain. Beat in sour cream, chives and 1/2 cup of the cheese. Spoon into baking dish. Sprinkle with remaining 1 cup cheese.

④ Bake uncovered 10 to 15 minutes or until thoroughly heated and cheese is melted.

DO-AHEAD DIRECTIONS: After beating sour cream, chives and 1/2 cup of the cheese into mashed potatoes, spoon into baking dish. Cover with foil; refrigerate up to 24 hours. Bake covered 30 minutes. Sprinkle with remaining 1 cup cheese. Bake uncovered 10 to 15 minutes longer or until thoroughly heated.

High Altitude (3500-6500 ft): In Step 3, do not sprinkle with remaining 1 cup cheese. In Step 4, bake 25 minutes; sprinkle with remaining cheese. Bake 5 minutes longer or until cheese is melted.

1 SERVING: Calories 130; Total Fat 6g (Saturated Fat 3.5g, Trans Fat 0g); Cholesterol 20mg; Sodium 250mg; Total Carbohydrate 16g (Dietary Fiber 2g); Protein 5g. EXCHANGES: 1 Starch, 1 Fat. CARBOHYDRATE CHOICES: 1.

tips&ideas

It is best not to use your electric mixer to mash the potatoes; they can quickly become gummy instead of smooth and creamy.

peas and onions alfredo

PREP TIME: 5 minutes • START TO FINISH: 15 minutes • MAKES: 6 servings

2 packages (9 oz each) Green Giant® frozen
    sweet peas & pearl onions
1 jar (2 oz) diced pimientos, drained
1/2 cup Alfredo pasta sauce (from 1-lb jar)
2 tablespoons shredded fresh Parmesan cheese

① Cook peas and onions as directed on
package.
② Place peas and onions in serving bowl. Stir in
pimientos and Alfredo sauce. Sprinkle with
shredded cheese.

VARIATION: If your family doesn't care for
onions, use two 9-ounce packages of frozen
Green Giant® Simply Steam® baby sweet peas.

High Altitude (3500-6500 ft): No change.

1 SERVING: Calories 125; Total Fat 7g (Saturated Fat
4g, Trans Fat nc); Cholesterol 20mg; Sodium 160mg;
Total Carbohydrate 10g (Dietary Fiber 3g); Protein 5g,
EXCHANGES: nc. CARBOHYDRATE CHOICES: 1/2.

green beans with glazed shallots in lemon-dill butter

PREP TIME: 15 minutes • START TO FINISH: 15 minutes • MAKES: 6 servings (about 1/2 cup each)

1 lb fresh green beans, trimmed
2 tablespoons butter
2 shallots, finely chopped
1/2 teaspoon sugar
1 teaspoon lemon juice
1 tablespoon chopped fresh dill weed
1/4 teaspoon salt

① In 4-quart Dutch oven, heat 1 to 2 inches water to boiling. Add beans; boil uncovered 8 to 10 minutes or until crisp-tender. Drain; return to Dutch oven.

② Meanwhile, in 10-inch skillet, melt butter over medium heat. Add shallots; cook 2 to 3 minutes, stirring occasionally, until crisp-tender. Stir in sugar. Cook 2 to 3 minutes longer, stirring occasionally, until shallots are glazed and brown. Stir in lemon juice, dill weed and salt.

③ Add shallot mixture to green beans; toss to coat.

High Altitude (3500-6500 ft): No change.

1 SERVING: Calories 60; Total Fat 4g (Saturated Fat 2.5g, Trans Fat 0g); Cholesterol 10mg; Sodium 130mg; Total Carbohydrate 5g (Dietary Fiber 2g); Protein 1g. EXCHANGES: 1 Vegetable, 1 Fat. CARBOHYDRATE CHOICES: 1/2.

tips&ideas

Shallots look like mini onions and taste like a mild mix of garlic and onion. You can usually find them near the onions in the produce section of the supermarket.

two-cheese potato gratin

PREP TIME: 30 minutes • START TO FINISH: 1 hour 35 minutes • MAKES: 12 servings (1/2 cup each)

1/2 cup butter or margarine
1/2 cup Gold Medal® all-purpose flour
3 cups milk
1 tablespoon Dijon mustard
1/2 teaspoon salt
10 cups thinly sliced (about 1/8 inch) Yukon gold potatoes (about 3 lb)
1-1/2 cups shredded Gruyère cheese (6 oz)
1-1/2 cups shredded Cheddar cheese (6 oz)

① Heat oven to 350°F. Grease 13x9-inch (3-quart) glass baking dish with shortening or cooking spray.

② In 2-quart saucepan, melt butter over medium heat. Stir in flour with wire whisk until smooth. Gradually stir in milk. Heat to boiling. Reduce heat to low; cook about 5 minutes, stirring frequently, until sauce is slightly thickened. Stir in mustard and salt.

③ Place half of the potatoes in baking dish; top with half of the sauce and half of each of the cheeses. Repeat layers.

④ Bake 50 to 55 minutes or until potatoes are tender and top is golden brown. Let stand 5 to 10 minutes before serving.

High Altitude (3500-6500 ft): Be sure to slice potatoes about 1/8 inch thick. In step 4, bake 1 hour to 1 hour 5 minutes.

1 SERVING: Calories 330; Total Fat 18g (Saturated Fat 11g, Trans Fat 0.5g); Cholesterol 55mg; Sodium 350mg; Total Carbohydrate 29g (Dietary Fiber 3g); Protein 12g. EXCHANGES: 1-1/2 Starch, 1/2 Other Carbohydrate, 1 High-Fat Meat, 2 Fat. CARBOHYDRATE CHOICES: 2.

tips&ideas

Yukon gold potatoes, with a yellow-gold color and creamy texture, hold their shape without being waxy.

company broccoli three-cheese bake

PREP TIME: 10 minutes • **START TO FINISH:** 1 hour • **MAKES:** 14 servings (1/2 cup each)

1 can (2.8 oz) French-fried onions
2 bags (24 oz each) Green Giant® frozen
  broccoli & three cheese sauce
1 package (3 oz) cream cheese, cut into cubes
1/4 cup chopped red bell pepper, if desired
1/2 teaspoon red pepper sauce

(1) Heat oven to 350°F. Reserve 1 cup French-fried onions for topping.

(2) In 5-quart Dutch oven, mix remaining onions, the broccoli, cream cheese, bell pepper and red pepper sauce. Cover; cook over medium-low heat about 20 minutes, stirring once halfway through cooking, until sauce chips are melted. Gently transfer to ungreased 2- to 3-quart casserole.

(3) Bake uncovered 20 to 25 minutes or until vegetables are tender. Sprinkle reserved onions around outer edge of casserole; bake 5 minutes longer.

High Altitude (3500-6500 ft): Heat oven to 375°F. In Step 2, cover and cook over medium heat 20 to 25 minutes, stirring every 5 minutes. In Step 3, bake 25 to 30 minutes.

1 SERVING: Calories 110; Total Fat 6g (Saturated Fat 2.5g, Trans Fat 1g); Cholesterol 10mg; Sodium 430mg; Total Carbohydrate 9g (Dietary Fiber 2g); Protein 3g. EXCHANGES: 1/2 Other Carbohydrate, 1 Vegetable, 1 Fat. CARBOHYDRATE CHOICES: 1/2.

green beans with lemon-herb butter

PREP TIME: 10 minutes • **START TO FINISH:** 20 minutes • **MAKES:** 4 servings

1 bag (12 oz) Green Giant® Fresh green beans
3 tablespoons butter (do not use margarine)
1 teaspoon grated lemon peel
1 teaspoon dried marjoram leaves
1/4 teaspoon salt
Lemon slices, if desired

① Cook green beans as directed on bag; drain.
② Meanwhile, in 2-quart saucepan, heat butter over medium heat until melted and beginning to brown; immediately remove from heat. Stir in lemon peel, marjoram and salt. Pour over beans; toss to coat. Garnish with lemon slices.

High Altitude (3500-6500 ft): No change.

1 SERVING: Calories 100; Total Fat 9g (Saturated Fat 4.5g, Trans Fat 0.5g); Cholesterol 25mg; Sodium 210mg; Total Carbohydrate 5g (Dietary Fiber 2g); Protein 1g. EXCHANGES: 1 Vegetable, 2 Fat. CARBOHYDRATE CHOICES: 1/2.

apple-gorgonzola salad with red wine vinaigrette

PREP TIME: 20 minutes • START TO FINISH: 20 minutes • MAKES: 6 servings

RED WINE VINAIGRETTE
- 1/3 cup olive or vegetable oil
- 1/4 cup red wine vinegar
- 2 tablespoons sugar
- 1 teaspoon Dijon mustard
- 1 clove garlic, finely chopped

SALAD
- 1 bag (10 oz) mixed baby greens or Italian-blend salad greens
- 1 medium red or green apple, chopped (1 cup)
- 1/2 cup crumbled Gorgonzola or blue cheese (2 oz)
- 1/3 cup chopped walnuts, toasted

① In small bowl, beat vinaigrette ingredients with wire whisk until smooth.

② In large bowl, toss salad ingredients with vinaigrette just before serving.

High Altitude (3500-6500 ft): No change.

1 SERVING: Calories 230; Total Fat 19g (Saturated Fat 4g, Trans Fat 0g); Cholesterol 5mg; Sodium 170mg; Total Carbohydrate 10g (Dietary Fiber 2g); Protein 4g. EXCHANGES: 1/2 Other Carbohydrate, 1/2 High-Fat Meat, 3 Fat. CARBOHYDRATE CHOICES: 1/2.

tips&ideas

This refreshing vinaigrette can be made up to 2 days ahead of time. Cover tightly and refrigerate until serving time.

asian tossed salad

PREP TIME: 20 minutes • **START TO FINISH:** 20 minutes • **MAKES:** 5 servings (1 cup each)

3 cups shredded romaine lettuce
1-1/2 cups (from 16-oz bag) coleslaw mix
(shredded cabbage and carrots)
1 cup fresh sugar snap peas, trimmed
1/2 cup shredded carrots
1/4 cup very thinly sliced red onion
1/4 cup fat-free mayonnaise or salad dressing
1/4 cup Chinese chicken salad dressing
1 tablespoon honey
2 tablespoons slivered almonds

(1) In large bowl, mix lettuce, coleslaw mix, peas, carrots and onion.

(2) In small bowl, mix mayonnaise, salad dressing and honey with wire whisk until smooth.

(3) Add dressing mixture to salad; toss to mix. Sprinkle with almonds.

High Altitude (3500-6500 ft): No change.

1 SERVING: Calories 110; Total Fat 6g (Saturated Fat 1g, Trans Fat 0g); Cholesterol 0mg; Sodium 240mg; Total Carbohydrate 12g (Dietary Fiber 2g); Protein 2g. EXCHANGES: 1/2 Other Carbohydrate, 1 Vegetable, 1 Fat. CARBOHYDRATE CHOICES: 1.

tips&ideas

If you can't find Chinese dressing, you can make your own by mixing 1/4 cup mayonnaise, 3 tablespoons citrus vinaigrette dressing, 1 tablespoon soy sauce and 1 tablespoon honey. For the best results, toss the dressing with the salad ingredients just before serving.

pomegranate and citrus broccoli salad

PREP TIME: 20 minutes • **START TO FINISH:** 20 minutes • **MAKES:** 9 servings (1/2 cup each)

1/2 cup mayonnaise or salad dressing

1/4 cup orange juice

1 teaspoon sugar

1/2 teaspoon salt

Dash of pepper

3 cups coarsely chopped broccoli florets (about 8 oz)

1 medium orange, peeled, cut into bite-size chunks (about 1 cup)

3/4 cup pomegranate seeds (from 1 pomegranate) or sweetened dried cranberries

1/3 cup roasted salted sunflower nuts

2 tablespoons sliced red onion

① In large serving bowl, mix mayonnaise, orange juice, sugar, salt and pepper.

② Add remaining ingredients; toss until well coated. Store covered in refrigerator.

High Altitude (3500-6500 ft): No change.

1 SERVING: Calories 150; Total Fat 13g (Saturated Fat 2g, Trans Fat 0g); Cholesterol 5mg; Sodium 240mg; Total Carbohydrate 7g (Dietary Fiber 2g); Protein 2g. EXCHANGES: 1/2 Other Carbohydrate, 2-1/2 Fat. CARBOHYDRATE CHOICES: 1/2.

apricot-glazed carrots

PREP TIME: 10 minutes • START TO FINISH: 10 hours 25 minutes • MAKES: 10 servings (1/2 cup each)

2 pounds baby-cut carrots
1 medium onion, cut in half and sliced
1/4 teaspoon salt
1/3 cup honey
1/3 cup apricot preserves
2 tablespoons chopped fresh parsley

① Place carrots and onion in 4- to 5-quart slow cooker. Sprinkle with salt.

② Cover and cook on Low heat setting 9 to 10 hours.

③ Discard liquid in cooker. Mix honey and preserves in small bowl; pour over carrots in cooker. Increase heat setting to High. Cover and cook 10 to 15 minutes or until hot. Sprinkle with parsley before serving. Carrots will hold on Low heat setting up to 2 hours; stir occasionally.

VARIATION: Peach, plum, pineapple or another flavor of preserves will lend these carrots a subtly different yet equally delicious fruit flavor.

High Altitude (3500-6500 ft): No change.

1 SERVING: Calories 110; Total Fat 0g (Saturated Fat 0g, Trans Fat 0g); Cholesterol 0mg; Sodium 95mg; Total Carbohydrate 27g (Dietary Fiber 3g); Protein 1g. EXCHANGES: 1-1/2 Other Carbohydrate, 1 Vegetable. CARBOHYDRATE CHOICES: 2.

tips&ideas

Carrots that are about the same size cook more evenly, so cut the thicker baby carrots lengthwise in half. Your results will be better.

spanish olive salad

PREP TIME: 15 minutes • START TO FINISH: 15 minutes • MAKES: 8 servings

About 1-1/2 heads red leaf lettuce, torn into bite-size pieces (8 cups tightly packed)

2 large oranges, peeled, sliced

1/3 cup assorted marinated olives, pitted

1/2 small red onion, thinly sliced into rings (about 1/2 cup)

1/2 cup balsamic vinaigrette dressing

① Divide lettuce among 8 salad plates. Top with orange slices, olives and onion rings.

② Just before serving, drizzle dressing over the salads.

High Altitude (3500-6500 ft): No change.

1 SERVING: Calories 100; Total Fat 8g (Saturated Fat 1g, Trans Fat 0g); Cholesterol 0mg; Sodium 250mg; Total Carbohydrate 7g (Dietary Fiber 2g); Protein 0g. EXCHANGES: 1 Vegetable, 1-1/2 Fat. CARBOHYDRATE CHOICES: 1/2.

mixed greens salad with warm walnut dressing

PREP TIME: 15 minutes • START TO FINISH: 15 minutes • MAKES: 8 servings

12 cups mixed field greens (about 10 oz)

3/4 cup olive or vegetable oil

1 cup walnut halves

6 tablespoons red wine vinegar

1/2 teaspoon salt

① Divide field greens among 8 salad bowls.

② Place 2 tablespoons of the oil in medium microwavable bowl. Add walnut halves; stir to coat. Microwave uncovered on High 2 minutes 30 seconds to 3 minutes, stirring about every 30 seconds, until walnuts are fragrant.

③ Stir in remaining oil and the vinegar. Microwave uncovered on High about 30 seconds or until dressing is warm but not boiling. Add salt; stir until dressing is well mixed. Pour over salads. Serve immediately.

High Altitude (3500-6500 ft): No change.

1 SERVING: Calories 280; Total Fat 28g (Saturated Fat 3.5g, Trans Fat 0g); Cholesterol 0mg; Sodium 160mg; Total Carbohydrate 3g (Dietary Fiber 1g); Protein 2g. EXCHANGES: 1/2 High-Fat Meat, 5 Fat. CARBOHYDRATE CHOICES: 0.

p. 124

p. 123

merry main dishes

Celebrate with the season's best entrees, from gorgeous stuffed turkeys to succulent beef tenderloins and more.

parsley, sage, rosemary and thyme turkey breast

PREP TIME: 10 minutes • **START TO FINISH:** 2 hours 40 minutes • **MAKES:** 8 servings

1/4 cup chopped fresh parsley
1 teaspoon dried sage leaves
1 teaspoon dried rosemary leaves, crushed
1 teaspoon dried thyme leaves
1 teaspoon salt
1/2 teaspoon pepper
1 bone-in whole turkey breast (5 to 6 lb)

1 Heat oven to 325°F. In small bowl, mix all ingredients except turkey. Gently lift skin slightly from turkey breast and pat seasoning mixture evenly over flesh. Pat skin down over seasoning mixture.

2 On rack in shallow roasting pan, place turkey breast. Insert ovenproof meat thermometer so tip is in thickest part of breast and does not touch bone. Roast uncovered 1 hour 45 minutes to 2 hours 30 minutes or until thermometer reads 170°F.

3 Cover with foil tent; let stand 10 minutes before carving. Remove skin before serving.

High Altitude (3500-6500 ft): No change.

1 SERVING: Calories 310; Total Fat 13g (Saturated Fat 3.5g, Trans Fat 0g); Cholesterol 130mg; Sodium 410mg; Total Carbohydrate 0g (Dietary Fiber 0g); Protein 48g. EXCHANGES: 4 Very Lean Meat, 3 Lean Meat. CARBOHYDRATE CHOICES: 0.

peppered beef tenderloin with mushroom sauce

PREP TIME: 25 minutes • START TO FINISH: 1 hour 30 minutes • MAKES: 12 servings (with 1/4 cup sauce each)

4 to 4-1/2 lb beef tenderloin roast
2 tablespoons olive or vegetable oil
2 teaspoons coarse ground black pepper
1/4 cup butter or margarine
1 medium onion, finely chopped (1/2 cup)
1 clove garlic, finely chopped
1 package (8 oz) sliced fresh mushrooms (3 cups)
2 tablespoons dry sherry, if desired
1 tablespoon cornstarch
1/4 cup cold water
2 teaspoons chopped fresh or 1/2 teaspoon dried thyme leaves
1/8 teaspoon pepper
1 can (10-1/2 oz) condensed beef consommé
1 teaspoon Dijon mustard
1 teaspoon tomato paste (from 6-oz can)

① Heat oven to 425°F. Rub beef with oil; sprinkle with pepper. Place beef on rack in shallow roasting pan, or place diagonally in 15x10x1-inch pan. Insert ovenproof meat thermometer so tip is in center of thickest part of beef.

② Bake uncovered 30 to 45 minutes or until thermometer reads 135°F. Cover beef loosely with tent of foil and let stand 15 to 20 minutes until thermometer reads 145°F (medium-rare doneness). (Temperature will continue to rise about 10°F and beef will be easier to carve.)

③ Meanwhile, in 12-inch nonstick skillet, melt butter over medium heat. Cook onion, garlic and mushrooms in butter 8 to 10 minutes, stirring occasionally, until mushrooms are completely tender and beginning to brown. Stir in sherry. In small bowl, mix cornstarch and water; slowly stir cornstarch mixture into mushroom mixture. Stir in thyme, pepper and beef consommé; cook and stir about 2 minutes or until slightly thickened and bubbly. Stir in mustard and tomato paste until well blended. Heat just until hot. Spoon sauce over sliced beef.

High Altitude (3500-6500 ft): In Step 3, increase second cook time to 4 minutes.

1 SERVING: Calories 270; Total Fat 15g (Saturated Fat 6g, Trans Fat 0.5g); Cholesterol 85mg; Sodium 240mg; Total Carbohydrate 3g (Dietary Fiber 0g); Protein 30g. EXCHANGES: 4-1/2 Lean Meat, 1/2 Fat. CARBOHYDRATE CHOICES: 0.

tips&ideas

Make the sauce up to a day ahead, then cover and refrigerate. Stir sauce; cover and microwave on High for 1 minute or until hot. Stir again.

basil salmon and julienne vegetables

PREP TIME: 15 minutes • **START TO FINISH:** 25 minutes • **MAKES:** 4 servings

Cooking spray
- 1 teaspoon olive, canola or soybean oil
- 1 bag (1 lb) frozen bell pepper and onion stir-fry
- 1 medium zucchini, cut into julienne (matchstick-size) strips
- 1 salmon fillet (1 lb), cut into 4 pieces
- 2 tablespoons chopped fresh basil leaves
- 1/2 teaspoon seasoned salt
- 1 teaspoon lemon-pepper seasoning
- 1/4 cup Progresso® chicken broth (from 32-oz carton)

① Spray 12-inch skillet with cooking spray; add oil and heat over medium heat. Add bell pepper stir-fry; cook 2 minutes, stirring occasionally. Stir in zucchini.

② Place salmon, skin side down, in skillet, pushing down into vegetables if necessary. Sprinkle salmon and vegetables with basil, seasoned salt and lemon-pepper seasoning. Pour broth over salmon and vegetables.

③ Reduce heat to medium-low. Cover; cook 8 to 10 minutes or until salmon flakes easily with fork. Remove salmon and vegetables from skillet with slotted spoon.

High Altitude (3500-6500 ft): No change.

1 SERVING: Calories 210; Total Fat 7g (Saturated Fat 2g, Trans Fat 0g); Cholesterol 65mg; Sodium 390mg; Total Carbohydrate 12g (Dietary Fiber 2g); Protein 23g. EXCHANGES: 1/2 Other Carbohydrate, 1 Vegetable, 3 Lean Meat. CARBOHYDRATE CHOICES: 1.

pork loin with apricot-rosemary glaze

PREP TIME: 10 minutes • **START TO FINISH:** 1 hour 50 minutes • **MAKES:** 10 servings

3 lb pork loin roast
1 teaspoon salt
1/4 teaspoon pepper
1 cup apricot preserves
1/4 cup dry sherry, cooking sherry or apple juice
2 teaspoons dried rosemary leaves, crumbled
2 cloves garlic, finely chopped

① Heat oven to 350°F. Trim fat from pork. Place pork in 13x9-inch glass baking dish. Sprinkle with salt and pepper.

② In 10-inch skillet, heat preserves, sherry, rosemary and garlic over medium heat, stirring frequently, until thickened. If necessary, mash apricot pieces with fork into small pieces. Spoon 1/4 cup apricot mixture onto pork (reserve remaining apricot mixture). Insert meat thermometer so tip is in center of thickest part of pork.

③ Bake uncovered 1 hour 15 minutes to 1 hour 30 minutes or until thermometer reads 155°F. Cover pork with foil; let stand 15 to 20 minutes or until thermometer reads 160°F. (Temperature will continue to rise about 5°F, and pork will be easier to carve.) Cut pork into slices. Heat remaining apricot mixture; serve with pork.

High Altitude (3500-6500 ft): No change.

1 SERVING: Calories 310; Total Fat 11g (Saturated Fat 3.5g, Trans Fat 0g); Cholesterol 85mg; Sodium 300mg; Total Carbohydrate 22g (Dietary Fiber 0g); Protein 30g. EXCHANGES: 1 Fruit, 1/2 Other Carbohydrate, 4 Lean Meat. CARBOHYDRATE CHOICES: 1-1/2.

tips&ideas

When checking the doneness of the roast, remove it from the oven when the thermometer reads 5°F less than the desired temperature. The roast will continue to cook as it stands, covered, before being sliced.

lemon-thyme turkey

PREP TIME: 15 minutes • **START TO FINISH:** 6 hours 15 minutes • **MAKES:** 8 servings (with 3 tablespoons sauce each)

4 to 5 lb bone-in turkey breast, thawed if frozen
2 teaspoons butter or margarine, melted
1 teaspoon grated lemon peel
1 clove garlic, finely chopped
1 teaspoon dried thyme leaves
1 teaspoon lemon-pepper seasoning
2 tablespoons cornstarch
1/4 cup water

① Spray 5- to 6-quart slow cooker with cooking spray. Place turkey in cooker. In small bowl, mix butter, lemon peel and garlic; rub over turkey breast. Sprinkle the turkey with thyme and lemon-pepper seasoning.

② Cover; cook on Low heat setting 6 to 7 hours.

③ Remove turkey from cooker; cover turkey to keep warm. If desired, skim fat from juices in cooker. Pour juices from cooker into 4-cup microwavable measuring cup. In small bowl, mix cornstarch and water until smooth; stir into juices in cup. Microwave uncovered on High 2 to 3 minutes, stirring every minute, until mixture thickens. Serve with sliced turkey.

High Altitude (3500-6500 ft): No change.

1 SERVING: Calories 290; Total Fat 13g (Saturated Fat 3.5g, Trans Fat 0g); Cholesterol 120mg; Sodium 150mg; Total Carbohydrate 2g (Dietary Fiber 0g); Protein 43g. EXCHANGES: 6 Very Lean Meat, 2 Fat. CARBOHYDRATE CHOICES: 0.

rosemary roast chicken

PREP TIME: 20 minutes • **START TO FINISH:** 2 hours 15 minutes • **MAKES:** 6 servings

3 to 3-1/2 lb whole broiler-fryer chicken
1-1/2 lb buttercup or acorn squash, peeled and cut into 1/2-inch rings or slices, then cut crosswise in half
2 medium onions, cut into 1-inch wedges (2 cups)
1/2 cup butter or margarine, melted
1/4 cup lemon juice
2 tablespoons honey
2 teaspoons dried rosemary leaves, crumbled
1 clove garlic, finely chopped

① Heat oven to 375°F. Fold wings of chicken under back. Tie or skewer drumsticks together. Place chicken, breast side up, on rack in shallow roasting pan. Arrange squash and onions around chicken.

② In small bowl, mix remaining ingredients; brush on chicken and vegetables just until evenly coated. Reserve remaining butter mixture. Insert meat thermometer in chicken so tip is in thickest part of inside thigh muscle and does not touch bone.

③ Roast uncovered 1 hour. Brush remaining butter mixture on chicken and vegetables. Cover loosely with foil to prevent overbrowning. Bake 45 to 55 minutes longer or until thermometer reads 180°F, juice of chicken is no longer pink when center of thigh is cut and squash is tender.

High Altitude (3500-6500 ft): No change.

1 SERVING: Calories 530; Total Fat 28g (Saturated Fat 13g, Trans Fat 1g); Cholesterol 190mg; Sodium 260mg; Total Carbohydrate 19g (Dietary Fiber 3g); Protein 50g. EXCHANGES: 1 Starch, 1 Vegetable, 6-1/2 Lean Meat, 1-1/2 Fat. CARBOHYDRATE CHOICES: 1

tips&ideas

Sweet butternut squash contains good-for-you fiber and is a great source of vitamins A and C.

sesame chicken

PREP TIME: 20 minutes • START TO FINISH: 20 minutes • MAKES: 4 servings

1-1/4 cups water
1/8 teaspoon salt
1 cup uncooked instant brown rice
2/3 cup water
3 tablespoons reduced-sodium soy sauce
2 teaspoons lemon juice
1 tablespoon cornstarch
1 teaspoon toasted sesame oil
2 teaspoons canola or olive oil
1 package (14 oz) uncooked chicken breast tenders (not breaded), pieces cut in half
1 bag (1 lb) frozen bell pepper and onion stir-fry, thawed, drained
1 tablespoon sesame seed

① In 2-quart saucepan, heat 1-1/4 cups water and the salt to boiling over high heat. Stir in rice. Reduce heat to low. Cover; simmer rice about 10 minutes or until the water is absorbed. Fluff with fork.

② Meanwhile, in small bowl, stir 2/3 cup water, the soy sauce, lemon juice, cornstarch and sesame oil; set aside.

③ Heat nonstick wok or 12-inch skillet over medium-high heat. Add canola oil; rotate wok to coat side. Add chicken; stir-fry 2 to 3 minutes. Add stir-fry vegetables; stir-fry 3 to 5 minutes or until chicken is no longer pink in center and vegetables are crisp-tender.

④ Stir soy sauce mixture into chicken mixture; heat to boiling. Cook and stir until sauce is thickened. Sprinkle with sesame seed. Serve with rice.

High Altitude (3500-6500 ft): In Step 3 after adding chicken, stir-fry 3 to 4 minutes. After adding vegetables, stir-fry 5 to 8 minutes.

1 SERVING: Calories 290; Total Fat 6g (Saturated Fat 0.5g, Trans Fat 0g); Cholesterol 45mg; Sodium 680mg; Total Carbohydrate 34g (Dietary Fiber 5g); Protein 26g. EXCHANGES: 2 Starch, 1 Vegetable, 2-1/2 Very Lean Meat, 1/2 Fat. CARBOHYDRATE CHOICES: 2.

tips&ideas

For a casual Christmas Eve dinner, serve this dish and a mixed green salad topped with pretty red sliced strawberries and dressing.

dijon and herb turkey breast with mushroom gravy

PREP TIME: 25 minutes • START TO FINISH: 3 hours 15 minutes • MAKES: 8 servings

1 tablespoon Dijon mustard
1 tablespoon butter or margarine, softened
1/2 teaspoon dried thyme leaves
1/2 teaspoon dried marjoram leaves
1/2 teaspoon salt
1/4 teaspoon coarse ground pepper
5 to 6 lb bone-in whole turkey breast, thawed if frozen
1 can (14 oz) chicken broth
8 oz small fresh whole mushrooms
1 medium onion, cut into 12 wedges
1/4 cup Gold Medal® all-purpose flour
1/4 cup cold water
Salt and pepper to taste, if desired

① Heat oven to 325°F. In small bowl, mix mustard, butter, thyme, marjoram, 1/2 teaspoon salt and 1/4 teaspoon pepper.

② In shallow roasting pan, place turkey breast, skin side up. Brush with mustard mixture. Place 1/2 cup of the broth in bottom of pan; refrigerate remaining broth. Insert ovenproof meat thermometer so tip is in thickest part of turkey breast and does not touch bone. Spray piece of foil with cooking spray; cover turkey. (Foil does not need to tightly cover turkey; secure foil to each end of pan.)

③ Bake 1 hour. Add mushrooms and onions to pan; spoon pan drippings over top. Bake uncovered 1 hour to 1 hour 30 minutes longer or until thermometer reads 170°F. Place turkey on platter; cover with foil to keep warm. Let stand 15 minutes for easiest carving.

④ Pour pan drippings (without vegetables) into measuring cup. Add remaining broth to drippings to equal 1-1/2 cups; pour into 2-quart saucepan. In small bowl, mix flour and cold water until smooth; stir into drippings in saucepan. Heat to boiling over medium-high heat, stirring constantly with wire whisk. Boil and stir about 1 minute or until mixture thickens. Stir in mushrooms and onions from pan. Simmer 5 minutes, stirring occasionally. Stir in salt and pepper to taste. Serve gravy with turkey.

High Altitude (3500-6500 ft): In Step 3, bake covered 1 hour 30 minutes. After adding mushrooms and onions, bake uncovered 1 hour longer or until thermometer reads 170°F. In Step 4, boil and stir drippings, flour and water about 3 minutes or until mixture thickens.

1 SERVING: Calories 400; Total Fat 17g (Saturated Fat 5g, Trans Fat 0g); Cholesterol 150mg; Sodium 550mg; Total Carbohydrate 6g (Dietary Fiber 0g); Protein 56g. EXCHANGES: 1/2 Starch, 7-1/2 Very Lean Meat, 2-1/2 Fat. CARBOHYDRATE CHOICES: 1/2.

french pork and bean casserole

PREP TIME: 25 minutes • START TO FINISH: 6 hours 55 minutes • MAKES: 5 servings (1-1/2 cups each)

2 slices bacon, chopped
1 lb boneless country-style pork ribs,
    cut into 3/4-inch pieces
1/2 cup finely chopped onion
1 cup shredded carrots
1 can (14.5 oz) diced tomatoes, undrained
1 can (8 oz) tomato sauce
1 teaspoon dried thyme leaves
1/2 teaspoon pepper
2 cans (15 to 16 oz each) great northern
    beans, drained
1/2 lb cooked kielbasa, cut into 1/2-inch pieces

1 In 10-inch skillet, cook bacon, pork pieces and onion over medium-high heat 8 to 10 minutes, stirring occasionally, until pork begins to brown.

2 Spray 3-1/2-to 4-quart slow cooker with cooking spray. In cooker, place pork mixture. Stir in remaining ingredients except beans and kielbasa. Layer beans over top.

3 Cover; cook on Low heat setting for about 6 to 7 hours.

4 Stir in kielbasa. Increase heat setting to High. Cover; cook 30 minutes longer or until thoroughly heated.

High Altitude (3500-6500 ft): No change.

1 SERVING: Calories 610; Total Fat 27g (Saturated Fat 10g, Trans Fat 0g); Cholesterol 90mg; Sodium 920mg; Total Carbohydrate 49g (Dietary Fiber 12g); Protein 41g. EXCHANGES: 2-1/2 Starch, 1/2 Other Carbohydrate, 1 Vegetable, 4-1/2 Medium-Fat Meat, 1/2 Fat. CARBOHYDRATE CHOICES: 3.

meatball lasagna

PREP TIME: 25 minutes • **START TO FINISH:** 9 hours 40 minutes • **MAKES:** 8 servings

1 jar (26 oz) tomato pasta sauce (any variety)
1 can (14.5 oz) diced tomatoes with Italian herbs, undrained
1 box (12 oz) frozen cooked Italian-style meatballs (12 meatballs), thawed, each cut in half
1-1/2 cups frozen bell pepper and onion stir-fry (from 1-lb bag), thawed, drained
1 container (15 oz) ricotta cheese
1 egg, beaten
2 tablespoons chopped fresh basil leaves
8 uncooked lasagna noodles
3 cups shredded mozzarella cheese (12 oz)
1/4 cup shredded Parmesan cheese (1 oz)

① Spray 13x9-inch (3-quart) glass baking dish with cooking spray. In large bowl, mix pasta sauce and tomatoes. Reserve 1/2 cup tomato mixture. Stir meatballs and stir-fry vegetables into remaining tomato mixture.

② In medium bowl, mix ricotta cheese, egg and basil.

③ Spoon and spread reserved 1/2 cup tomato mixture in bottom of baking dish. Top with 4 noodles. Top with about half of the ricotta mixture and half of the meatball mixture. Layer with remaining 4 noodles, remaining ricotta mixture, 1 cup mozzarella cheese and remaining meatball mixture. Sprinkle with remaining 2 cups mozzarella cheese and the Parmesan cheese. Spray sheet of foil with cooking spray; cover baking dish with foil. Refrigerate for 8 hours or overnight.

④ Heat oven to 350°F. Bake covered lasagna 45 minutes. Uncover; bake 15 to 20 minutes longer or until bubbly, edges are golden brown and cheese is melted. Let stand 10 minutes before cutting.

High Altitude (3500-6500 ft): Heat oven to 375°F. Bake covered 1 hour 5 minutes. Uncover and bake 15 to 20 minutes longer.

1 SERVING: Calories 540; Total Fat 24g (Saturated Fat 12g, Trans Fat 0.5g); Cholesterol 115mg; Sodium 1260mg; Total Carbohydrate 48g (Dietary Fiber 3g); Protein 32g. EXCHANGES: 2 Starch, 1 Other Carbohydrate, 3-1/2 Medium-Fat Meat, 1 Fat. CARBOHYDRATE CHOICES: 3.

tips&ideas

Thaw the meatballs in the refrigerator overnight, or thaw them in the microwave following the directions on the box.

maple-sage pork roast

PREP TIME: 30 minutes • **START TO FINISH:** 8 hours 30 minutes • **MAKES:** 8 servings

1 boneless pork shoulder roast (2 to 3 lb)
2 tablespoons real maple syrup or maple-flavored syrup
1 clove garlic, finely chopped
2 teaspoons dried sage leaves
1/2 teaspoon beef bouillon granules
1/2 cup water
2 cups 1-1/2-inch cubes peeled butternut squash
2 cups ready-to-eat baby-cut carrots, cut in half lengthwise
2 small onions, cut into wedges
3 tablespoons cornstarch
1/2 cup water

① Spray 4- to 5-quart slow cooker with cooking spray. If pork roast comes in netting or is tied, remove netting or strings. Place pork in slow cooker. In small bowl, mix syrup, garlic, sage, bouillon granules and 1/2 cup water; spoon over pork. Arrange squash, carrots and onions around pork.

② Cover; cook on Low heat setting for 8 to 9 hours.

③ Remove pork and vegetables from cooker; cover to keep warm. If desired, skim fat from liquid in cooker. Pour liquid into 4-cup microwavable measuring cup. In small bowl, mix cornstarch and 1/2 cup water until smooth; stir into liquid in cup. Microwave uncovered on High 2 to 3 minutes, stirring every minute, until mixture thickens. Serve with pork and vegetables.

High Altitude (3500-6500 ft): No change.

1 SERVING: Calories 280; Total Fat 14g (Saturated Fat 5g, Trans Fat 0g); Cholesterol 75mg; Sodium 110mg; Total Carbohydrate 14g (Dietary Fiber 2g); Protein 25g. EXCHANGES: 1/2 Starch, 1/2 Other Carbohydrate, 3-1/2 Lean Meat, 1/2 Fat. CARBOHYDRATE CHOICES: 1.

tips&ideas

Fresh whole carrots, quartered by length then cut crosswise into 2-inch sections, can be substituted for the baby carrots.

seafood enchiladas

PREP TIME: 30 minutes • START TO FINISH: 1 hour 5 minutes • MAKES: 8 servings

2 tablespoons butter or margarine

1 medium onion, chopped (1/2 cup)

2 cloves garlic, finely chopped

3 tablespoons Gold Medal® all-purpose flour

1 can (14 oz) chicken broth

1 container (8 oz) sour cream

2 cups shredded Mexican cheese blend (8 oz)

1 can (4.5 oz) Old El Paso® chopped green chiles, undrained

3 cans (6 oz each) crabmeat, drained, rinsed

1 package (8 oz) frozen cooked peeled shrimp, thawed (45 to 50 count)

1 package (11.5 oz) Old El Paso® flour tortillas for burritos (8 tortillas)

1 ripe avocado, pitted, peeled and chopped

2 tablespoons fresh lime juice

1 small plum (Roma) tomato, chopped (1/3 cup)

3 tablespoons chopped fresh cilantro

① Heat oven to 350°F. In 2-quart saucepan, melt butter over medium-high heat. Cook onion and garlic in butter 3 to 4 minutes, stirring frequently, until softened. Stir in flour until all flour is blended with butter. Stir in broth and sour cream until smooth. Heat to boiling; cook about 2 minutes, stirring constantly, until sauce is thickened. Remove from heat. Stir in cheese until melted. Stir in chiles.

② In medium bowl, mix 1 cup of cheese sauce, the crabmeat and shrimp. In 13x9-inch (3-quart) glass baking dish, spoon 1 cup of the cheese sauce over bottom. Spoon about 1/2 cup seafood mixture onto each tortilla. Roll up tortillas; place seam sides down on sauce in dish. Pour remaining sauce over enchiladas.

③ Cover baking dish with foil. Bake 30 to 35 minutes or until bubbly.

④ In medium bowl, toss remaining ingredients. Just before serving, spoon avocado mixture down center of enchiladas.

High Altitude (3500-6500 ft): Heat oven to 375°F. Cover and bake 35 minutes. Uncover and bake 10 to 15 minutes longer.

1 SERVING: Calories 480; Total Fat 26g (Saturated Fat 13g, Trans Fat 0.5g); Cholesterol 155mg; Sodium 1050mg; Total Carbohydrate 29g (Dietary Fiber 2g); Protein 30g. EXCHANGES: 2 Starch, 3-1/2 Lean Meat, 3 Fat. CARBOHYDRATE CHOICES: 2.

tips&ideas

To change up the taste, use Cheddar or Monterey Jack instead of the cheese blend.

herb-scented roast turkey & cornbread stuffing

PREP TIME: 45 minutes • START TO FINISH: 5 hours 50 minutes • MAKES: 16 servings

CORNBREAD STUFFING

1/2 cup butter or margarine
3 medium celery stalks, chopped (1-1/2 cups)
3/4 cup chopped onion
9 cups 1/2-inch cubes cornbread or soft bread
1-1/2 teaspoons chopped fresh or 1/2 teaspoon dried sage leaves, crumbled
1-1/2 teaspoons chopped fresh or 1/2 teaspoon dried thyme leaves
1 teaspoon salt
1/8 teaspoon pepper

TURKEY

1 whole turkey (12 lb), thawed if frozen
1 tablespoon chopped fresh or 2 teaspoons dried rosemary leaves, crumbled
1 tablespoon chopped fresh or 2 teaspoons dried sage leaves, crumbled
1 teaspoon salt
1/4 teaspoon pepper
2 cloves garlic, finely chopped
1/4 cup butter or margarine, melted

FOOLPROOF GRAVY

1/2 cup turkey drippings (fat and juices from roasted turkey)
1/2 cup Gold Medal® all-purpose flour
3 cups liquid (juices from roasted turkey or chicken broth)
Browning sauce, if desired
1/2 teaspoon salt
1/4 teaspoon pepper

① Heat oven to 325°F. In 10-inch skillet, melt butter over medium heat. Cook celery and onion in butter about 2 minutes, stirring occasionally, until crisp-tender; remove from heat. In large bowl, mix celery mixture and remaining stuffing ingredients until well blended.

② Stuff turkey just before roasting, not ahead of time. Fill wishbone area lightly with stuffing. Fasten neck skin to back with skewer. Fold wings across back with tips touching. Fill body cavity lightly. (Do not pack because stuffing will expand while cooking.) Tuck drumsticks under band of skin at tail, or tie together with heavy string, then tie to tail.

③ In small bowl, mix rosemary, 1 tablespoon sage, 1 teaspoon salt, 1/4 teaspoon pepper and the garlic; rub into turkey skin. Place turkey, breast side up, on rack in shallow roasting pan. Brush with 1/4 cup butter. Do not add water. Place meat thermometer in thickest part of inside thigh muscle so thermometer does not touch bone.

④ Roast uncovered 4 to 5 hours, brushing with pan juices every 30 minutes, until thermometer reads 165°F and drumsticks move easily when lifted or twisted. Thermometer placed in center of stuffing should read 165°F.

⑤ Place foil loosely over turkey when it begins to turn golden. When turkey is two-thirds done, cut band of skin, or remove string or skewer holding legs. When turkey is done, place on warm platter and cover with foil to keep warm. Let stand about 20 minutes for easiest carving. While turkey is standing, prepare Foolproof Gravy if desired.

⑥ To serve, garnish turkey with fresh herb sprigs, if desired.

METHOD FOR FOOLPROOF GRAVY:

① Pour drippings from roasting pan into bowl, leaving brown particles in pan. Return 1/2 cup drippings to roasting pan. (Measure accurately because too little fat makes gravy lumpy.)

② Stir in flour with wire whisk. (Measure accurately so gravy is not greasy.) Cook over medium heat, stirring constantly, until mixture is smooth and bubbly. Remove from heat.

③ Stir in liquid. Heat to boiling, stirring constantly. Boil and stir 1 minute. Stir in a few drops of browning sauce. Stir in salt and pepper. Strain if desired.

High Altitude (3500-6500 ft): For gravy, in Step 3, boil and stir 2 to 3 minutes.

1 SERVING: Calories 830; Total Fat 50g (Saturated Fat 19g, Trans Fat 2g); Cholesterol 235mg; Sodium 1440mg; Total Carbohydrate 43g (Dietary Fiber 4g); Protein 51g. EXCHANGES: 2 Starch, 1 Other Carbohydrate, 6-1/2 Lean Meat, 6 Fat. CARBOHYDRATE CHOICES: 3.

beef tenderloin with red wine sauce

PREP TIME: 20 minutes • START TO FINISH: 1 hour 35 minutes • MAKES: 8 servings

① Heat oven to 400°F. If necessary, trim fat from beef. Turn small end of beef under about 6 inches. Tie turned-under portion with string at about 1-1/2 inch intervals. Place in shallow roasting pan. Sprinkle with salt and cracked black pepper. Carefully insert ovenproof meat thermometer so tip is in center of thickest part of beef.

② For medium-rare, roast uncovered 30 to 40 minutes or until thermometer reads 135°F. Cover loosely with foil; let stand 15 to 20 minutes until thermometer reads 145°F. (Temperature will continue to rise about 10°F, and beef will be easier to carve.) For medium, roast uncovered 40 to 50 minutes or until thermometer reads 150°F. Cover loosely with foil; let stand 15 to 20 minutes until the thermometer reads 160°F.

③ Meanwhile, in 8-inch skillet, melt 2 tablespoons of the butter over medium-high heat. Add shallots; cook about 1 minute, stirring frequently. Add wine; cook about 4 minutes until reduced slightly. Stir in broth. Heat to boiling. Reduce heat to medium-low; cook about 10 minutes longer, stirring occasionally, until reduced to about 1 cup. Beat in remaining 4 tablespoons butter, 1 tablespoon at a time, with wire whisk. Beat in 1/2 teaspoon pepper.

④ Remove string from beef before carving. Serve sauce with beef.

High Altitude (3500-6500 ft): No change.

1 SERVING: Calories 350; Total Fat 20g (Saturated Fat 10g, Trans Fat 1g); Cholesterol 95mg; Sodium 390mg; Total Carbohydrate 1g (Dietary Fiber 0g); Protein 40g. EXCHANGES: 6 Lean Meat, 1/2 Fat. CARBOHYDRATE CHOICES: 0.

BEEF

- 1 beef tenderloin roast (3 lb)
- 1/2 teaspoon salt
- 1/2 teaspoon freshly cracked black pepper

SAUCE

- 6 tablespoons butter or margarine
- 1/2 cup finely chopped shallots (3 medium)
- 1 cup dry red wine or marsala cooking wine
- 1 cup beef broth
- 1/2 teaspoon pepper

tips&ideas

Add 1/4 cup ruby port to the sauce for a more intense wine flavor.

lemon-chicken rigatoni with broccoli

PREP TIME: 20 minutes • **START TO FINISH:** 45 minutes • **MAKES:** 4 servings (1-1/2 cups each)

2 tablespoons butter or margarine
2 cloves garlic, finely chopped
2 cups uncooked rigatoni pasta (6 oz)
2 cups chicken broth
2 cups Green Giant® frozen broccoli cuts
2 cups chopped deli rotisserie chicken
  (from 2- to 2-1/2-lb chicken)
1-1/2 teaspoons grated lemon peel
1/4 cup shredded Parmesan cheese

(1) In 12-inch skillet, melt butter over medium heat. Cook garlic in butter about 1 minute, stirring occasionally, until softened.

(2) Stir in uncooked pasta and broth. Heat to boiling, stirring occasionally; reduce heat to medium-low. Cover; simmer for 11 minutes. Stir well.

(3) Spread broccoli and chicken over pasta. Cover; cook 12 to 14 minutes longer or until pasta is tender.

(4) Stir in lemon peel. Top with cheese.

High Altitude (3500-6500 ft): Increase chicken broth to 2-1/4 cups. In Step 1, melt butter over medium-high heat. In Step 2, cover and simmer 20 minutes.

1 SERVING: Calories 410; Total Fat 14g (Saturated Fat 6g, Trans Fat 0.5g); Cholesterol 80mg; Sodium 1010mg; Total Carbohydrate 38g (Dietary Fiber 5g); Protein 32g. EXCHANGES: 2-1/2 Starch, 3-1/2 Very Lean Meat, 2 Fat. CARBOHYDRATE CHOICES: 2-1/2.

sage and garlic roast turkey

PREP TIME: 15 minutes • START TO FINISH: 5 hours • MAKES: 12 to 14 servings

12 to 14 lb turkey, thawed if frozen
2 tablespoons butter or margarine, melted
1-1/2 teaspoons parsley flakes
1 teaspoon dried sage leaves
1/2 teaspoon paprika
1/2 teaspoon seasoned salt
1/2 teaspoon garlic powder
1/2 teaspoon coarse ground pepper
1 cup water
Fresh sage and small apples, if desired

① Heat oven to 325°F. Fasten neck skin to back of turkey with skewer. Fold wings across back of turkey so tips are touching. In small bowl, mix remaining ingredients except water, fresh sage and apples.

② On rack in shallow roasting pan, place turkey, breast side up. Brush with butter mixture. Insert ovenproof meat thermometer so tip is in thickest part of inside thigh and does not touch bone. Add water to roasting pan.

③ Cover turkey loosely with foil or roaster cover; roast 3 hours. Uncover; roast 45 minutes to 1 hour 30 minutes longer. Turkey is done when thermometer reads 180°F and legs move easily when lifted or twisted. Place turkey on warm platter; cover with foil to keep warm. Let stand 15 minutes for easiest carving. Garnish with sage and apples.

High Altitude (3500-6500 ft): No change.

1 SERVING: Calories 400; Total Fat 24g (Saturated Fat 7g, Trans Fat 1g); Cholesterol 150mg; Sodium 200mg; Total Carbohydrate 0g (Dietary Fiber 0g); Protein 45g. EXCHANGES: 6-1/2 Lean Meat, 1 Fat. CARBOHYDRATE CHOICES: 0.

tips&ideas _____

Frozen turkeys will keep in the freezer for up to 6 months, so try to purchase yours when it's at a bargain price.

orange salmon and rice

PREP TIME: 15 minutes • **START TO FINISH:** 1 hour 5 minutes • **MAKES:** 4 servings

1 package (6 oz) original-flavor long grain and wild rice mix
1/4 cup chopped pecans
1-1/2 cups water
1 to 1-1/2 lb salmon fillet
2 tablespoons orange marmalade
2 teaspoons soy sauce
1/4 teaspoon ground ginger
1/4 cup chopped fresh parsley

① Heat oven to 400°F. Spray 11x7-inch (2-quart) glass baking dish with cooking spray. In baking dish, mix rice, seasoning packet from rice mix, pecans and water.

② Remove skin from salmon with sharp knife. Cut salmon into 4 serving-size pieces. Place salmon on rice mixture. In small bowl, mix marmalade, soy sauce and ginger; brush over salmon. Cover baking dish with foil.

③ Bake 40 to 50 minutes or until salmon flakes easily with fork and rice is tender. Sprinkle with parsley.

High Altitude (3500-6500 ft): Cover and bake 45 to 50 minutes.

1 SERVING: Calories 290; Total Fat 12g (Saturated Fat 2.5g, Trans Fat 0g); Cholesterol 75mg; Sodium 230mg; Total Carbohydrate 20g (Dietary Fiber 1g); Protein 26g. EXCHANGES: 1 Starch, 1/2 Other Carbohydrate, 3-1/2 Lean Meat. CARBOHYDRATE CHOICES: 1.

chicken cacciatore

PREP TIME: 15 minutes • START TO FINISH: 8 hours 25 minutes • MAKES: 6 servings

2-1/2 lb boneless skinless chicken thighs (about 12)

1 jar (4.5 oz) Green Giant® sliced mushrooms, drained

2 cans (6 oz each) Italian-style tomato paste

1-3/4 cups Progresso® chicken broth (from 32-oz carton)

1/2 cup white wine, if desired

1-1/2 teaspoons dried basil leaves

1/2 teaspoon salt

1 dried bay leaf

12 oz uncooked linguine

1/4 teaspoon dried thyme leaves

1 tablespoon cornstarch

Shredded Parmesan cheese, if desired

1 Spray 3- to 4-quart slow cooker with cooking spray. In cooker, place chicken. Add mushrooms, tomato paste, broth, wine, basil, salt and bay leaf; gently stir to mix.

2 Cover; cook on Low heat setting for 8 to 10 hours.

3 About 15 minutes before serving, cook and drain linguine as directed on package. Remove chicken from cooker; cover to keep warm. Stir thyme into sauce in cooker. Increase heat setting to High. In small bowl, mix 1/4 cup sauce from cooker and the cornstarch until smooth; stir into remaining sauce in cooker.

4 Cover; cook 10 minutes longer, stirring frequently. Remove bay leaf before serving. Serve chicken and sauce over linguine. Sprinkle with cheese.

High Altitude (3500-6500 ft): No change.

1 SERVING: Calories 620; Total Fat 17g (Saturated Fat 5g, Trans Fat 0g); Cholesterol 120mg; Sodium 1110mg; Total Carbohydrate 63g (Dietary Fiber 6g); Protein 53g. EXCHANGES: 2 Starch, 2 Other Carbohydrate, 1 Vegetable, 6 Lean Meat. CARBOHYDRATE CHOICES: 4.

tips&ideas

One 26-ounce jar of tomato pasta sauce can be substituted for the tomato paste, chicken broth and white wine.

country french beef stew

PREP TIME: 25 minutes • **START TO FINISH:** 7 hours 55 minutes • **MAKES:** 12 servings

 6 slices bacon, cut into 1/2-inch pieces
 1 boneless beef chuck roast (3 lb), trimmed of fat, cut into 1-inch pieces
 1 large onion, cut into 1/2-inch wedges
 3 cups ready-to-serve baby-cut carrots
 1 cup red Zinfandel wine or nonalcoholic red wine
3/4 cup Progresso® beef flavored broth (from 32-oz carton)
 3 tablespoons Gold Medal® all-purpose flour
 1 teaspoon dried basil leaves
1/2 teaspoon dried thyme leaves
1/2 teaspoon salt
1/4 teaspoon pepper
 1 can (14.5 oz) diced tomatoes, undrained
 1 package (8 oz) sliced fresh mushrooms
1/2 cup dry-pack julienne-cut sun-dried tomatoes
Hot cooked egg noodles, if desired
Chopped fresh parsley or basil leaves, if desired

① Spray 5- to 6-quart slow cooker with cooking spray. In 12-inch nonstick skillet, cook bacon over medium-high heat, stirring occasionally, until crisp. Place bacon in cooker. Discard all but 1 tablespoon bacon fat in skillet. Cook beef in bacon fat over medium-high heat 2 to 3 minutes, stirring occasionally, until brown. Stir onion into beef. Cook 1 minute, stirring occasionally. Spoon mixture into cooker.

② Stir carrots, wine, broth, flour, basil, thyme, salt, pepper and canned diced tomatoes into mixture in cooker.

③ Cover; cook on Low heat setting for 7 to 8 hours.

④ Stir in mushrooms and sun-dried tomatoes. Cover; cook on Low heat setting 20 to 30 minutes longer or until sun-dried tomatoes are tender. Serve beef mixture over noodles; sprinkle with parsley.

High Altitude (3500-6500 ft): No change.

1 SERVING: Calories 270; Total Fat 15g (Saturated Fat 6g, Trans Fat 0.5g); Cholesterol 70mg; Sodium 430mg; Total Carbohydrate 9g (Dietary Fiber 2g); Protein 25g. EXCHANGES: 1 Vegetable, 3-1/2 Lean Meat, 1 Fat. CARBOHYDRATE CHOICES: 1/2.

tips&ideas

If you cannot find the julienne-cut tomatoes, cut sun-dried tomato halves with a kitchen scissors.

bow-ties and shrimp casserole

PREP TIME: 15 minutes • **START TO FINISH:** 1 hour • **MAKES:** 4 servings (1-1/2 cups each)

3 cups uncooked farfalle (bow-tie) pasta (6 oz)
1 package (1.8 oz) leek soup, dip and recipe mix
2 cups fat-free (skim) milk
1 lb cooked peeled deveined medium shrimp, thawed if frozen and tails peeled
1-1/2 cups Green Giant® SELECT® frozen baby sweet peas
1/2 cup shredded Havarti cheese (2 oz)
1/4 teaspoon paprika

① Heat oven to 350°F. Spray 2-quart casserole with cooking spray. Cook and drain pasta as directed on package. Place pasta in casserole.

② In same saucepan, heat soup mix and milk over medium heat just to boiling, stirring constantly. Pour over pasta. Add shrimp and peas to casserole; stir gently to mix. Sprinkle with cheese and paprika.

③ Cover and bake 35 to 45 minutes or until thoroughly heated and bubbly around edges.

High Altitude (3500-6500 ft): No change.

1 SERVING: Calories 450; Total Fat 10g (Saturated Fat 5g, Trans Fat 0g); Cholesterol 245mg; Sodium 1570mg; Total Carbohydrate 54g (Dietary Fiber 5g); Protein 40g. EXCHANGES: 3 Starch, 1/2 Low-Fat Milk, 4 Very Lean Meat, 1/2 Fat. CARBOHYDRATE CHOICES: 3.

citrus salmon

PREP TIME: 15 minutes • **START TO FINISH:** 40 minutes • **MAKES:** 8 servings

1 salmon fillet (3 lb)
1/2 teaspoon salt
1/4 cup finely chopped fresh parsley
1/4 cup finely chopped fresh tarragon leaves
1/4 cup grated lemon peel
1/2 cup orange juice
2 tablespoons white balsamic vinegar
1 tablespoon olive or vegetable oil

① Heat oven to 375°F. Spray 13x9-inch (3-quart) glass baking dish with cooking spray. Pat salmon dry with paper towel. Place salmon, skin side down, in pan. Sprinkle with salt.

② In small bowl, mix parsley, tarragon and lemon peel. Press mixture evenly on salmon.

③ In same bowl, mix orange juice, vinegar and oil; set aside.

④ Bake 10 minutes. Pour juice mixture over salmon; bake 10 to 15 minutes longer or until salmon flakes easily with fork. Serve salmon with orange sauce from pan.

High Altitude (3500-6500 ft): No change.

1 SERVING: Calories 230; Total Fat 10g (Saturated Fat 2.5g, Trans Fat 0g); Cholesterol 95mg; Sodium 240mg; Total Carbohydrate 3g (Dietary Fiber 0g); Protein 31g. EXCHANGES: 4 Lean Meat. CARBOHYDRATE CHOICES: 0.

brined whole turkey

PREP TIME: 15 minutes • START TO FINISH: 12 hours 30 minutes • MAKES: 12 to 14 servings

2 gallons cold water
2 cups kosher salt or 1 cup table salt
12 to 14 lb turkey (not prebasted), thawed if frozen
1 medium onion, cut into fourths
1 medium carrot, coarsely chopped
1 medium celery stalk, coarsely chopped
1 teaspoon dried thyme leaves
3 tablespoons unsalted butter, melted

① Do not rub cavities of turkey with salt. In a large clean bucket or stockpot (noncorrosive), mix cold water and salt, stirring until salt is dissolved. Add turkey. Cover and refrigerate 8 to 12 hours.

② Heat oven to 325°F. Remove turkey from brine; discard brine. Thoroughly rinse turkey under cool running water, gently rubbing outside and inside of turkey to release salt. Pat skin and both interior cavities dry with paper towels.

③ Fasten neck skin to back of turkey with skewer. Fold wings across back of turkey so tips are touching. In medium bowl, toss onion, carrot, celery and thyme with 1 tablespoon of the melted butter; place in turkey cavity.

④ On rack in large shallow roasting pan, place turkey, breast side down. Brush entire back side of turkey with 1 tablespoon melted butter. Turn turkey over. Brush entire breast side of turkey with remaining 1 tablespoon melted butter. Insert ovenproof meat thermometer so tip is in thickest part of inside thigh and does not touch bone. (Do not add water or cover turkey.)

⑤ Roast uncovered 3 hours 30 minutes to 4 hours, brushing twice with pan drippings during last 30 minutes of roasting. After roasting about 2 hours when turkey begins to turn golden, place a tent of foil loosely over turkey.

⑥ Turkey is done when thermometer reads 180°F and legs move easily when lifted or twisted. If a meat thermometer is not used, begin testing for doneness after about 3 hours. Remove vegetables from cavity; discard. Place turkey on warm platter; cover with foil to keep warm. Let stand 15 minutes for easiest carving.

High Altitude (3500-6500 ft): No change.

1 SERVING: Calories 400; Total Fat 25g (Saturated Fat 8g, Trans Fat 1g); Cholesterol 150mg; Sodium 680mg; Total Carbohydrate 0g (Dietary Fiber 0g); Protein 45g. EXCHANGES: 6-1/2 Lean Meat, 1 Fat. CARBOHYDRATE CHOICES: 0.

sausage and shrimp paella

PREP TIME: 25 minutes • **START TO FINISH:** 1 hour • **MAKES:** 8 servings

2 cans (14 oz each) chicken broth
1 teaspoon saffron threads
1 lb cooked smoked chorizo sausage, sliced
1 medium red bell pepper, cut into thin strips
1 medium green bell pepper, cut into thin strips
1 medium onion, chopped (1/2 cup)
2 cloves garlic, finely chopped
1 can (14.5 oz) diced tomatoes with herbs, undrained
2-1/4 cups uncooked Arborio or regular long-grain rice
1 cup dry white wine or nonalcoholic white wine
1/2 lb cooked peeled deveined medium shrimp, thawed if frozen, tail shells removed
1 cup Green Giant® frozen sweet peas (from 1-lb bag)
2 tablespoons chopped fresh parsley

① In 2-quart saucepan, heat broth to boiling. Stir in saffron; set aside.

② Meanwhile, in large paella pan or 3-inch deep 12-inch ovenproof skillet, cook sausage over medium heat about 5 minutes, stirring occasionally, until brown. Move sausage to one side of pan. Add bell peppers and onion to pan. Cook about 5 minutes, stirring occasionally, until crisp-tender. Stir in garlic and tomatoes; heat to boiling. Stir in rice, wine and heated broth mixture; heat to boiling. Reduce heat. Cover and simmer 15 minutes; remove pan from heat.

③ Stir in shrimp and peas. Cover and simmer about 10 minutes or until rice is tender. Sprinkle with parsley.

High Altitude (3500-6500 ft): After stirring in shrimp and peas, cover and heat to boiling. Reduce heat and simmer about 10 minutes.

1 SERVING: Calories 540; Total Fat 23g (Saturated Fat 9g, Trans Fat 0g); Cholesterol 105mg; Sodium 1420mg; Total Carbohydrate 56g (Dietary Fiber 2g); Protein 28g. EXCHANGES: 3-1/2 Starch, 2-1/2 High-Fat Meat. CARBOHYDRATE CHOICES: 4.

tips&ideas

The saffron stirred into the bubbly hot broth gives this paella its classic look and flavor.

shrimp alfredo primavera

PREP TIME: 20 minutes • **START TO FINISH:** 20 minutes • **MAKES:** 4 servings (1-1/2 cups each)

3 cups uncooked bow-tie (farfalle) pasta (8 oz)
2 slices bacon, cut into 1/2-inch pieces
1-1/2 cups Green Giant® frozen sweet peas
1/4 cup water
1 lb uncooked peeled deveined medium shrimp, thawed if frozen, tail shells removed
3/4 cup refrigerated Alfredo sauce (from 10-oz container)
2 tablespoons chopped fresh chives

(1) Cook and drain pasta as directed on package.

(2) Meanwhile, in 12-inch nonstick skillet, cook bacon over medium heat 4 to 5 minutes, stirring occasionally, until crisp. Stir in peas; cook 2 minutes, stirring occasionally. Add water; cover and cook 3 to 5 minutes or until peas are tender and water has evaporated. Add shrimp; cook 2 to 3 minutes, stirring occasionally, until shrimp are pink and firm.

(3) Stir in Alfredo sauce and pasta. Cook over medium-low heat, stirring occasionally, until thoroughly heated. Sprinkle with chives.

High Altitude (3500-6500 ft): No change.

1 SERVING: Calories 510; Total Fat 20g (Saturated Fat 10g, Trans Fat 0.5g); Cholesterol 215mg; Sodium 720mg; Total Carbohydrate 54g (Dietary Fiber 5g); Protein 32g. EXCHANGES: 3 Starch, 1 Vegetable, 3 Very Lean Meat, 3-1/2 Fat. CARBOHYDRATE CHOICES: 3.

grilled garlic-sage pork roast

PREP TIME: 20 minutes • **START TO FINISH:** 1 hour 5 minutes • **MAKES:** 6 servings

8 cloves garlic, finely chopped
3 tablespoons chopped fresh sage leaves
2 tablespoons olive or canola oil
1/2 teaspoon salt
1/4 teaspoon pepper
1-1/2 pound boneless center-cut pork loin roast

1 Brush grill rack with vegetable oil. Heat coals or gas grill for direct heat.

2 Stir together garlic, sage, oil, salt and pepper in small bowl. Rub garlic mixture over pork.

3 Cover and grill pork 4 to 5 inches from medium heat 35 to 40 minutes, turning occasionally, until meat thermometer inserted into center of pork reads 155°F. Cover and let stand 5 minutes until thermometer reads 160°F.

4 To serve, cut pork across grain into thin slices. Garnish with additional fresh sage leaves if desired.

VARIATION: To roast, heat oven to 400°F. Place pork on rack in shallow roasting pan. Insert meat thermometer so tip is in thickest part of pork and does not rest in fat. Bake 50 to 60 minutes or until meat thermometer reads 155°F. Cover and let stand 5 minutes until thermometer reads 160°F.

High Altitude (3500-6500 ft): No change.

1 SERVING: Calories 220; Total Fat 12g (Saturated Fat 3.5g, Trans Fat 0g); Cholesterol 75mg; Sodium 180mg; Total Carbohydrate 0g (Dietary Fiber 0g); Protein 26g. EXCHANGES: 3-1/2 Lean Meat, 1/2 Fat. CARBOHYDRATE CHOICES: 0.

stuffed chicken parmesan

PREP TIME: 20 minutes • **START TO FINISH:** 55 minutes • **MAKES:** 6 servings

6 boneless skinless chicken breasts
(about 5 oz each)
1 box (9 oz) Green Giant® frozen chopped
spinach, thawed, well drained
2 oz cream cheese, softened
1/4 cup shredded Parmesan cheese
1/2 teaspoon dried basil leaves
1 clove garlic, finely chopped
1 egg
12 stone-ground wheat crackers, crushed
(about 1/2 cup)
1 teaspoon dried basil leaves
1/2 teaspoon pepper
2 cups Muir Glen® organic Italian herb pasta sauce
(from 25.5-oz jar)
1/4 cup shredded mozzarella cheese (1 oz)

① Heat oven to 375°F. Spray 13x9-inch
(3-quart) glass baking dish with cooking spray.
Between pieces of plastic wrap or waxed paper,
place each chicken breast smooth side down;
gently pound with flat side of meat mallet or
rolling pin until about 1/4 inch thick.

② In medium bowl, mix spinach, cream cheese,
Parmesan cheese, 1/2 teaspoon basil and the
garlic until blended. Spread about 1 tablespoon
spinach mixture over each chicken breast; roll
up tightly. If necessary, secure with toothpicks.

③ In small shallow dish, beat egg with fork
until foamy. In another small shallow dish, mix
cracker crumbs, 1 teaspoon basil and the
pepper. Dip each chicken breast into beaten egg,
then roll in crumb mixture to coat. Place seam
side down in baking dish.

④ Bake uncovered 20 minutes. Pour pasta
sauce over chicken; sprinkle with mozzarella
cheese. Bake 10 to 15 minutes longer or until
thermometer inserted in center of chicken
reads 165°F. Carefully remove toothpicks from
chicken before eating.

High Altitude (3500-6500 ft): Bake uncovered
25 minutes. Add sauce and cheese; bake for
8 to 12 minutes.

1 SERVING: Calories 330; Total Fat 13g (Saturated Fat
5g, Trans Fat 0g); Cholesterol 135mg; Sodium 550mg;
Total Carbohydrate 14g (Dietary Fiber 2g); Protein 38g.
EXCHANGES: 1/2 Starch, 1/2 Other Carbohydrate, 5 Lean
Meat. CARBOHYDRATE CHOICES: 1.

tips&ideas

Another easy way to flatten chicken breasts is to place one at a time in a
freezer food storage bag, not sealed, before pounding.

bavarian-style beef roast and sauerkraut

PREP TIME: 15 minutes • **START TO FINISH:** 8 hours 45 minutes • **MAKES:** 10 servings

1 tablespoon vegetable oil
1 boneless beef tip roast (3 lb), trimmed of fat
2 teaspoons caraway seed
1/2 teaspoon salt
1 bag (16 oz) frozen small whole onions
1 can (16 oz) Bavarian-style sauerkraut, undrained
1/2 cup dark beer or beef broth
1/4 cup Gold Medal® all-purpose flour
1 tablespoon stone-ground mustard

1 In 12-inch skillet, heat oil over medium-high heat. Add beef; cook about 5 minutes or until brown on all sides. Sprinkle with caraway seed and salt.

2 In 5- to 6-quart slow cooker, place beef; place onions, sauerkraut and 1/4 cup of the beer around beef.

3 Cover and cook on Low heat setting for 6 to 8 hours.

4 About 30 minutes before serving, remove beef from cooker; cover to keep warm. In small bowl, mix flour, remaining 1/4 cup beer and the mustard until smooth; gradually stir into juices in cooker. Increase heat setting to High; cover and cook 15 to 30 minutes or until slightly thickened. Serve beef with juices.

High Altitude (3500-6500 ft): No change.

1 SERVING: Calories 180; Total Fat 6g (Saturated Fat 1.5g, Trans Fat 0g); Cholesterol 65mg; Sodium 480mg; Total Carbohydrate 9g (Dietary Fiber 2g); Protein 26g. EXCHANGES: 1 Vegetable, 3-1/2 Very Lean Meat, 1 Fat. CARBOHYDRATE CHOICES: 1/2.

tips&ideas

Go ethnic around the holidays. Create a full German meal with this beef roast, buttered egg noodles, a spinach salad with hot bacon dressing and fresh, crusty rolls.

herbed beef stroganoff

PREP TIME: 10 minutes • **START TO FINISH:** 8 hours 15 minutes • **MAKES:** 8 servings

2 lb beef stew meat
1 package (8 oz) sliced fresh mushrooms
1 large onion, cut lengthwise in half, then cut crosswise into slices
1/4 teaspoon pepper
1 tablespoon beef bouillon granules
1 bag (16 oz) wide egg noodles
1 container (8 oz) sour cream
1 teaspoon dried thyme leaves
1 tablespoon Gold Medal® all-purpose flour
1 large tomato, chopped (1 cup)

① In 3-1/2 to 4 quart slow cooker, place beef, mushrooms, onion, pepper and bouillon granules.

② Cover and cook on Low heat setting for 8 to 9 hours.

③ About 20 minutes before serving, cook and drain noodles as directed on package. Gently stir sour cream and thyme into drained noodles.

④ Sprinkle flour over beef mixture in cooker; gently stir into mixture. Increase heat setting to High. Cover and cook 3 minutes. Serve beef mixture over noodles; top with tomato.

High Altitude (3500-6500 ft): In Step 4, cover and cook 5 to 7 minutes.

1 SERVING: Calories 490; Total Fat 21g (Saturated Fat 9g, Trans Fat 1g); Cholesterol 140mg; Sodium 400mg; Total Carbohydrate 43g (Dietary Fiber 3g); Protein 33g. EXCHANGES: 3 Starch, 3-1/2 Medium-Fat Meat. CARBOHYDRATE CHOICES: 3.

tips&ideas

For a hot sandwich you can hold in your hand, spoon about 1/2 cup stroganoff into pita bread halves and top with the chopped tomato.

apricot-bourbon glazed ham

PREP TIME: 10 minutes • **START TO FINISH:** 1 hour 55 minutes • **MAKES:** 10 servings

1/2 cup apricot preserves
2 teaspoons ground ginger
1/4 cup bourbon or pineapple juice
6 to 8 lb fully cooked smoked bone-in ham

① Heat oven to 325°F. In small bowl, mix preserves, ginger and bourbon until smooth.

② Place ham on rack in shallow roasting pan. Make cuts about 1/2 inch apart and 1/4 inch deep in diamond pattern around top and sides of ham. Brush with 3 tablespoons of the preserves mixture. Insert ovenproof meat thermometer in thickest part of ham.

③ Bake uncovered 45 minutes. Brush remaining preserves mixture over ham. Bake about 45 minutes longer or until thermometer reads 140°F. Remove ham from oven, cover with tent of foil and let stand 10 to 15 minutes for easier carving.

High Altitude (3500-6500 ft): No change.

1 SERVING: Calories 250; Total Fat 8g (Saturated Fat 2.5g, Trans Fat 0g); Cholesterol 80mg; Sodium 1770mg; Total Carbohydrate 13g (Dietary Fiber 0g); Protein 31g. EXCHANGES: 1 Other Carbohydrate, 4-1/2 Very Lean Meat, 1 Fat. CARBOHYDRATE CHOICES: 1.

italian beef short ribs

PREP TIME: 10 minutes • **START TO FINISH:** 2 hours 40 minutes • **MAKES:** 6 servings

4 lb beef short ribs, cut into serving pieces
2 medium onions, cut into 1-inch wedges (2 cups)
1 package (8 oz) fresh whole mushrooms, cut in half
1 jar (14 oz) tomato pasta sauce (any variety)

① Heat oven to 350°F. Place ribs and onions in ungreased 13x9-inch (3-quart) glass baking dish. Cover and bake 1 hour. Drain and discard fat.

② Add mushrooms to ribs and onions in dish. Pour pasta sauce over all. Cover tightly with foil and bake about 1 hour 30 minutes longer or until ribs are tender. If desired, skim off and discard any excess fat from top.

High Altitude (3500-6500 ft): No change.

1 SERVING: Calories 340; Total Fat 20g (Saturated Fat 7g, Trans Fat 1g); Cholesterol 70mg; Sodium 380mg; Total Carbohydrate 17g (Dietary Fiber 2g); Protein 24g. EXCHANGES: 1/2 Starch, 2 Vegetable, 2-1/2 Medium-Fat Meat, 1-1/2 Fat. CARBOHYDRATE CHOICES: 1.

chicken paprika shepherd's pie

PREP TIME: 20 minutes • **START TO FINISH:** 55 minutes • **MAKES:** 4 servings

1 pouch Betty Crocker® roasted garlic mashed potatoes (from 7.2-oz box)
1 cup hot water
1/2 cup milk
3 tablespoons butter or margarine
1 lb boneless skinless chicken breasts, cut into 1/2-inch pieces
1 medium onion, chopped (1/2 cup)
1-1/2 cups Green Giant® frozen mixed vegetables
1 jar (12 oz) home-style chicken gravy
2-1/4 teaspoons paprika
1/2 cup sour cream

① Heat oven to 350°F. Spray 2-quart shallow casserole or 8-inch square glass baking dish with cooking spray. Make mashed potatoes as directed on box for 4 servings—except use 1 cup hot water, 1/2 cup milk and 2 tablespoons of the butter.

② Meanwhile, in 12-inch nonstick skillet, melt remaining 1 tablespoon butter over medium-high heat. Cook chicken and onion in butter for 4 to 6 minutes, stirring frequently, until chicken is no longer pink in center. Stir in mixed vegetables, gravy and 2 teaspoons of the paprika. Cover; cook over medium-low heat for 5 minutes, stirring frequently to prevent sticking.

③ Stir in sour cream. Spoon into casserole. Spoon or pipe potatoes in 8 mounds around edge of casserole. Sprinkle potatoes with remaining paprika.

④ Bake uncovered 25 to 35 minutes or until mixture bubbles around edge of casserole.

High Altitude (3500-6500 ft): No change.

1 SERVING: Calories 500; Total Fat 25g (Saturated Fat 11g, Trans Fat 1.5g); Cholesterol 115mg; Sodium 1000mg; Total Carbohydrate 36g (Dietary Fiber 5g); Protein 33g. EXCHANGES: 2 Starch, 1/2 Other Carbohydrate, 4 Very Lean Meat, 4 Fat. CARBOHYDRATE CHOICES: 2-1/2.

tips&ideas

To add a slightly smoky flavor to the casserole, add about 1/4 pound of sliced smoked kielbasa sausage when you stir in the vegetables.

quinoa pilaf with salmon and asparagus

PREP TIME: 30 minutes • **START TO FINISH:** 30 minutes • **MAKES:** 4 servings (3/4 cup each)

1 cup uncooked quinoa
6 cups water
1 vegetable bouillon cube
1 lb salmon fillets
2 tablespoons butter or margarine
20 stalks fresh asparagus, cut diagonally
into 2-inch pieces (2 cups)
4 medium green onions, sliced (1/4 cup)
1 cup Green Giant® frozen sweet peas thawed
1/2 cup halved grape tomatoes
1/2 cup vegetable or chicken broth
1 teaspoon lemon-pepper seasoning
2 teaspoons chopped fresh or 1/2 teaspoon
dried dill weed

① Rinse quinoa thoroughly by placing in a fine-mesh strainer and holding under cold running water until water runs clear; drain well.

② In 2-quart saucepan, heat 2 cups of the water to boiling over high heat. Add quinoa; reduce heat to low. Cover; simmer 10 to 12 minutes or until water is absorbed.

③ Meanwhile, in 12-inch skillet, heat remaining 4 cups water and bouillon cube to boiling over high heat. Add salmon, skin side up; reduce heat to low. Cover; simmer 10 to 12 minutes or until fish flakes easily with fork. Remove with slotted spoon to plate; let cool. Discard water. Remove skin from salmon; break into large pieces.

④ Meanwhile, rinse and dry skillet. Melt butter in skillet over medium heat. Add asparagus; cook 5 minutes, stirring frequently. Stir in onions; cook 1 minute, stirring frequently. Stir in peas, tomatoes and broth; cook 1 minute.

⑤ Gently stir quinoa, salmon, lemon-pepper seasoning and dill weed into asparagus mixture. Cover; cook about 2 minutes or until hot.

High Altitude (3500-6500 ft): No change.

tips&ideas

When shopping, choose asparagus spears that are firm but tender, are tightly closed and have a dark green or purple tinge on the tips.

1 SERVING: Calories 420; Total Fat 15g (Saturated Fat 6g, Trans Fat 0g); Cholesterol 90mg; Sodium 650mg; Total Carbohydrate 39g (Dietary Fiber 5g); Protein 33g. EXCHANGES: 1-1/2 Starch, 1 Other Carbohydrate, 1 Vegetable, 3-1/2 Lean Meat, 1/2 Fat. CARBOHYDRATE CHOICES: 2-1/2.

garlic chicken and broccoli stir-fry

PREP TIME: 20 minutes • **START TO FINISH:** 20 minutes • **MAKES:** 4 servings (1-1/2 cups each)

2 tablespoons vegetable oil
4 cloves garlic, peeled, sliced
  (about 2 tablespoons)
4 cups fresh broccoli florets (about 1 lb)
1/2 cup ready-to-eat baby-cut carrots,
  cut in half lengthwise
1 can (8 oz) sliced water chestnuts, drained
1/4 cup water
1/2 cup teriyaki baste and glaze (from 12-oz bottle)
2 cups bite-size strips deli rotisserie chicken
  (from 2- to 2-1/2-lb chicken)
Hot cooked rice, if desired

① In 12-inch nonstick skillet or wok, heat oil over medium-high heat. Cook garlic in oil about 1 minute, stirring constantly and being careful that garlic doesn't burn, until golden brown.

② Add broccoli, carrots, water chestnuts and water to skillet. Cook 7 to 9 minutes, stirring occasionally, until vegetables are crisp-tender and water has evaporated.

③ Gently stir in teriyaki glaze and chicken. Cook 1 to 2 minutes or until chicken is thoroughly heated. Serve over rice.

High Altitude (3500-6500 ft): No change.

1 SERVING: Calories 310; Total Fat 12g (Saturated Fat 2.5g, Trans Fat 0g); Cholesterol 60mg; Sodium 1170mg; Total Carbohydrate 26g (Dietary Fiber 5g); Protein 25g. EXCHANGES: 1 Starch, 1/2 Other Carbohydrate, 1 Vegetable, 3 Lean Meat, 1/2 Fat. CARBOHYDRATE CHOICES: 2.

parmesan breaded pork chops

PREP TIME: 5 minutes • **START TO FINISH:** 20 minutes • **MAKES:** 4 servings

1/3 cup Progresso® Italian Style dry bread crumbs
2 tablespoons grated Parmesan cheese
4 pork boneless butterfly loin chops, 1/2 inch thick (about 1-1/4 lb)
1 egg, beaten
1 can (14-1/2 oz) chunky tomatoes with olive oil, garlic and spices, undrained
1 can (8 oz) tomato sauce
1 small green bell pepper, chopped (1/2 cup)

① Mix bread crumbs and cheese. Dip pork in egg, then coat with crumb mixture.

② Spray 12-inch nonstick skillet with cooking spray; heat over medium heat. Cook the pork in skillet about 5 minutes, turning once, until brown.

③ Stir in remaining ingredients. Heat to boiling; reduce heat to low. Cover and simmer 10 to 12 minutes, stirring occasionally, until pork is slightly pink in center.

High Altitude (3500-6500 ft): No change.

1 SERVING: Calories 260; Total Fat 10g (Saturated Fat 4g, Trans Fat nc); Cholesterol 110mg; Sodium 810mg; Total Carbohydrate 19g (Dietary Fiber 2g); Protein 25g. EXCHANGES: 1/2 Starch, 2 Vegetable, 3 Lean Meat. CARBOHYDRATE CHOICES: nc.

turkey and stuffing bake

PREP TIME: 20 minutes • **START TO FINISH:** 1 hour • **MAKES:** 8 servings

3 cups chopped cooked turkey
1 bag (14 oz) Green Giant Select® frozen broccoli
  florets, thawed and drained
1 can (10.75 oz) cream of chicken soup
1/2 cup sour cream
1-1/2 cups shredded Swiss cheese (6 oz)
1 package (6 oz) stuffing mix for turkey
3/4 cup hot water

① Heat oven to 350°F. Spread turkey in ungreased 13x9-inch glass baking dish. Top with broccoli.

② In medium bowl, stir together soup, sour cream and cheese; spread over broccoli. In large bowl, stir together stuffing mix and hot water; sprinkle over casserole.

③ Bake uncovered 35 to 40 minutes or until hot and bubbly.

High Altitude (3500-6500 ft): No change.

1 SERVING: Calories 340; Total Fat 16g (Saturated Fat 7g, Trans Fat 0.5g); Cholesterol 75mg; Sodium 720mg; Total Carbohydrate 23g (Dietary Fiber 2g); Protein 26g. EXCHANGES: 1 Starch, 1 Vegetable, 3 Lean Meat, 1-1/2 Fat. CARBOHYDRATE CHOICES: 1-1/2.

tips&ideas

You can also use chicken in this recipe. Simply substitute chicken for the turkey, and use chicken stuffing mix.

provençal pork roast

PREP TIME: 15 minutes • **START TO FINISH:** 9 hours 30 minutes • **MAKES:** 8 servings

3 to 3-1/2 lb pork boneless loin roast
1 teaspoon seasoned salt
1/2 teaspoon garlic pepper
6 to 8 small red potatoes, cut into fourths
1 can (14.5 oz) diced tomatoes with Italian seasonings, undrained
2 tablespoons Gold Medal® all-purpose flour
1 medium zucchini, cut lengthwise in half, then cut crosswise into slices (2 cups)
1/2 cup halved pitted ripe olives, if desired

① Spray 12-inch nonstick skillet with cooking spray. If pork roast comes in netting or is tied, do not remove. Sprinkle pork with seasoned salt and garlic pepper. Cook pork in skillet over medium-high heat 5 to 6 minutes, turning occasionally, until brown on all sides.

② Spray 5- to 6-quart slow cooker with cooking spray. Place pork in cooker. Arrange potatoes around pork. Mix tomatoes and flour in small bowl; pour over pork and potatoes.

③ Cover and cook on Low heat setting for about 8 to 9 hours.

④ Place pork and potatoes on platter; cover to keep warm. Add zucchini and olives to sauce in cooker. Increase heat setting to High. Cover and cook 10 to 15 minutes or until zucchini is tender. Remove netting or strings from pork. Serve pork with zucchini mixture.

High Altitude (3500-6500 ft): No change.

1 SERVING: Calories 360; Total Fat 13g (Saturated Fat 4.5g, Trans Fat 0g); Cholesterol 110mg; Sodium 380mg; Total Carbohydrate 20g (Dietary Fiber 3g); Protein 40g. EXCHANGES: 1 Starch, 1 Vegetable, 5 Lean Meat. CARBOHYDRATE CHOICES: 1.

tips&ideas

For a burst of fresh flavor, add 2 to 3 tablespoons chopped fresh basil or Italian parsley while cooking the zucchini.

crispy herbed fish fillets

PREP TIME: 25 minutes • **START TO FINISH:** 25 minutes • **MAKES:** 4 servings

1 lb flounder fillets (about 1/2 inch thick),
  cut into 4 serving pieces
2 eggs
1-1/4 cups Progresso® panko crispy bread crumbs
1 teaspoon grated lemon peel
1 teaspoon dried marjoram leaves
1/2 teaspoon salt
1/4 teaspoon pepper
1/4 cup olive or vegetable oil

① Dry fish well on paper towels. In shallow dish, beat eggs with fork or wire whisk until well mixed. In another shallow dish, mix bread crumbs, lemon peel, marjoram, salt and pepper.

② In 12-inch nonstick skillet, heat 2 tablespoons of the oil over medium heat.

Dip fish in eggs, then coat well with crumb mixture. Add about half of the fish in single layer to oil. Cook 3 to 4 minutes, carefully turning once, until outside is browned and crisp and the fish flakes easily with a fork.

③ Remove cooked fish from skillet to plate; cover to keep warm. Repeat with remaining oil and fish.

High Altitude (3500-6500 ft): No change.

1 SERVING: Calories 310; Total Fat 17g (Saturated Fat 3g, Trans Fat 0g); Cholesterol 160mg; Sodium 440mg; Total Carbohydrate 14g (Dietary Fiber 0g); Protein 25g. EXCHANGES: 1 Starch, 3 Very Lean Meat, 3 Fat. CARBOHYDRATE CHOICES: 1.

chicken risotto

PREP TIME: 15 minutes • START TO FINISH: 6 hours 30 minutes • MAKES: 4 servings (1-1/2 cups each)

1-1/4 lb boneless skinless chicken breasts, cut into 3/4-inch cubes
1/2 cup finely chopped onion
1/2 cup shredded carrot
1 clove garlic, finely chopped
2 cups water
2 cups uncooked instant white rice
2 tablespoons butter or margarine
1 can (10-3/4 oz) condensed cream of chicken soup
1/2 cup grated Parmesan cheese

① In 3- to 4-quart slow cooker, mix chicken, onion, carrot, garlic and water.

② Cover; cook on Low heat setting for 6 to 7 hours.

③ Stir in rice and butter. Increase heat setting to High. Cover; cook 5 minutes until rice is tender. Stir in soup and cheese. Cover; cook 10 to 15 minutes or until thoroughly heated. Serve immediately.

High Altitude (3500-6500 ft): Add up to 1/2 cup additional water if mixture becomes too thick.

1 SERVING: Calories 580; Total Fat 20g (Saturated Fat 8g, Trans Fat 0.5g); Cholesterol 115mg; Sodium 900mg; Total Carbohydrate 57g (Dietary Fiber 2g); Protein 43g. EXCHANGES: 3-1/2 Starch, 4-1/2 Very Lean Meat, 3 Fat. CARBOHYDRATE CHOICES: 4.

garlic and mushroom beef roast

PREP TIME: 10 minutes • **START TO FINISH:** 11 hours 10 minutes • **MAKES:** 6 servings

3 to 4 lb beef boneless rump or tip roast
1 teaspoon salt
2 cloves garlic, finely chopped
8 ounces small whole fresh mushrooms
1/2 cup sun-dried tomatoes in oil, drained and chopped
1/2 cup light Italian dressing

① Spray 12-inch nonstick skillet with cooking spray. If beef roast comes in netting or is tied, do not remove. Sprinkle beef with salt and garlic. Cook beef in skillet over medium-high heat 5 to 6 minutes, turning occasionally, until brown on all sides.

② Spray 4- to 5-quart slow cooker with cooking spray. Place mushrooms in cooker. Place beef on mushrooms. Spread tomatoes over beef. Pour dressing over mixture in cooker.

③ Cover and cook on Low heat setting for 9 to 11 hours.

④ Place beef on cutting board; remove netting or strings. Slice beef. Serve mushrooms and juices with beef.

High Altitude (3500-6500 ft): No change.

1 SERVING: Calories 320; Total Fat 12g (Saturated Fat 3g, Trans Fat 0g); Cholesterol 120mg; Sodium 760mg; Total Carbohydrate 5g (Dietary Fiber 1g); Protein 47g.
EXCHANGES: 1 Vegetable, 6 Very Lean Meat, 1-1/2 Fat
CARBOHYDRATE CHOICES: 1/2.

tips&ideas _____

For great comfort food, use this beef for hot roast beef sandwiches. Or serve it thinly sliced on hearty bread with mayo, Dijon mustard, sliced red onion and crispy lettuce.

ginger beef roast

PREP TIME: 15 minutes • **START TO FINISH:** 8 hours 35 minutes • **MAKES:** 8 servings

1 boneless beef chuck roast (3 lb)
1 teaspoon peppered seasoned salt
3/4 cup classic-style stir-fry sauce
2 tablespoons ketchup
2 tablespoons rice vinegar
2 teaspoons grated gingerroot
  or 1 teaspoon ground ginger
1 bag (1 lb) frozen bell pepper and onion stir-fry, thawed

① Spray 12-inch nonstick skillet with cooking spray. If beef roast comes in netting or is tied, do not remove. Sprinkle beef with peppered seasoned salt. Cook beef in skillet over medium-high heat 5 to 6 minutes, turning once, until brown on both sides.

② Spray 5- to 6-quart slow cooker with cooking spray. Place beef in cooker (if necessary, cut beef in half to fit in cooker). In small bowl, mix stir-fry sauce, ketchup, vinegar and gingerroot; pour over beef.

③ Cover and cook on Low heat setting for 8 to 9 hours.

④ Place beef on platter; cover to keep warm. Add stir-fry vegetables to mixture in cooker. Increase heat setting to High. Cover and cook 15 to 20 minutes or until peppers are tender. Remove netting or strings from beef. Serve pepper mixture with beef.

High Altitude (3500-6500 ft): No change.

1 SERVING: Calories 370; Total Fat 20g (Saturated Fat 7g, Trans Fat 1g); Cholesterol 105mg; Sodium 1290mg; Total Carbohydrate 10g (Dietary Fiber 0g); Protein 37g. EXCHANGES: 1/2 Starch, 1 Vegetable, 5 Lean Meat, 1 Fat. CARBOHYDRATE CHOICES: 1/2.

tips&ideas

Although it's tempting, avoid peeking in the slow cooker during cooking. Lifting the lid lets steam escape, and steam helps with the cooking.

fiery orange-glazed pork tenderloin

PREP TIME: 5 minutes • **START TO FINISH:** 50 minutes • **MAKES:** 3 servings

1 pork tenderloin (about 3/4 lb)
1/2 teaspoon seasoned salt
1/2 teaspoon pepper
1/3 cup orange marmalade
1/2 teaspoon crushed red pepper flakes

① Heat oven to 400°F. Sprinkle pork with seasoned salt and pepper. On rack in shallow pan, place pork. Insert ovenproof meat thermometer so tip is in thickest part of pork. Bake uncovered for 18 minutes.

② Meanwhile, in small bowl, mix orange marmalade and red pepper. Reserve half the marmalade mixture. Brush or spoon remaining marmalade mixture over pork.

③ Bake uncovered 15 to 20 minutes longer or until thermometer reads 155°F. Cover pork loosely with foil; let stand 10 minutes or until thermometer reads 160°F.

④ Cut pork into 1/2-inch slices. Serve with reserved marmalade mixture.

High Altitude (3500-6500 ft): No change.

1 SERVING: Calories 240; Total Fat 4.5g (Saturated Fat 1.5g, Trans Fat 0g); Cholesterol 70mg; Sodium 290mg; Total Carbohydrate 25g (Dietary Fiber 0g); Protein 25g. EXCHANGES: 1-1/2 Other Carbohydrate, 3-1/2 Very Lean Meat, 1/2 Fat. CARBOHYDRATE CHOICES: 1-1/2.

roasted rosemary pork chops and potatoes

PREP TIME: 20 minutes • START TO FINISH: 1 hour 5 minutes • MAKES: 4 servings

2 tablespoons Dijon mustard

2 tablespoons olive or vegetable oil

1/2 teaspoon dried rosemary leaves, crushed

1/2 teaspoon garlic-pepper blend

1/2 teaspoon seasoned salt

1/2 teaspoon paprika

3 Yukon gold potatoes, cut into 1-inch pieces (about 4 cups)

1 medium red onion, cut into 1/2-inch-wide wedges

4 bone-in loin pork chops, 1/2 inch thick

① Heat oven to 425°F. Spray 15x10x1-inch pan with cooking spray. In large bowl, mix mustard, oil, rosemary, garlic-pepper blend, seasoned salt and paprika. Reserve 1 tablespoon of the mustard mixture.

② Add potatoes and onion to remaining mustard mixture in bowl; toss to coat. Place vegetables in pan.

③ Roast uncovered 25 minutes. Turn and stir potato mixture. Brush pork chops with reserved 1 tablespoon mustard mixture. Add pork chops to corners of pan.

④ Roast uncovered 15 to 20 minutes longer or until pork is no longer pink when cut near bone and vegetables are tender.

High Altitude (3500-6500 ft): No change.

1 SERVING: Calories 360; Total Fat 15g (Saturated Fat 4g, Trans Fat 0g); Cholesterol 65mg; Sodium 410mg; Total Carbohydrate 29g (Dietary Fiber 4g); Protein 27g. EXCHANGES: 2 Starch, 3 Lean Meat, 1 Fat. CARBOHYDRATE CHOICES: 2.

speedy mediterranean chicken

PREP TIME: 30 minutes • **START TO FINISH:** 30 minutes • **MAKES:** 4 servings

1 tablespoon olive or vegetable oil
2 teaspoons curry powder
1 jar (16 oz) Old El Paso® Thick 'n Chunky salsa
1/2 cup sliced green olives
1/4 cup golden raisins
1/4 cup honey
1 deli rotisserie chicken (2 to 2-1/2 lb), cut into 6 to 8 pieces, skin removed if desired

(1) In 12-inch nonstick skillet, heat oil over medium heat. Stir in curry powder. Cook over medium heat 1 minute, stirring constantly.

(2) Stir in remaining ingredients except chicken. Add chicken; turn to coat.

(3) Cover; cook over medium-high heat 5 to 6 minutes, turning chicken occasionally, until sauce is bubbly and chicken is thoroughly heated.

High Altitude (3500-6500 ft): No change.

1 SERVING: Calories 430; Total Fat 15g (Saturated Fat 3.5g, Trans Fat 0g); Cholesterol 110mg; Sodium 1740mg; Total Carbohydrate 37g (Dietary Fiber 1g); Protein 36g. EXCHANGES: 2-1/2 Other Carbohydrate, 5 Lean Meat. CARBOHYDRATE CHOICES: 2-1/2.

smothered chicken

PREP TIME: 30 minutes • **START TO FINISH:** 30 minutes • **MAKES:** 4 servings

2 tablespoons butter or margarine
1 medium onion, sliced (about 1 cup)
1 package (8 oz) sliced fresh mushrooms (3 cups)
2 teaspoons sugar
1 jar (12 oz) chicken gravy
1 tablespoon dry sherry, if desired
1 deli rotisserie chicken (2 to 2-1/2 lb), cut into serving pieces, skin removed if desired
1 tablespoon chopped fresh parsley

(1) In 12-inch skillet, melt butter over medium heat. Cook onion and mushrooms in butter 8 to 10 minutes, stirring occasionally, until onions are tender and beginning to brown. Stir in

sugar. Cook about 3 minutes, stirring occasionally, until vegetables are very brown.

(2) Stir gravy and sherry into vegetables. Add chicken to skillet; spoon sauce over chicken.

(3) Cover; cook 5 to 10 minutes, turning chicken after half the cooking time, until thoroughly heated. Sprinkle with parsley.

High Altitude (3500-6500 ft): No change.

1 SERVING: Calories 390; Total Fat 20g (Saturated Fat 7g, Trans Fat 0.5g); Cholesterol 125mg; Sodium 1150mg; Total Carbohydrate 13g (Dietary Fiber 2g); Protein 39g. EXCHANGES: 1 Starch, 5 Lean Meat, 1 Fat. CARBOHYDRATE CHOICES: 1.

turkey and green chile stuffing casserole

PREP TIME: 25 minutes • START TO FINISH: 1 hour 40 minutes • MAKES: 6 servings

2 tablespoons butter or margarine
1 medium onion, chopped (1/2 cup)
1 small red bell pepper, chopped (1/2 cup)
4 cups seasoned cornbread stuffing mix
1 cup Green Giant® Niblets® frozen corn
1 can (4.5 oz) Old El Paso® chopped green chiles, undrained
1-1/2 cups water
2 turkey breast tenderloins (about 3/4 lb each)
1/2 teaspoon chili powder
1/2 teaspoon peppered seasoned salt

① Heat oven to 350°F. Spray an 11x7-inch (2-quart) glass baking dish with cooking spray. In 12-inch nonstick skillet, melt butter over medium-high heat. Cook onion and bell pepper in butter 2 to 3 minutes, stirring frequently, until tender. Stir in the stuffing mix, corn, chiles and water. Spread stuffing mixture in baking dish.

② Sprinkle both sides of turkey tenderloins with chili powder and peppered seasoned salt. Place on stuffing, pressing into stuffing mixture slightly. Spray sheet of foil with cooking spray. Cover baking dish with foil, sprayed side down.

③ Bake 1 hour. Uncover and bake 10 to 15 minutes longer or until juice of turkey is no longer pink when centers of thickest pieces are cut.

High Altitude (3500-6500 ft): No change.

1 SERVING: Calories 360; Total Fat 7g (Saturated Fat 3g, Trans Fat 0.5g); Cholesterol 85mg; Sodium 990mg; Total Carbohydrate 43g (Dietary Fiber 3g); Protein 33g. EXCHANGES: 3 Starch, 3-1/2 Very Lean Meat, 1/2 Fat. CARBOHYDRATE CHOICES: 3.

tips&ideas

Look for the cornbread stuffing mix in bags near the other packages of stuffing at the grocery store.

puff pastry-topped chicken pie

PREP TIME: 35 minutes • **START TO FINISH:** 35 minutes • **MAKES:** 12 servings

1 package (17.3 oz) frozen puff pastry sheets, thawed

1 egg, beaten

6 tablespoons butter or margarine

4 medium stalks celery, thinly sliced (2 cups)

2 medium onions, chopped (1 cup)

1 cup Gold Medal® all-purpose flour

1 carton (32 oz) chicken broth

3 cups half-and-half

1/2 cup dry white wine, if desired

2 lb Green Giant® frozen mixed vegetables, thawed, drained

6 cups bite-size pieces cooked chicken

2 teaspoons dried tarragon leaves

1 teaspoon salt

1/4 teaspoon pepper

① Heat oven to 400°F. On lightly floured surface, unfold pastry sheets, pressing fold marks flat and sealing any tears. Measure diameter of soup plate or bowl to be used as serving dishes. Using small sharp knife, cut 12 Christmas tree shapes from pastry, about 4 to 5 inches tall and wide, to fit in soup plate. Reroll cut dough to 1/4-inch thickness as necessary to cut all trees.

② On ungreased cookie sheets, arrange pastry trees 1/2 inch apart. Brush with egg. Bake about 8 minutes or until puffed and golden brown.

③ Meanwhile, in 4-quart Dutch oven, melt butter over medium heat. Cook celery and onions in butter 5 to 7 minutes, stirring occasionally, until vegetables are crisp-tender but not browned.

④ Stir in flour until no lumps remain. Slowly add broth, half-and-half and wine, stirring constantly. Heat to boiling, stirring constantly; cook 2 to 3 minutes or until slightly thickened.

⑤ Stir in mixed vegetables, chicken, tarragon, salt and pepper; cook 2 to 3 minutes longer or until hot. Remove from heat. Spoon about 1-1/4 cups chicken mixture into each soup plate. Top with pastry tree.

High Altitude (3500-6500 ft): No change.

1 SERVING: Calories 600; Total Fat 35g (Saturated Fat 14g, Trans Fat 2.5g); Cholesterol 165mg; Sodium 790mg; Total Carbohydrate 41g (Dietary Fiber 5g); Protein 30g. EXCHANGES: 2 Starch, 1/2 Other Carbohydrate, 3-1/2 Lean Meat, 4-1/2 Fat. CARBOHYDRATE CHOICES: 3.

dijon chicken smothered in mushrooms

PREP TIME: 20 minutes • START TO FINISH: 20 minutes • MAKES: 4 servings

4 boneless skinless chicken breasts (about 1-1/4 lb)
1/4 cup Gold Medal® all-purpose flour
1/2 teaspoon salt
1/4 teaspoon pepper
2 tablespoons olive or canola oil
1/2 cup roasted garlic-seasoned chicken broth (from 14-oz can)
1 jar (4.5 oz) Green Giant® sliced mushrooms, drained
1-1/2 tablespoons Dijon mustard
Chopped fresh thyme, if desired

1 Between pieces of plastic wrap or waxed paper, place chicken breast half with smooth side down; gently pound with flat side of meat mallet or rolling pin until about 1/4 inch thick. Repeat with remaining chicken. In shallow pan, stir together flour, salt and pepper.

2 Heat oil in 12-inch nonstick skillet over medium-high heat. Coat both sides of chicken with flour mixture. Cook chicken in hot oil 6 to 8 minutes, turning once, until chicken is no longer pink in center. Remove chicken to serving plate; cover to keep warm.

3 Stir broth into skillet. Heat to boiling over medium-high heat. Stir in mushrooms and mustard. Cook 2 to 3 minutes, stirring frequently, until slightly thickened. Spoon sauce over chicken. Sprinkle with thyme.

High Altitude (3500-6500 ft): No change.

1 SERVING: Calories 270; Total Fat 12g (Saturated Fat 2.5g, Trans Fat 0g); Cholesterol 85mg; Sodium 760mg; Total Carbohydrate 8g (Dietary Fiber 1g); Protein 33g. EXCHANGES: 1/2 Starch, 4-1/2 Very Lean Meat, 1-1/2 Fat. CARBOHYDRATE CHOICES: 1/2.

asian pork stew

2 lb boneless country-style pork ribs,
   cut into 2-inch pieces
3 medium carrots, cut into 1-inch slices
2 medium onions, cut into 1-inch wedges
1 package (8 oz) fresh whole mushrooms,
   cut in half if large
1 can (8 oz) whole water chestnuts, drained
1 can (8 oz) bamboo shoots, drained
3/4 cup hoisin sauce
1/3 cup reduced-sodium soy sauce
4 large cloves garlic, finely chopped
1 tablespoon finely chopped gingerroot
4 cups water
2 cups uncooked regular long-grain white rice
2 tablespoons cornstarch
3 tablespoons water
1/3 cup lightly packed coarsely chopped cilantro

① Spray 5- to 6-quart slow cooker with cooking spray. In cooker, layer pork, carrots, onions, mushrooms, water chestnuts and bamboo shoots. In small bowl, stir together 1/2 cup of the hoisin sauce, the soy sauce, garlic and gingerroot; pour into cooker.

② Cover; cook on Low heat setting for 7 to 9 hours.

③ During last hour of cooking, in 3-quart saucepan, heat 4 cups water and the rice to boiling over high heat. Reduce heat to low. Cover; simmer 15 to 20 minutes or until rice is tender and water is absorbed.

④ Gently remove pork and vegetables with slotted spoon to large bowl; cover to keep warm. Skim any fat from liquid in cooker. Pour liquid into 1-quart saucepan. Stir remaining 1/4 cup hoisin sauce into liquid; heat to boiling. In small bowl, mix cornstarch and 3 tablespoons water; stir into liquid. Cook, stirring constantly, until thickened; pour over pork mixture and gently stir. Sprinkle cilantro over stew. Serve over rice.

High Altitude (3500-6500 ft): No change.

1 SERVING: Calories 510; Total Fat 15g (Saturated Fat 5g, Trans Fat 0g); Cholesterol 70mg; Sodium 810mg; Total Carbohydrate 63g (Dietary Fiber 3g); Protein 30g. EXCHANGES: 3 Starch, 1 Other Carbohydrate, 1 Vegetable, 2-1/2 Medium-Fat Meat. CARBOHYDRATE CHOICES: 4.

tips&ideas

Hoisin sauce is often used in Chinese cuisine. The reddish brown sauce, flavored with soybeans, garlic, chiles and numerous spices, tastes spicy and sweet.

honey-orange ham

PREP TIME: 15 minutes • **START TO FINISH:** 5 hours • **MAKES:** 12 servings

1 orange
1/3 cup honey
1 teaspoon ground mustard
1 fully cooked bone-in half-ham (6 to 9 pounds)
Whole cloves, if desired

① Grate 1 tablespoon peel from orange; squeeze juice. Mix peel and juice with honey and mustard in small bowl. Pierce surface of ham at 2-inch intervals with metal skewer; place in 2-gallon resealable plastic food-storage bag. Pour honey mixture over ham; seal bag. Refrigerate 2 hours.

② Heat oven to 325°. Place ham, fat side up, on rack in shallow roasting pan. Discard marinade. Insert cloves in ham. Insert meat thermometer so tip is in thickest part of ham and does not touch bone or rest in fat.

③ Bake uncovered 1 hour. Cover loosely with aluminum foil so ham does not overbrown. Bake 1 hour to 1 hour 30 minutes longer or until thermometer reads 135° to 140°. Let ham stand loosely covered 10 to 15 minutes for easier carving.

High Altitude (3500-6500 ft): No change.

1 SERVING: Calories 170; Total Fat 6g (Saturated Fat 2g, Trans Fat nc); Cholesterol 60mg; Sodium 1310mg; Total Carbohydrate 6g (Dietary Fiber 0g); Protein 23g. EXCHANGES: 3 Lean Meat. CARBOHYDRATE CHOICES: 1/2.

tips&ideas

The honey marinade soaks into the ham, giving the ham great flavor and a deep golden brown glaze.

african groundnut stew with chicken

PREP TIME: 20 minutes • **START TO FINISH:** 8 hours 20 minutes • **MAKES:** 8 servings (1-1/2 cups each)

6 boneless skinless chicken thighs (about 1 lb)

3 boneless skinless chicken breasts (about 3/4 lb)

1 medium onion, chopped (1 cup)

3/4 cup peanut butter

1 can (28 oz) diced tomatoes, undrained

1-3/4 cups Progresso® chicken broth (from 32-oz carton)

2 tablespoons grated gingerroot

2 tablespoons tomato paste

2 teaspoons curry powder

1 teaspoon crushed red pepper flakes

1/2 teaspoon salt

1-1/2 lb dark-orange sweet potatoes (3 medium), peeled, cubed (about 4 cups)

1 lb small red potatoes (about 12), cut into eighths (about 2-1/2 cups)

① Spray 5- to 6-quart slow cooker with cooking spray. In cooker, layer all ingredients, spooning peanut butter in dollops.

② Cover; cook on Low heat setting for 8 to 10 hours. Break up chicken before serving.

High Altitude (3500-6500 ft): No change.

1 SERVING: Calories 420; Total Fat 19g (Saturated Fat 4.5g, Trans Fat 0g); Cholesterol 60mg; Sodium 710mg; Total Carbohydrate 32g (Dietary Fiber 6g); Protein 31g. EXCHANGES: 1-1/2 Starch, 1/2 Other Carbohydrate, 1 Vegetable, 3-1/2 Lean Meat, 1 Fat. CARBOHYDRATE CHOICES: 2.

p. 161

p. 166

casual winter entertaining

Even if the weather outside is frightful, your company will feel delightful eating these simple pleasures.

cheesy chicken quesadillas

PREP TIME: 25 minutes • START TO FINISH: 25 minutes • MAKES: 32 servings (1 wedge each)

1 cup chopped cooked chicken
1/4 cup fat-free ranch dressing
2 teaspoons chili powder
1/2 teaspoon grated lime peel
4 flour tortillas (8 to 10 inch)
1/2 cup shredded Mexican cheese blend (2 oz)
2 medium green onions, thinly sliced (2 tablespoons)
1 tablespoon vegetable oil
Sour cream, if desired

① Heat gas or charcoal grill. In medium bowl, mix chicken, dressing, chili powder and lime peel. Spread chicken mixture over half of each tortilla; sprinkle with cheese and onions. Fold tortilla over and press down. Brush top of each with oil.

② Place quesadillas, oil sides down, on grill over medium-low heat. Brush tops with remaining oil. Cover grill; cook 4 to 6 minutes, turning once, until both sides are golden brown and cheese is melted. Cut each into 8 wedges. Serve with sour cream.

VARIATION: To cook in skillet: Heat 12-inch skillet over medium-high heat. Place quesadilla, oil side down, in skillet. Brush top with oil. Cook 2 to 3 minutes, turning once, until both sides are golden brown and cheese is melted. Repeat with remaining quesadillas.

High Altitude (3500-6500 ft): No change.

1 SERVING: Calories 40; Total Fat 2g (Saturated Fat 0.5g, Trans Fat 0g); Cholesterol 5mg; Sodium 70mg; Total Carbohydrate 4g (Dietary Fiber 0g); Protein 2g. EXCHANGES: 1/2 Starch. CARBOHYDRATE CHOICES: 0.

tips & ideas

Purchase a cooked chicken breast at the deli; then remove the skin and bones. This will yield about 1 cup of cooked chicken.

beef and onion soup with cheesy biscuit croutons

PREP TIME: 25 minutes • START TO FINISH: 30 minutes • MAKES: 4 servings (1-1/2 cups each)

SOUP
- 1 lb lean (at least 80%) ground beef
- 1 package onion soup and dip mix (from 2-oz box)
- 1/4 teaspoon pepper
- 1-3/4 cups Progresso® beef flavored broth (from 32-oz carton)
- 3 cups water
- 1 tablespoon packed brown sugar
- 1 tablespoon Worcestershire sauce

CROUTONS
- 1 cup Original Bisquick® mix
- 3 tablespoons grated Parmesan cheese
- 1/4 cup water
- 3/4 cup finely shredded Swiss cheese (3 oz)

Italian (flat-leaf) parsley, if desired

VARIATION: A blue-veined cheese, such as blue, Gorgonzola or Stilton, would be tasty on the croutons. Use about 3/4 cup crumbled cheese instead of the Swiss cheese.

High Altitude (3500-6500 ft): No change.

1 SERVING: Calories 460; Total Fat 24g (Saturated Fat 11g, Trans Fat 2g); Cholesterol 95mg; Sodium 1640mg; Total Carbohydrate 30g (Dietary Fiber 1g); Protein 31g. EXCHANGES: 1 Starch, 1 Other Carbohydrate, 4 Medium-Fat Meat, 1/2 Fat. CARBOHYDRATE CHOICES: 2.

① In 3-quart saucepan, cook beef, onion soup mix and pepper over medium-high heat 5 to 7 minutes, stirring occasionally, until beef is thoroughly cooked; drain. Stir in broth, water, brown sugar and Worcestershire sauce. Heat to boiling. Reduce heat to medium-low; cook uncovered for 10 minutes. Cover and remove from heat.

② Meanwhile, heat oven to 425°F. Spray cookie sheet with cooking spray. In medium bowl, stir Bisquick mix, Parmesan cheese and water until soft dough forms. Place dough on surface sprinkled with Bisquick mix; roll in Bisquick mix to coat. Shape into a ball; knead 10 times. On cookie sheet, press or roll dough into 12x6-inch rectangle, 1/4 inch thick. Cut into 8 squares, but do not separate. Bake 6 to 8 minutes or until golden brown. Remove from oven.

③ Set oven control to broil. Sprinkle croutons with Swiss cheese. Cut and separate squares slightly. Broil with tops 4 to 6 inches from heat 2 to 3 minutes or until cheese is bubbly and slightly browned.

④ Float 2 croutons in each bowl of soup. Garnish with parsley.

philly beef squares

PREP TIME: 15 minutes • START TO FINISH: 1 hour 5 minutes • MAKES: 6 servings

1-1/2 teaspoons dried minced onion
1 lb lean (at least 80%) ground beef
3/4 cup cheese dip (from 15-oz jar)
2 cups Original Bisquick® mix
1 cup milk
1 egg
2 cups frozen bell pepper and onion stir-fry
(from 1-lb bag), thawed, drained

(1) Heat oven to 375°F. Spray 8-inch square pan or 2-quart glass baking dish with cooking spray. In small bowl, cover onion with hot water.

(2) In 10-inch skillet, cook beef over medium-high heat 5 to 7 minutes, stirring occasionally, until brown; drain. Stir in cheese dip. Cook 2 to 3 minutes or until hot.

(3) In medium bowl, mix Bisquick mix, milk and egg until blended. Pour half of the batter into pan. Top with beef mixture and bell pepper mixture. Pour remaining batter evenly over top. Drain onion; sprinkle over batter.

(4) Bake 40 to 45 minutes or until golden brown and center is set. Let stand 5 minutes before cutting into squares. If desired, heat leftover cheese dip as directed on jar and spoon over each serving.

High Altitude (3500-6500 ft): Bake 42 to 47 minutes.

1 SERVING: Calories 390; Total Fat 20g (Saturated Fat 8g, Trans Fat 1.5g); Cholesterol 95mg; Sodium 810mg; Total Carbohydrate 32g (Dietary Fiber 1g); Protein 21g. EXCHANGES: 1-1/2 Starch, 1/2 Other Carbohydrate, 2-1/2 Medium-Fat Meat, 1-1/2 Fat. CARBOHYDRATE CHOICES: 2.

turkey-green chile enchiladas

PREP TIME: 20 minutes • **START TO FINISH:** 1 hour 5 minutes • **MAKES:** 8 servings

SAUCE

- 2 tablespoons vegetable oil
- 1 large onion, finely chopped (1 cup)
- 2 cloves garlic, finely chopped
- 1 cup chicken broth
- 2 tablespoons semisweet chocolate chips
- 1 tablespoon ground ancho chiles
- 1 teaspoon ground cumin
- 1/2 teaspoon salt
- 1 can (28 oz) fire-roasted crushed tomatoes, undrained

ENCHILADAS

- 2 cups shredded cooked turkey
- 1 cup sour cream
- 1-1/2 cups shredded Cheddar cheese (6 oz)
- 2 cans (4.5 oz each) Old El Paso® chopped green chiles, undrained
- 1 package (11.5 oz) Old El Paso® flour tortillas for burritos (8 tortillas)
- 1 cup shredded pepper Jack cheese (4 oz)

① Heat oven to 350°F. Lightly spray 13x9-inch (3-quart) glass baking dish with cooking spray.

② In 12-inch skillet, heat oil over medium-high heat. Add onion and garlic; cook about 1 minute, stirring frequently, until onion is tender. Stir in remaining sauce ingredients. Heat to boiling. Reduce heat to low; cook uncovered 15 minutes, stirring occasionally.

③ In medium bowl, mix all enchilada ingredients except tortillas and pepper Jack cheese. Spread about 1/2 cup turkey mixture over each tortilla; top with 2 tablespoons sauce. Roll up tortillas; arrange seam sides down in baking dish. Pour remaining sauce over tortillas. Top with pepper Jack cheese.

④ Spray sheet of foil with cooking spray; place sprayed side down over baking dish. Bake 30 to 45 minutes or until thoroughly heated.

High Altitude (3500-6500 ft): Bake 45 to 50 minutes.

1 SERVING: Calories 470; Total Fat 27g (Saturated Fat 13g, Trans Fat 0.5g); Cholesterol 85mg; Sodium 1520mg; Total Carbohydrate 33g (Dietary Fiber 2g); Protein 24g. EXCHANGES: 1-1/2 Starch, 1/2 Other Carbohydrate, 3 Lean Meat, 3-1/2 Fat. CARBOHYDRATE CHOICES: 2.

tips&ideas

Chocolate chips are used in this recipe to add depth to the flavor of the sauce.

salsa chicken fiesta

PREP TIME: 15 minutes • **START TO FINISH:** 45 minutes • **MAKES:** 6 servings

2/3 cup Bisquick Heart Smart™ mix
2 tablespoons water
1/4 cup fat-free egg product or 2 egg whites
1-1/2 cups shredded reduced-fat Cheddar cheese (6 oz)
3 boneless skinless chicken breasts, cut into 1/2-inch pieces
1-1/4 cups Old El Paso® Thick 'n Chunky salsa

① Heat oven to 400°F. Spray 8- or 9-inch square pan with cooking spray. In small bowl, stir Bisquick® mix, water and egg product until well blended; spread in pan. Sprinkle with 1-1/4 cups of the cheese.

② In 10-inch nonstick skillet, cook chicken over medium-high heat, stirring frequently, until outsides turn white; drain. Stir in salsa; heat until hot. Spoon over batter in pan to within 1/2 inch of edges.

③ Bake 22 to 25 minutes or until edges are dark golden brown. Sprinkle with remaining 1/4 cup cheese. Bake 1 to 3 minutes longer or until cheese is melted; loosen from sides of pan.

High Altitude (3500-6500 ft): Do not use 8-inch pan. Increase Bisquick Heart Smart™ mix to 3/4 cup. Increase first bake time to 25 to 30 minutes.

1 SERVING: Calories 190; Total Fat 5g (Saturated Fat 2g, Trans Fat 0g); Cholesterol 45mg; Sodium 850mg; Total Carbohydrate 15g (Dietary Fiber 0g); Protein 22g. EXCHANGES: 1 Starch, 2-1/2 Very Lean Meat, 1/2 Fat. CARBOHYDRATE CHOICES: 1.

tips&ideas

Serve with bowls of shredded lettuce, chopped tomatoes, chopped onions, sliced black olives and fat-free sour cream.

asian barbecue pulled-pork sandwiches with asian slaw

PREP TIME: 15 minutes • **START TO FINISH:** 8 hours 55 minutes • **MAKES:** 13 sandwiches

1 boneless pork shoulder roast (3 lb),
   trimmed of fat

1/2 teaspoon seasoned salt

1 cup barbecue sauce

1/2 cup teriyaki marinade and sauce
   (from 11-oz bottle)

4 cups coleslaw mix (from 1-lb bag)

3 medium green onions, sliced (2 tablespoons)

1 tablespoon sugar

1/4 cup rice vinegar

3 tablespoons water

1-1/2 teaspoons seasoned salt

13 sandwich buns, split

① Remove netting or strings from pork roast; cut pork into 3-inch pieces. Place pork in 5- to 6-quart slow cooker. Sprinkle with 1/2 teaspoon seasoned salt; toss to coat.

② Cover and cook on Low heat setting about 8 to 10 hours.

③ Remove pork from cooker, using slotted spoon; place on cutting board. Discard liquid in cooker. Shred pork, using 2 forks. Return to cooker. Mix barbecue sauce and teriyaki marinade in small bowl; pour over pork and mix well. Increase heat setting to High. Cover and cook 30 to 40 minutes or until hot.

④ Mix remaining ingredients except buns in large bowl. To serve, spoon 1/3 cup pork mixture into each bun and top with 1/4 cup coleslaw. Pork mixture will hold on Low heat setting up to 2 hours; stir occasionally.

VARIATION: Instead of the teriyaki marinade, you can use an additional 1/2 cup of the barbecue sauce.

High Altitude (3500-6500 ft): No change.

1 SANDWICH: Calories 330; Total Fat 13g (Saturated Fat 4.5g, Trans Fat 0g); Cholesterol 55mg; Sodium 500mg; Total Carbohydrate 30g (Dietary Fiber 2g); Protein 23g. EXCHANGES: 2 Starch, 3 Medium-Fat Meat. CARBOHYDRATE CHOICES: 2.

tips&ideas

To continue the fun Asian theme, you could serve two salads: one of melon chunks drizzled with a citrus dressing, the other a pasta salad tossed with Thai peanut dressing.

make-ahead cheeseburger lasagna

PREP TIME: 35 minutes • **START TO FINISH:** 10 hours 5 minutes • **MAKES:** 8 servings

1-1/2 lb lean (at least 80%) ground beef
   3 tablespoons instant minced onion
   1 can (15 oz) tomato sauce
1-1/2 cups water
  1/2 cup ketchup
   1 tablespoon yellow mustard
   1 egg
   1 container (15 oz) ricotta cheese
   2 cups shredded Cheddar-American cheese
     blend (8 oz)
  12 uncooked lasagna noodles
   1 cup shredded Cheddar cheese (4 oz)
   1 cup shredded lettuce
   1 medium tomato, sliced
  1/2 cup dill pickle slices

① Spray 13x9-inch (3-quart) glass baking dish with cooking spray. In 12-inch nonstick skillet, cook beef and onion over medium-high heat for 5 to 7 minutes, stirring frequently, until beef is brown; drain. Stir in tomato sauce, water, ketchup and mustard. Simmer 5 minutes, stirring occasionally.

② Meanwhile, in medium bowl, beat egg with fork or wire whisk. Stir in ricotta cheese and 2 cups of the cheese blend.

③ Spread 1 cup beef mixture over bottom of baking dish. Top with 4 uncooked noodles. Spread half of the ricotta mixture over noodles; top with 1-1/2 cups beef mixture. Repeat layers once with 4 noodles, remaining ricotta mixture and 1-1/2 cups beef mixture. Top with remaining 4 noodles, beef mixture and 1 cup Cheddar cheese. Cover with foil; refrigerate at least 8 hours or overnight.

④ Heat oven to 350°F. Bake lasagna, covered, 45 minutes. Uncover and bake 25 to 35 minutes longer or until bubbly. Remove from oven. Cover with foil; let stand 5 to 10 minutes before cutting.

⑤ Just before serving, top with lettuce, tomato and pickles. Serve with additional ketchup if desired.

High Altitude (3500-6500 ft): Use 1-3/4 cups water.

1 SERVING: Calories 590; Total Fat 32g (Saturated Fat 17g, Trans Fat 1g); Cholesterol 135mg; Sodium 1050mg; Total Carbohydrate 38g (Dietary Fiber 3g); Protein 39g. EXCHANGES: 2 Starch, 1/2 Other Carbohydrate, 5 Medium-Fat Meat, 1 Fat. CARBOHYDRATE CHOICES: 2-1/2.

jerk pork sandwiches

PREP TIME: 20 minutes • **START TO FINISH:** 9 hours 20 minutes • **MAKES:** 8 sandwiches

1 boneless pork shoulder roast (2-1/2 to 3 lb)
1 medium onion, chopped (1/2 cup)
3 tablespoons Caribbean jerk seasoning
1/2 cup chili sauce
1/2 cup purchased corn relish
2 tablespoons chopped fresh cilantro
1 cup shredded lettuce
8 pita fold breads

① Spray 3- to 4-quart slow cooker with cooking spray. Carefully remove netting or strings from pork roast; cut pork into 2-inch pieces. Place pork and onion in cooker. Sprinkle with jerk seasoning; gently toss to coat. Pour chili sauce over top.

② Cover and cook on Low heat setting about 9 to 11 hours.

③ Place pork on cutting board; use 2 forks to pull pork into shreds. Return pork to cooker. Mix corn relish and cilantro in small bowl. To serve, layer lettuce, pork mixture and corn relish in pita fold breads.

High Altitude (3500-6500 ft): No change.

1 SANDWICH: Calories 450; Total Fat 18g (Saturated Fat 6g, Trans Fat 0g); Cholesterol 90mg; Sodium 760mg; Total Carbohydrate 36g (Dietary Fiber 3g); Protein 36g. EXCHANGES: 2-1/2 Starch, 4 Lean Meat, 1/2 Fat. CARBOHYDRATE CHOICES: 2-1/2.

tips&ideas

Caribbean jerk seasoning, sometimes called Jamaican jerk seasoning, is a blend of many spices that may include chiles, thyme, garlic, cinnamon and ginger. You'll find it by the other spices.

thai peanut chicken

PREP TIME: 10 minutes • **START TO FINISH:** 5 hours 10 minutes • **MAKES:** 6 servings

8 boneless skinless chicken thighs (2 lb)
1 bottle (13.5 oz) Thai peanut sauce
2 medium carrots, sliced (3/4 cup)
4 medium green onions, sliced (1/2 cup)
1 cup uncooked converted white rice
2-1/4 cups water
1/4 cup chopped cocktail peanuts
2 tablespoons chopped fresh cilantro
1/2 cup chopped red bell pepper, if desired

① Spray 3- to 4-quart slow cooker with cooking spray. In cooker, place chicken thighs. In medium bowl, mix peanut sauce, carrots and onions; pour over chicken.

② Cover; cook on Low heat setting about 5 to 6 hours.

③ Cook rice in water as directed on package; spoon onto serving platter. With slotted spoon, remove chicken from cooker; place over rice. Pour sauce from cooker over chicken. Sprinkle with peanuts, cilantro and red bell pepper.

High Altitude (3500-6500 ft): No change.

1 SERVING: Calories 490; Total Fat 21g (Saturated Fat 3g, Trans Fat 0g); Cholesterol 60mg; Sodium 1370mg; Total Carbohydrate 46g (Dietary Fiber 1g); Protein 29g. EXCHANGES: 2 Starch, 1 Other Carbohydrate, 3 Lean Meat, 2 Fat. CARBOHYDRATE CHOICES: 3.

layered mexican party salad

PREP TIME: 20 minutes • **START TO FINISH:** 30 minutes • **MAKES:** 12 servings (1 cup each)

1 box (7.75 oz) Betty Crocker® Suddenly Salad® classic pasta salad mix
3 tablespoons cold water
2 tablespoons vegetable oil
1 teaspoon ground cumin
1 can (15 oz) Progresso® black beans, drained, rinsed
1 can (15.25 oz) Green Giant® whole kernel corn, drained
4 cups torn romaine lettuce
1 container (12 oz) refrigerated guacamole dip
1-1/2 cups finely shredded Mexican 4-cheese blend (6 oz)
3 plum (Roma) tomatoes, chopped
1 can (2-1/4 oz) sliced ripe olives, drained
3 cups nacho-flavored tortilla chips

① Empty pasta mix into 3-quart saucepan 2/3 full of boiling water. Gently boil uncovered about 12 minutes, stirring occasionally. Drain pasta; rinse with cold water. Shake to drain well.

② In medium bowl, stir together seasoning mix, water, oil and cumin. Stir in pasta, beans and corn.

③ In 4-quart glass salad bowl or 13x9-inch glass baking dish, layer lettuce and pasta mixture. Carefully spread guacamole evenly over top. Sprinkle with cheese and tomatoes; top with olives.

④ Just before serving, arrange chips around edge of bowl. Serve immediately, or refrigerate.

High Altitude (3500-6500 ft): Make pasta mix following High Altitude directions on box.

1 SERVING: Calories 300; Total Fat 13g (Saturated Fat 4g, Trans Fat 0g); Cholesterol 15mg; Sodium 700mg; Total Carbohydrate 36g (Dietary Fiber 7g); Protein 9g. EXCHANGES: 1-1/2 Starch, 1 Other Carbohydrate, 1/2 High-Fat Meat, 1-1/2 Fat. CARBOHYDRATE CHOICES: 2-1/2.

chile-chicken enchilada casserole

PREP TIME: 25 minutes • START TO FINISH: 1 hour 30 minutes • MAKES: 8 servings

2 cups diced cooked chicken
3 cups shredded Colby-Monterey Jack cheese (12 oz)
1 can (4.5 oz) Old El Paso® chopped green chiles, undrained
3/4 cup sour cream
1 package (11.5 oz) Old El Paso® flour tortillas for burritos (8 tortillas)
1 can (16 oz) Old El Paso® refried beans
1 can (10 oz) Old El Paso® enchilada sauce
4 medium green onions, sliced (1/4 cup)
1 cup shredded lettuce
1 medium tomato, chopped (3/4 cup)

① Heat oven to 350°F. Spray 13x9-inch (3-quart) glass baking dish with cooking spray. In medium bowl, mix chicken, 1-1/2 cups of the cheese, the green chiles and sour cream.

② Layer 3 tortillas in baking dish, overlapping as necessary and placing slightly up sides of dish (cut third tortilla in half). Spread about half of the beans over tortillas. Top with about half of the chicken mixture and half of the enchilada sauce. Layer with 3 more tortillas and remaining beans and chicken mixture. Place remaining 2 tortillas over chicken mixture, overlapping slightly (do not place up sides of dish). Pour remaining enchilada sauce over top. Sprinkle with remaining 1-1/2 cups cheese. Cover baking dish with foil.

③ Bake 45 to 55 minutes or until bubbly and thoroughly heated. Let stand 5 to 10 minutes before cutting. Garnish casserole or individual servings with onions, lettuce and tomato.

High Altitude (3500-6500 ft): Heat oven to 375°F.

1 SERVING: Calories 470; Total Fat 25g (Saturated Fat 13g, Trans Fat 0.5g); Cholesterol 85mg; Sodium 1080mg; Total Carbohydrate 34g (Dietary Fiber 3g); Protein 27g. EXCHANGES: 2-1/2 Starch, 2-1/2 Medium-Fat Meat, 2 Fat. CARBOHYDRATE CHOICES: 2

tips&ideas

This is a perfect dinner option for when you anticipate a busy day. Make the casserole in the morning (or up to 8 hours in advance), then cover and refrigerate it until it's time to bake it.

cheesy scalloped potatoes with ham

PREP TIME: 50 minutes • **START TO FINISH:** 50 minutes • **MAKES:** 6 servings (1 cup each)

2 tablespoons butter or margarine
1 clove garlic, finely chopped
2 lb round white potatoes (about 4 medium), peeled and thinly sliced
1/2 lb fully cooked ham, cut into 1/2-inch pieces (about 2 cups)
1 cup shredded American-Cheddar cheese blend (4 oz)
3 tablespoons Gold Medal® all-purpose flour
1/4 teaspoon pepper
1 pint (2 cups) half-and-half

① In 4-quart Dutch oven, melt butter over medium heat. Cook garlic in butter 1 minute, stirring occasionally, until softened. Remove from heat. Stir in potatoes, ham, cheese, flour and pepper.

② Pour half-and-half over potato mixture. Heat to boiling over medium-high heat; reduce heat to low. Cover and simmer about 30 minutes, stirring occasionally, until potatoes are tender.

High Altitude (3500-6500 ft): No change.

1 SERVING: Calories 430; Total Fat 24g (Saturated Fat 13g, Trans Fat 0.5g); Cholesterol 85mg; Sodium 850mg; Total Carbohydrate 34g (Dietary Fiber 3g); Protein 20g. EXCHANGES: 2 Starch, 2 Medium-Fat Meat, 2-1/2 Fat. CARBOHYDRATE CHOICES: 2

tips&ideas

We do not recommend using low-fat or nonfat milk instead of the half-and-half in this recipe because it can curdle when heated.

philly cheese steak sandwiches

PREP TIME: 15 minutes • **START TO FINISH:** 6 hours 15 minutes • **MAKES:** 6 sandwiches

1 boneless beef round steak, 1 inch thick (2 lb), trimmed of fat, cut into bite-size strips

2 medium onions, sliced

1 tablespoon garlic-pepper blend

2 tablespoons water

1 tablespoon beef bouillon granules

2 large green bell peppers, cut into bite-size strips

6 slices (3/4 oz each) American cheese, cut in half

6 hoagie buns, split

① Spray 3- to 4-quart slow cooker with cooking spray. In medium bowl, sprinkle beef and onions with garlic-pepper blend; stir to coat evenly. Spoon mixture into cooker.

② In measuring cup, stir water and bouillon granules until granules are dissolved. Pour over mixture in cooker.

③ Cover; cook on Low heat setting 6 to 8 hours. About 20 minutes before serving, stir in bell peppers.

④ Place 2 cheese pieces on bottom of each bun. Using slotted spoon, spoon beef mixture over cheese. Cover with tops of buns. Beef mixture can be kept warm on Low heat setting up to 2 hours.

VARIATION: Cheddar or mozzarella cheese can be used in place of the American cheese.

High Altitude (3500-6500 ft): No change.

1 SANDWICH: Calories 550; Total Fat 14g (Saturated Fat 7g, Trans Fat 1g); Cholesterol 105mg; Sodium 1360mg; Total Carbohydrate 56g (Dietary Fiber 4g); Protein 49g. EXCHANGES: 2 Starch, 1 Other Carbohydrate, 1 Vegetable, 6 Very Lean Meat, 2 Fat. CARBOHYDRATE CHOICES: 4.

chipotle salsa ribs

PREP TIME: 10 minutes • START TO FINISH: 6 hours 10 minutes • MAKES: 6 servings

SOUTHWESTERN RUB

1 tablespoon packed brown sugar
1 teaspoon chili powder
1 teaspoon paprika
1/2 teaspoon ground cumin
1/2 teaspoon seasoned salt
1/2 teaspoon garlic pepper
1/4 teaspoon ground ginger

RIBS

4 pounds pork loin back ribs
(not cut into serving pieces)
1/2 cup chipotle salsa
1/4 cup chili sauce
2 tablespoons orange marmalade

① Combine all ingredients for rub and mix well. Rub mixture over ribs. Wrap tightly in plastic wrap and refrigerate at least 4 hours but no longer than 12 hours.

② If using charcoal grill, place drip pan directly under grilling area, and arrange coals around edge of firebox. Heat coals or gas grill for indirect heat. Cover and grill ribs over drip pan or over unheated side of gas grill and 4 to 6 inches from medium heat 1 hour 30 minutes to 2 hours, turning occasionally, until tender.

③ Mix salsa, chili sauce and marmalade in small bowl. Brush over ribs during last 10 to 15 minutes of grilling. Heat remaining salsa mixture to boiling; boil and stir 1 minute. Cut ribs into serving-size pieces. Serve salsa mixture with ribs.

High Altitude (3500-6500 ft): No change.

1 SERVING: Calories 610; Total Fat 44g (Saturated Fat 16g, Trans Fat 0g); Cholesterol 175mg; Sodium 500mg; Total Carbohydrate 11g (Dietary Fiber 1g); Protein 43g. EXCHANGES: 1 Other Carbohydrate, 6 Medium-Fat Meat, 2-1/2 Fat. CARBOHYDRATE CHOICES: 1.

tips&ideas

Pork loin back ribs are the leanest and most tender ribs, but you also could use pork spareribs. Plan on cooking them for the same amount of time.

hot veggie and cheese hoagies

PREP TIME: 30 minutes • **START TO FINISH:** 45 minutes • **MAKES:** 8 sandwiches

8 soft sub or hoagie buns (about 6 to 7 inch), split
1 tablespoon olive or vegetable oil
1 medium onion, halved, thinly sliced
1 medium red bell pepper, coarsely chopped
4 cups small broccoli florets
3 cups sliced fresh mushrooms (8 oz)
1 teaspoon dried basil leaves
1/2 teaspoon seasoned salt
1 tablespoon water
1/4 cup Italian dressing
8 slices (3/4 oz each) Havarti cheese
8 slices (3/4 oz each) Cheddar cheese

① Heat oven to 375°F. On ungreased cookie sheet, place buns, cut sides up. Bake 5 to 8 minutes or until toasted.

② Meanwhile, in 12-inch nonstick skillet, heat oil over medium-high heat. Cook onion and bell pepper in oil 3 minutes, stirring constantly. Add broccoli and mushrooms; sprinkle with basil and seasoned salt; add water. Cover; cook 3 to 5 minutes, stirring occasionally, until broccoli is crisp-tender.

③ Cut eight 16x12-inch pieces of foil. Spray foil with cooking spray. Drizzle dressing over cut sides of toasted buns. Cut cheese slices to fit sandwiches. Layer Havarti cheese, vegetable mixture and Cheddar cheese in buns. Wrap each sandwich in foil.

④ Bake 10 to 15 minutes or until warm and cheese is melted.

High Altitude (3500-6500 ft): No change.

1 SANDWICH: Calories 520; Total Fat 23g (Saturated Fat 11g, Trans Fat 1g); Cholesterol 45mg; Sodium 1050mg; Total Carbohydrate 58g (Dietary Fiber 5g); Protein 21g. EXCHANGES: 3 Starch, 1/2 Other Carbohydrate, 1 Vegetable, 1-1/2 High-Fat Meat, 2 Fat. CARBOHYDRATE CHOICES: 4.

tips&ideas

Instead of using cooking spray to spray the foil, try the new nonstick foil available in grocery stores. It's a great convenience product.

mexican chicken chili

PREP TIME: 10 minutes • **START TO FINISH:** 7 hours 10 minutes • **MAKES:** 6 servings (1-2/3 cups each)

1-3/4 lb boneless skinless chicken thighs
1 medium onion, chopped (1/2 cup)
2 medium stalks celery, sliced (3/4 cup)
2 cans (14.5 oz each) stewed tomatoes with garlic and onion, undrained
2 cans (15 to 16 oz each) pinto beans, undrained
1 can (10 oz) Old El Paso® enchilada sauce
2 teaspoons chili powder
1 teaspoon ground cumin
1/3 cup sour cream
2 tablespoons chopped fresh cilantro, if desired
Scoop-shaped corn chips, if desired

① Spray 4- to 5-quart slow cooker with cooking spray. In cooker, mix all ingredients except sour cream, cilantro and corn chips.

② Cover; cook on Low heat setting for about 7 to 8 hours.

③ Stir mixture to break up chicken. Top each serving with sour cream and cilantro. Serve with corn chips.

High Altitude (3500-6500 ft): No change.

1 SERVING: Calories 410; Total Fat 11g (Saturated Fat 4g, Trans Fat 0g); Cholesterol 60mg; Sodium 860mg; Total Carbohydrate 47g (Dietary Fiber 13g); Protein 31g. EXCHANGES: 2 Starch, 1 Other Carbohydrate, 3-1/2 Lean Meat. CARBOHYDRATE CHOICES: 3.

tips&ideas

Instead of using the canned stewed tomatoes with garlic and onion, use regular stewed tomatoes and add a teaspoon of finely chopped garlic.

turkey salad sandwiches

PREP TIME: 20 minutes • **START TO FINISH:** 20 minutes • **MAKES:** 4 sandwiches

1-1/2 cups diced cooked turkey
1/2 cup diced unpeeled apple
1/2 cup mayonnaise or salad dressing
1-1/2 teaspoons curry powder
1/4 teaspoon ground ginger
1/4 teaspoon pepper
1 medium stalk celery, chopped (1/2 cup)
2 green onions, chopped (2 tablespoons)
8 slices whole grain bread

① In medium bowl, mix all of the ingredients except bread.

② Spread turkey mixture on 4 slices bread. Top with remaining bread.

High Altitude (3500-6500 ft): No change.

1 SANDWICH: Calories 460; Total Fat 28g (Saturated Fat 5g, Trans Fat 0.5g); Cholesterol 55mg; Sodium 510mg; Total Carbohydrate 31g (Dietary Fiber 5g); Protein 21g. EXCHANGES: 2 Starch, 2 Lean Meat, 4 Fat. CARBOHYDRATE CHOICES: 2.

turkey taco pizza

PREP TIME: 20 minutes • **START TO FINISH:** 30 minutes • **MAKES:** 4 servings (2 wedges each)

1 package (10 oz) prebaked thin Italian
   pizza crust (12 inch)
1/2 cup Old El Paso® taco sauce
2 cups chopped cooked turkey
1-1/2 cups shredded mozzarella and Cheddar
   cheese blend (6 oz)
1/2 cup sour cream
1 cup shredded lettuce
1 medium tomato, seeded, chopped (3/4 cup)
1/2 cup crushed nacho-flavored tortilla chips

① Heat oven to 450°F. On cookie sheet, place pizza crust. In small bowl, stir the taco sauce and turkey.

② Spread turkey mixture over pizza crust, leaving 1-inch border. Top with cheese. Bake 8 to 10 minutes or until cheese is melted and pizza is thoroughly heated.

③ Drop sour cream by teaspoonfuls over pizza. Top with lettuce, tomato and tortilla chips. Cut into 8 wedges.

High Altitude (3500-6500 ft): No change.

1 SERVING: Calories 580; Total Fat 29g (Saturated Fat 14g, Trans Fat 1g); Cholesterol 125mg; Sodium 960mg; Total Carbohydrate 43g (Dietary Fiber 2g); Protein 38g. EXCHANGES: 2-1/2 Starch, 1/2 Other Carbohydrate, 4 Lean Meat, 3 Fat. CARBOHYDRATE CHOICES: 3.

greek turkey burgers with yogurt sauce

PREP TIME: 20 minutes • **START TO FINISH:** 20 minutes • **MAKES:** 4 servings

YOGURT SAUCE
1/2 cup plain fat-free yogurt
1/4 cup chopped red onion
1/4 cup chopped cucumber

BURGERS
1 lb lean ground turkey
1/2 cup plain fat-free yogurt
1 teaspoon dried oregano leaves
1/2 teaspoon garlic powder
1/2 teaspoon salt
1/2 teaspoon pepper
4 whole wheat hamburger buns

① In small bowl, mix all sauce ingredients; refrigerate until ready to serve.

② Set oven control to broil. In medium bowl, mix all burger ingredients except buns. Shape mixture into 4 patties, each about 1/2 inch thick and 5 inches in diameter. Place patties on rack in broiler pan.

③ Broil burgers about 6 inches from heat 8 to 10 minutes, turning after 5 minutes, until thermometer inserted in center reads 165°F. Place burgers on buns. Serve with sauce.

High Altitude (3500-6500 ft): No change.

1 SERVING: Calories 310; Total Fat 8g (Saturated Fat 2g, Trans Fat 0.5g); Cholesterol 75mg; Sodium 640mg; Total Carbohydrate 26g (Dietary Fiber 3g); Protein 33g. EXCHANGES: 1-1/2 Starch, 4 Very Lean Meat, 1 Fat. CARBOHYDRATE CHOICES: 2.

tips&ideas
This flavorful yogurt sauce tastes great on pita bread wedges or as a dip for veggies. The red onion and cucumber supply a fresh burst of flavor.

latin-style flank steak with spicy parsley pesto

1 lb beef flank steak
1/4 teaspoon pepper
1/4 teaspoon salt
1/2 cup chopped fresh flat-leaf or
    curly-leaf parsley
2 teaspoons red wine vinegar
5 or 6 drops red pepper sauce
1/8 teaspoon ground cumin

① Place oven rack in second position from the top. Set oven control to broil.

② On rack in broiler pan, place beef. Sprinkle with pepper and half of the salt. Broil with top 4 to 6 inches from heat 10 to 12 minutes, turning once, until desired doneness.

③ In small bowl, mix parsley, vinegar, pepper sauce, cumin and remaining half of the salt.

④ Cut beef across grain into thin strips. Serve beef with parsley pesto.

High Altitude (3500-6500 ft): No change.

1 SERVING: Calories 210; Total Fat 13g (Saturated Fat 5g, Trans Fat 0.5g); Cholesterol 70mg; Sodium 210mg; Total Carbohydrate 0g (Dietary Fiber 0g); Protein 23g. EXCHANGES: 3 Medium-Fat Meat. CARBOHYDRATE CHOICES: 0.

tips&ideas

For easy cleanup, line broiler pan with foil. Roasted Vegetables (page 89) are a good accompaniment to the steak.

gingered chicken and fruit salad

PREP TIME: 25 minutes • START TO FINISH: 25 minutes • MAKES: 4 servings

DRESSING

1/2 teaspoon grated lime peel
2 tablespoons fresh lime juice
2 tablespoons canola oil
1 tablespoon water
2 teaspoons honey
1/2 teaspoon ground ginger

SALAD

6 cups fresh baby spinach leaves
2 cups cubed cooked chicken breast
1 ripe medium mango, seed removed,
   peeled and cubed
1 cup red seedless grapes, halved
2 medium green onions, sliced (2 tablespoons)
2 tablespoons coarsely chopped pecans, toasted

① In container with tight-fitting lid, shake dressing ingredients until well mixed.

② Divide spinach leaves among 4 serving plates. Top each with chicken, mango, grapes, onions and pecans. Drizzle with dressing.

High Altitude (3500-6500 ft): No change.

1 SERVING: Calories 290; Total Fat 13g (Saturated Fat 1.5g, Trans Fat 0g); Cholesterol 55mg; Sodium 90mg; Total Carbohydrate 22g (Dietary Fiber 3g); Protein 23g. EXCHANGES: 1/2 Fruit, 1 Other Carbohydrate, 3 Lean Meat, 1 Fat. CARBOHYDRATE CHOICES: 1-1/2.

tips & ideas

If you poach your own fresh chicken breasts in reduced-sodium chicken broth instead of using packaged cooked cubed chicken, you'll reduce the overall sodium in this recipe.

cheesy potato soup

PREP TIME: 15 minutes • **START TO FINISH:** 6 hours 45 minutes • **MAKES:** 6 servings (1-1/2 cups each)

1 bag (32 oz) frozen southern-style diced hash brown potatoes, thawed

1/2 cup frozen chopped onion (from 12-oz bag), thawed

1 medium stalk celery, diced (1/2 cup)

3-1/2 cups Progresso® chicken broth (from 32-oz carton)

1 cup water

3 tablespoons Gold Medal® all-purpose flour

1 cup milk

1 bag (8 oz) shredded American-Cheddar cheese blend (2 cups)

1/4 cup real bacon pieces (from 2.8-oz package)

4 medium green onions, sliced (1/4 cup)

① Spray 3- to 4-quart slow cooker with cooking spray. In cooker, mix potatoes, onion, celery, broth and water.

② Cover; cook on Low heat setting for about 6 to 8 hours.

③ In small bowl, mix flour and milk; stir into potato mixture. Increase heat setting to High. Cover; cook 20 to 30 minutes longer or until mixture thickens. Stir in cheese until melted. Garnish servings of soup with bacon and green onions. Sprinkle with pepper if desired.

High Altitude (3500-6500 ft): No change.

1 SERVING: Calories 410; Total Fat 15g (Saturated Fat 9g, Trans Fat 0g); Cholesterol 45mg; Sodium 1210mg; Total Carbohydrate 50g (Dietary Fiber 5g); Protein 19g. EXCHANGES: 3-1/2 Starch, 1 High-Fat Meat, 1 Fat. CARBOHYDRATE CHOICES: 3.

tips&ideas

Instead of using purchased bacon pieces, cook 2 slices of bacon until crisp, then drain and crumble.

cheesy chicken and artichoke pizza

PREP TIME: 20 minutes • START TO FINISH: 35 minutes • MAKES: 4 servings (2 wedges each)

1 package (10 oz) prebaked thin Italian pizza crust (12 inch)
1/4 cup reduced-fat mayonnaise
1/4 cup grated Parmesan cheese
1 can (14 oz) artichoke hearts, drained, coarsely chopped
1-1/2 cups shredded Monterey Jack cheese (6 oz)
1 cup chopped deli rotisserie chicken (from 2 to 2-1/2 lb chicken)
3 medium green onions, chopped (3 tablespoons)

① Heat oven to 450°F. On cookie sheet, place pizza crust. In medium bowl, mix mayonnaise, Parmesan cheese and artichokes.

② Spread artichoke mixture over pizza crust, leaving 1-inch border. Top with 1 cup of the cheese, the chicken and onions. Top with remaining 1/2 cup cheese.

③ Bake 8 to 10 minutes or until cheese is melted and pizza is thoroughly heated. Cut into 8 wedges.

High Altitude (3500-6500 ft): No change.

1 SERVING: Calories 550; Total Fat 27g (Saturated Fat 12g, Trans Fat 0.5g); Cholesterol 85mg; Sodium 1250mg; Total Carbohydrate 43g (Dietary Fiber 7g); Protein 34g. EXCHANGES: 3 Starch, 3-1/2 Lean Meat, 3 Fat. CARBOHYDRATE CHOICES: 3.

tips & ideas

Add a southwestern kick by putting 2 tablespoons Old El Paso® chopped green chiles in the chicken mixture.

creamy fruit salad

PREP TIME: 20 minutes • **START TO FINISH:** 20 minutes • **MAKES:** 4 servings (1 cup each)

DRESSING

1 container (6 oz) Yoplait® Original 99% Fat Free lemon burst or French vanilla yogurt

1 tablespoon light mayonnaise

1/4 teaspoon grated orange peel

2 tablespoons orange juice

SALAD

2 large unpeeled red apples, cubed (about 3 cups)

1 medium orange, peeled, cut into bite-size pieces

2 tablespoons golden raisins

4 leaves Bibb lettuce

2 tablespoons coarsely chopped walnuts

① In small bowl, mix dressing ingredients until well blended.

② In medium bowl, mix apples, orange and raisins. Pour dressing over fruit; toss gently to coat.

③ Divide lettuce leaves among 4 serving plates. Spoon fruit mixture into lettuce leaves; sprinkle with walnuts.

High Altitude (3500-6500 ft): No change.

1 SERVING: Calories 180; Total Fat 4.5g (Saturated Fat 0.5g, Trans Fat 0g); Cholesterol 0mg; Sodium 45mg; Total Carbohydrate 32g (Dietary Fiber 4g); Protein 2g. EXCHANGES: 1 Fruit, 1 Other Carbohydrate, 1/2 High-Fat Meat. CARBOHYDRATE CHOICES: 2.

tips&ideas

Golden raisins come from the same grape as regular raisins, but golden raisins are treated with sulphur dioxide to prevent darkening. The raisins are then dried with artificial heat to give a plumper, moister raisin that gets its name from its pale gold color.

chicken-gorgonzola pasta salad

PREP TIME: 20 minutes • **START TO FINISH:** 20 minutes • **MAKES:** 12 servings (1-1/2 cups each)

7 cups uncooked radiatore (nuggets) pasta (about 19 oz)

4-1/2 cups cubed cooked chicken breast (about 20 oz)

1 package (2.1 oz) refrigerated precooked bacon (about 15 slices), cut into small pieces

1 can (14.5 oz) Muir Glen® organic fire roasted diced tomatoes, drained

2 cups lightly packed fresh baby spinach leaves

1 jar (16 oz) refrigerated ranch dressing

1 cup crumbled Gorgonzola cheese (4 oz)

Bibb lettuce, if desired

① Cook and drain pasta as directed on package.

② In large bowl, mix cooked pasta, chicken, bacon, tomatoes and spinach. Pour dressing over pasta mixture; toss until coated. Fold in cheese. Cover and refrigerate until serving. To serve, line bowl with lettuce and spoon in salad.

High Altitude (3500-6500 ft): No change.

1 SERVING: Calories 530; Total Fat 28g (Saturated Fat 7g, Trans Fat 0g); Cholesterol 70mg; Sodium 790mg; Total Carbohydrate 42g (Dietary Fiber 3g); Protein 28g. EXCHANGES: 2 Starch, 1 Other Carbohydrate, 3 Lean Meat, 3-1/2 Fat. CARBOHYDRATE CHOICES: 3.

chicken caesar sandwiches

PREP TIME: 20 minutes • **START TO FINISH:** 7 hours 55 minutes • **MAKES:** 12 sandwiches

2 lb boneless skinless chicken thighs
1 envelope (1.2 oz) Caesar dressing mix
1 can (10-3/4 oz) condensed cream of chicken soup
1/3 cup shredded Parmesan cheese
1/4 cup chopped fresh parsley
1/2 teaspoon coarsely ground pepper
2 cups shredded romaine lettuce
12 "dollar" buns (about 2-1/2 inches in diameter)

① Place chicken in 3- to 4-quart slow cooker.

② Cover and cook on Low heat setting for 6 to 7 hours.

③ Remove chicken from cooker, using slotted spoon; place on cutting board. Discard liquid in cooker. Shred chicken, using 2 forks. Mix dressing mix (dry), soup, cheese, parsley and pepper in cooker; gently fold in chicken. Increase heat setting to High. Cover and cook 30 to 35 minutes or until mixture is hot.

④ To serve, spoon 1/4 cup chicken mixture onto lettuce in each bun. Chicken mixture will hold on Low heat setting up to 2 hours; stir occasionally.

VARIATION: Instead of the Caesar dressing mix, try ranch dressing mix to give the sauce a buttermilk-herb twist.

High Altitude (3500-6500 ft): No change.

1 SANDWICH: Calories 250; Total Fat 11g (Saturated Fat 3.5g, Trans Fat 0g); Cholesterol 50mg; Sodium 610mg; Total Carbohydrate 19g (Dietary Fiber 1g); Protein 20g. EXCHANGES: 1 Starch, 2-1/2 Lean Meat, 1 Fat. CARBOHYDRATE CHOICES: 1.

tips&ideas

Caesar salad never tasted so good! Serve the warm chicken mixture over crunchy chopped romaine lettuce and sprinkle with chopped tomatoes.

smoked sausage and bean soup

PREP TIME: 15 minutes • **START TO FINISH:** 8 hours 45 minutes • **MAKES:** 7 servings (1-1/2 cups each)

1 lb small red potatoes, each cut into 8 pieces
  (about 3 cups)
4 medium carrots, sliced (2 cups)
1 medium onion, chopped (1/2 cup)
1 medium stalk celery, sliced (1/2 cup)
2 cans (15 oz each) navy or cannellini beans,
  drained, rinsed
3-1/2 cups Progresso® chicken broth
  (from 32-oz carton)
1 teaspoon dried thyme leaves
1/2 teaspoon seasoned salt
1 lb cooked kielbasa, cut in half lengthwise, then cut
  crosswise into 1/4-inch slices
2 tablespoons chopped fresh parsley

① Spray 3- to 4-quart slow cooker with cooking spray. In cooker, mix all ingredients except sausage and parsley.

② Cover; cook on Low heat setting for about 8 to 9 hours.

③ Stir in sausage and parsley. Cover; cook on Low heat setting 30 minutes longer or until sausage is hot.

VARIATION: Diced cooked ham can be used in place of the sausage.

High Altitude (3500-6500 ft): No change.

1 SERVING: Calories 440; Total Fat 19g (Saturated Fat 7g, Trans Fat 0.5g); Cholesterol 40mg; Sodium 1220mg; Total Carbohydrate 47g (Dietary Fiber 14g); Protein 20g. EXCHANGES: 2-1/2 Starch, 1 Vegetable, 1-1/2 High-Fat Meat, 1 Fat. CARBOHYDRATE CHOICES: 3.

tips&ideas

If the red potatoes are very small, be sure to cut them in half to help prevent overcooking.

p. 201

p. 188

christmas breakfast & brunch

Whether your family time is early morning or nearly lunchtime, make it special with these delicious choices.

brunch potatoes alfredo with roasted peppers

PREP TIME: 10 Minutes • **START TO FINISH:** 50 Minutes • **MAKES:** 10 servings

7 cups frozen country-style shredded hash brown potatoes (from 30-oz bag), thawed

3/4 cup chopped drained roasted red bell peppers (from 7-oz jar)

4 medium green onions, sliced (1/4 cup)

1 container (10 oz) refrigerated Alfredo pasta sauce

1-1/2 cups shredded Swiss cheese (6 oz)

Additional sliced green onion tops

① Heat oven to 350°F. Spray 11x7-inch or 12x8-inch glass baking dish with cooking spray. Place potatoes, bell peppers and green onions in baking dish; mix lightly. Top with Alfredo sauce; sprinkle with cheese.

② Bake uncovered 40 to 45 minutes or until golden brown. Sprinkle with additional green onion tops and chopped roasted red bell peppers if desired just before serving.

High Altitude (3500-6500 ft): Bake 45 to 50 minutes.

1 SERVING: Calories 300; Total Fat 14g (Saturated Fat 9g, Trans Fat 0.5g); Cholesterol 45mg; Sodium 570mg; Total Carbohydrate 32g (Dietary Fiber 3g, Sugars 2g); Protein 10g. EXCHANGES: 2 Starch, 1/2 High-Fat Meat, 2 Fat. CARBOHYDRATE CHOICES: 2.

tiramisu waffles

PREP TIME: 15 Minutes • START TO FINISH: 30 Minutes • MAKES: 12 servings (1 waffle each plus topping)

1 package (8 oz) cream cheese, softened
1/2 cup sugar
1/2 cup chocolate-flavor syrup
1 container (8 oz) frozen whipped topping, thawed
1-1/2 cups Original Bisquick® mix
1 cup sugar
1/3 cup unsweetened baking cocoa
3/4 cup water
2 tablespoons vegetable oil
2 eggs
1 cup hot coffee
Additional unsweetened baking cocoa, if desired

① To make Tiramisu Topping, beat cream cheese, 1/2 cup sugar and the chocolate syrup in large bowl with electric mixer on medium speed until smooth. Gently stir in whipped topping until blended. Refrigerate while making waffles.

② Heat waffle iron; grease if necessary.

③ Stir remaining ingredients except coffee and additional cocoa until blended. Pour batter by slightly less than 1 cupfuls onto center of hot waffle iron.

④ Bake about 5 minutes or until steaming stops. Carefully remove waffle. Drizzle coffee over waffles. Spoon Tiramisu Topping onto waffles; sprinkle with cocoa.

High Altitude (3500-6500 ft): No change.

1 SERVING: Calories 305; Total Fat 13g (Saturated Fat 6g, Trans Fat nc); Cholesterol 60mg; Sodium 300mg; Total Carbohydrate 44g (Dietary Fiber 1g, Sugars nc); Protein 4g. EXCHANGES: 1-1/2 Starch, 1-1/2 Fruit, 2 Fat. CARBOHYDRATE CHOICES: 0.

tips & ideas

To soften cream cheese quickly, remove the foil wrapper and place cream cheese on waxed paper or microwavable plate; microwave uncovered on Medium (50%) for 1 minute to 1 minute 30 seconds.

berry french toast bake

PREP TIME: 25 minutes • START TO FINISH: 1 hour 45 minutes • MAKES: 10 servings

FRENCH TOAST BAKE

6 eggs
1-1/2 cups half-and-half
2 teaspoons vanilla
1/2 cup Gold Medal® all-purpose flour
1/4 cup sugar
1/4 teaspoon salt
1 loaf (1 lb) soft French bread, cut into 1-inch cubes (8 cups)
1-1/2 cups frozen unsweetened mixed berries (from two 14-oz bags)

BERRY SAUCE

1/2 cup sugar
1-1/2 teaspoons cornstarch
2 tablespoons orange juice
1 cup frozen unsweetened mixed berries
1-1/2 cups fresh strawberries, cut in half

① Grease bottom and sides of 13x9-inch (3-quart) glass baking dish with butter.

② In large bowl, beat eggs, half-and-half, vanilla, flour, 1/4 cup sugar and the salt with wire whisk until smooth. Stir in bread and 1-1/2 cups mixed berries. Spoon into baking dish. Cover tightly; refrigerate at least 1 hour but no longer than 24 hours.

③ Heat oven to 400°F. Uncover bread mixture; bake 25 to 35 minutes or until golden brown and knife inserted in center comes out clean.

④ Meanwhile, in 1-1/2 quart saucepan, stir together 1/2 cup sugar and the cornstarch. Stir in orange juice until smooth. Stir in 1 cup mixed berries. Heat to boiling over medium heat, stirring constantly. Cook about 4 minutes, stirring constantly, until slightly thickened; remove from heat. Just before serving, stir in strawberry halves. Serve warm over French toast bake.

High Altitude (3500-6500 ft): No change.

1 SERVING: Calories 330; Total Fat 9g (Saturated Fat 4g, Trans Fat 0g); Cholesterol 140mg; Sodium 380mg; Total Carbohydrate 54g (Dietary Fiber 5g); Protein 10g. EXCHANGES: 2 Starch, 1 Fruit, 1/2 Other Carbohydrate, 1/2 High-Fat Meat, 1 Fat. CARBOHYDRATE CHOICES: 3.

tips & ideas

This recipe is great to serve guests for breakfast since you can make it the night before.

orange pancakes with raspberry sauce

PREP TIME: 30 minutes • **START TO FINISH:** 30 minutes • **MAKES:** 8 servings

RASPBERRY SAUCE
3 tablespoons sugar
1 tablespoon cornstarch
2/3 cup orange juice
1 box (10 oz) frozen raspberries in syrup, thawed, undrained

PANCAKES
2 large eggs
1-1/2 cups milk
1/4 cup vegetable oil
2 cups all-purpose flour
2 tablespoons sugar
2 teaspoons baking powder
2 teaspoons grated orange peel
1 teaspoon vanilla
1/4 teaspoon salt

① In 1-quart saucepan, mix 3 tablespoons sugar and the cornstarch. Stir in orange juice and raspberries. Cook over medium heat, stirring constantly, until mixture thickens and boils. Boil and stir 1 minute. Remove from heat.

② Heat griddle or skillet over medium-high heat (375°F). Brush with vegetable oil if necessary (or spray with cooking spray before heating).

③ In large bowl, beat eggs with wire whisk until well beaten. Beat in remaining ingredients just until smooth.

④ For each pancake, pour slightly less than 1/4 cup batter from cup or pitcher onto hot griddle. Cook pancakes 1 to 2 minutes or until bubbly on top, puffed and dry around edges. Turn; cook other sides 1 to 2 minutes or until golden brown. Serve with raspberry sauce.

High Altitude (3500-6500 ft): No change.

1 SERVING: Calories 300; Total Fat 9g (Saturated Fat 2g, Trans Fat 0g); Cholesterol 55mg; Sodium 230mg; Total Carbohydrate 49g (Dietary Fiber 3g); Protein 7g. EXCHANGES: 2 Starch, 1-1/2 Other Carbohydrate, 1-1/2 Fat. CARBOHYDRATE CHOICES: 3.

tips&ideas

To keep the pancakes warm, place them in a single layer on a paper towel-lined cookie sheet in a 200 degree oven. Do not stack warm pancakes or they will become limp and soggy.

tex-mex sausage and egg bake

PREP TIME: 20 minutes • START TO FINISH: 9 hours 25 minutes • MAKES: 10 servings

12 oz bulk spicy pork sausage

5 cups frozen southern-style hash brown potatoes (from 32-oz bag)

1 can (4.5 oz) Old El Paso® chopped green chiles, undrained

3 cups shredded Colby-Monterey Jack cheese (12 oz)

6 eggs

1-1/2 cups milk

1/4 teaspoon salt

1 cup Old El Paso® Thick 'n Chunky salsa

1 Spray 13x9-inch (3-quart) glass baking dish with cooking spray. In 10-inch skillet, cook sausage over medium heat 8 to 10 minutes, stirring occasionally, until no longer pink. Drain on paper towel.

2 Spread frozen potatoes in baking dish. Sprinkle with sausage, green chiles and 1-1/2 cups of the cheese. In medium bowl, beat eggs, milk and salt with fork or wire whisk until well blended. Pour over potato mixture. Sprinkle with remaining 1-1/2 cups cheese. Cover; refrigerate at least 8 hours but no longer than 12 hours.

3 Heat oven to 350°F. Bake uncovered 50 to 60 minutes or until knife inserted near center comes out clean. Let stand 10 minutes before cutting into squares. Serve with salsa.

High Altitude (3500-6500 ft): No change.

1 SERVING: Calories 350; Total Fat 20g (Saturated Fat 10g, Trans Fat 0g); Cholesterol 175mg; Sodium 1120mg; Total Carbohydrate 25g (Dietary Fiber 3g); Protein 19g. EXCHANGES: 1-1/2 Starch, 2 High-Fat Meat, 1 Fat. CARBOHYDRATE CHOICES: 1-1/2.

egg-topped biscuits florentine

PREP TIME: 30 minutes • **START TO FINISH:** 30 minutes • **MAKES:** 6 servings

1 cup Gold Medal® all-purpose flour
1-1/2 teaspoons baking powder
1 teaspoon sugar
1/2 teaspoon salt
1/2 cup whipping (heavy) cream
3 tablespoons butter or margarine, melted
6 eggs
1 box (10 oz) Green Giant® frozen creamed spinach
6 slices Canadian-style bacon
Freshly ground pepper, if desired

① Heat oven to 425°F. In medium bowl, mix flour, baking powder, sugar and salt. Stir in whipping cream just until dough forms. On lightly floured surface, knead dough 1 minute. Press dough into 6x4-inch rectangle, 1/2 inch thick. Cut into six 2-inch square biscuits.

② Pour melted butter into shallow dish. Dip all sides of each biscuit into butter. On ungreased cookie sheet, place biscuits 2 inches apart. Bake 10 to 15 minutes or until golden brown.

③ Meanwhile, in 12-inch skillet, heat 1-1/2 to 2 inches of water to boiling; reduce to simmering. Break each egg, one at a time, into custard cup or saucer. Holding dish close to water's surface, carefully slip egg into water. Cook 3 to 5 minutes or until whites and yolks are firm, not runny. Remove eggs with slotted spoon. Meanwhile, cook spinach as directed on package.

④ On microwavable plate, place Canadian bacon. Cover loosely and microwave on High about 1 minute or until hot.

⑤ For each serving, split 1 biscuit and place on serving plate. Top each serving with 1 slice Canadian bacon, about 2 tablespoons creamed spinach and 1 poached egg. Sprinkle eggs lightly with pepper.

High Altitude (3500-6500 ft): Add 1 to 2 tablespoons more cream if dough is too dry. Bake 11 to 13 minutes.

1 SERVING: Calories 350; Total Fat 22g (Saturated Fat 10g, Trans Fat 1g); Cholesterol 270mg; Sodium 900mg; Total Carbohydrate 21g (Dietary Fiber 1g); Protein 16g. EXCHANGES: 1 Starch, 1/2 Other Carbohydrate, 2 Lean Meat, 3 Fat. CARBOHYDRATE CHOICES: 1-1/2.

tips & ideas

In today's cooking world, the term "Florentine" generally means the recipe contains spinach.

stuffed french toast strata with orange syrup

PREP TIME: 15 minutes • START TO FINISH: 7 hours • MAKES: 6 servings

FRENCH TOAST STRATA

  12 slices raisin-cinnamon bread
  1/2 cup pineapple cream cheese spread
    (from 8-ounce container)
  1/2 cup orange marmalade
    2 tablespoons butter or margarine, softened
    4 eggs
1-1/2 cups milk
    1 teaspoon vanilla

ORANGE SYRUP

  3/4 cup light corn syrup
  1/4 cup frozen orange juice concentrate

① Spray rectangular baking dish, 13x9x2 inches, with cooking spray. Toast 6 slices of the bread; place in pan. Spread each slice toast evenly with cream cheese and marmalade. Butter remaining bread slices; place butter sides up on toast.

② Beat eggs, milk and vanilla in medium bowl with wire whisk until blended. Pour over bread. Cover with aluminum foil and refrigerate at least 6 hours or overnight.

③ Heat oven to 350°. Uncover and bake 35 to 45 minutes or until deep golden brown and slightly puffed. Cut between bread slices.

④ Meanwhile, in a small microwavable bowl, mix corn syrup and orange juice concentrate. Microwave uncovered on High about 1 minute or until heated. Serve warm over Stuffed French Toast Strata.

VARIATION: For a sweet treat, try the Orange Syrup poured over vanilla ice cream.

High Altitude (3500-6500 ft): Bake 40 to 50 minutes.

1 SERVING: Calories 535; Total Fat 17g (Saturated Fat 9g, Trans Fat nc); Cholesterol 180mg; Sodium 490mg; Total Carbohydrate 84g (Dietary Fiber 2g); Protein 12g. EXCHANGES: 4 Starch, 3 Fat. CARBOHYDRATE CHOICES: 5-1/2.

tips & ideas

When a recipe contains the word "strata" in the title, it refers to a layered casserole, often including bread and eggs for brunch.

make-ahead sausage-potato egg bake

PREP TIME: 30 minutes • START TO FINISH: 10 hours 15 minutes • MAKES: 12 servings

1 lb smoked spicy sausage (andouille, chorizo or kielbasa), cut into 3/8-inch slices
1 large onion, chopped (3/4 cup)
1 medium red bell pepper, chopped (1 cup)
1 medium green bell pepper, chopped (1 cup)
3 cloves garlic, finely chopped
1 bag (20 oz) refrigerated home-style potato slices
1/2 teaspoon salt
1/2 teaspoon pepper
3 cups shredded sharp Cheddar cheese (12 oz)
12 eggs
3/4 cup milk

tips & ideas

This dish needs to be refrigerated for at least 8 hours before baking, so it's a great do-ahead recipe.

① Spray 13x9-inch (3-quart) glass baking dish with cooking spray. In 12-inch skillet, cook sausage over medium heat 5 to 7 minutes, stirring occasionally, until sausage begins to brown; drain if necessary. Add onion; cook 2 to 3 minutes or until slightly softened. Add both bell peppers; cook and stir 1 minute. Add garlic; cook and stir 30 seconds or until softened.

② Spread half of potatoes in bottom of baking dish. Sprinkle with 1/4 teaspoon each of the salt and pepper. Layer with half of sausage mixture and half of cheese. Repeat layers.

③ In large bowl, beat eggs and milk with wire whisk. Pour over layers in baking dish. Cover; refrigerate 8 hours or overnight but no longer than 24 hours.

④ Heat oven to 350°F. Loosely cover baking dish with sheet of nonstick foil or regular foil sprayed with cooking spray (nonstick- or sprayed-side down). Bake 1 hour 30 minutes to 1 hour 40 minutes or until set and potatoes are tender when pierced with a fork. Remove from oven; let stand 5 minutes before cutting.

High Altitude (3500-6500 ft): No change.

1 SERVING: Calories 420; Total Fat 30g (Saturated Fat 13g, Trans Fat 0g); Cholesterol 275mg; Sodium 870mg; Total Carbohydrate 14g (Dietary Fiber 1g); Protein 24g. EXCHANGES: 1 Starch, 3 High-Fat Meat, 1 Fat. CARBOHYDRATE CHOICES: 1.

upside-down banana-walnut french toast

PREP TIME: 15 minutes • START TO FINISH: 2 hours • MAKES: 10 servings

1-1/2 cups packed brown sugar
1/2 cup butter or margarine, melted
1/4 cup corn syrup
1/2 cup chopped walnuts
3 medium bananas, sliced
1 loaf (about 1 lb) sliced unfrosted firm cinnamon bread
6 eggs
1-1/2 cups milk
1 teaspoon vanilla

① Spray bottom and sides of 13x9-inch (3-quart) glass baking dish with cooking spray or grease with shortening. In large bowl, stir together brown sugar, butter, corn syrup and walnuts until smooth. Gently stir in bananas. Spoon banana mixture into baking dish.

② Reserve heels of bread for another use. Arrange 2 layers of bread on banana mixture, tearing bread to fit if needed.

③ In medium bowl, beat eggs, milk and vanilla with wire whisk until well mixed. Pour over bread. Cover tightly; refrigerate at least 1 hour but no longer than 24 hours.

④ Heat oven to 325°F. Uncover bread mixture; bake 45 to 55 minutes or until knife inserted in center comes out clean. Serve portions upside down, spooning sauce from bottom of dish over each serving.

High Altitude (3500-6500 ft): Heat oven to 350°F. Bake 40 to 45 minutes.

1 SERVING: Calories 490; Total Fat 19g (Saturated Fat 7g, Trans Fat 1g); Cholesterol 155mg; Sodium 380mg; Total Carbohydrate 72g (Dietary Fiber 2g); Protein 10g. EXCHANGES: 3 Starch, 2 Other Carbohydrate, 3-1/2 Fat. CARBOHYDRATE CHOICES: 5.

ham and hash brown casserole

PREP TIME: 15 minutes • START TO FINISH: 1 hour 10 minutes • MAKES: 6 servings (1-1/4 cups each)

1 bag (1 lb 4 oz) refrigerated hash brown potatoes
1-1/2 cups diced cooked ham
2 cups shredded Colby or mild Cheddar cheese (8 oz)
1 cup chive-and-onion sour cream potato topper
1-1/2 cups milk
1/2 teaspoon peppered seasoned salt

① Heat oven to 350°F. Spray 8-inch square (2-quart) glass baking dish with cooking spray.

② In large bowl, mix potatoes, ham and 1-1/2 cups of the cheese. Spread in baking dish. In same bowl, mix sour cream, milk and seasoned salt with wire whisk until well blended. Spoon over potato mixture; stir to mix. Cover baking dish with foil.

③ Bake 45 minutes. Sprinkle with remaining 1/2 cup cheese. Bake uncovered about 10 minutes longer or until casserole is bubbly and thoroughly heated.

High Altitude (3500-6500 ft): No change.

1 SERVING: Calories 450; Total Fat 23g (Saturated Fat 14g, Trans Fat 0g); Cholesterol 70mg; Sodium 1030mg; Total Carbohydrate 39g (Dietary Fiber 3g); Protein 23g. EXCHANGES: 2 Starch, 1/2 Other Carbohydrate, 2-1/2 Lean Meat, 3 Fat. CARBOHYDRATE CHOICES: 2-1/2.

sausage oven pancake square

PREP TIME: 20 minutes • **START TO FINISH:** 50 minutes • **MAKES:** 6 servings

1 package (12 oz) bulk pork sausage
1 cup shredded American-Cheddar cheese blend (4 oz)
1 egg
1/4 cup milk
2 tablespoons maple-flavored syrup
1 tablespoon vegetable oil
1/2 cup Gold Medal® all-purpose flour
1 teaspoon baking powder
1/8 teaspoon salt
3/4 cup maple-flavored syrup

① Heat oven to 350°F. In 10-inch skillet, cook sausage over medium-high heat 5 to 7 minutes, stirring frequently, until no longer pink. Drain sausage on paper towels. In ungreased 8-inch or 9-inch square pan, spread cooked sausage. Sprinkle cheese over sausage.

② In large bowl, beat egg, milk, 2 tablespoons maple syrup and the oil with wire whisk until well blended. Beat in flour, baking powder and salt. Pour batter evenly over sausage and cheese.

③ Bake uncovered 25 to 30 minutes or until golden brown. Serve topped with 3/4 cup maple syrup.

High Altitude (3500-6500 ft): No change.

1 SERVING: Calories 390; Total Fat 18g (Saturated Fat 7g, Trans Fat 0g); Cholesterol 75mg; Sodium 740mg; Total Carbohydrate 44g (Dietary Fiber 0g); Protein 12g. EXCHANGES: 1 Starch, 2 Other Carbohydrate, 1-1/2 High-Fat Meat, 1 Fat. CARBOHYDRATE CHOICES: 3.

dreamy orange waffles

PREP TIME: 30 minutes • START TO FINISH: 30 minutes
MAKES: 6 servings (two 4-inch waffles, 1/3 cup orange syrup and 2 tablespoons topping each)

ORANGE SYRUP
1 cup packed brown sugar
2 tablespoons cornstarch
1 cup orange juice
1 can (11 oz) mandarin orange segments, drained

WAFFLES
2 cups Original Bisquick® mix
1-1/4 cups milk
2 tablespoons butter or margarine, melted
1 tablespoon grated orange peel
1 egg

TOPPING
1 cup frozen (thawed) whipped topping

① In 1-quart saucepan, heat brown sugar, cornstarch and orange juice to boiling over medium-high heat, stirring frequently. Boil and stir 1 to 2 minutes or until syrup is slightly thickened and mixture is clear. Remove from heat; stir in orange segments. Keep warm.

② Heat waffle maker. (Waffle makers without a nonstick coating may need to be brushed with vegetable oil or sprayed with cooking spray.) In medium bowl, stir waffle ingredients with wire whisk or fork until blended.

③ For each waffle, pour batter onto center of hot waffle iron. (Check manufacturer's directions for recommended amount of batter.) Close lid of waffle maker. Bake 3 to 5 minutes or until steaming stops. Carefully remove waffle.

④ Serve waffles with syrup and topping.

High Altitude (3500-6500 ft): No change.

1 SERVING: Calories 460; Total Fat 13g (Saturated Fat 7g, Trans Fat 1.5g); Cholesterol 50mg; Sodium 570mg; Total Carbohydrate 78g (Dietary Fiber 2g); Protein 7g.
EXCHANGES: 2 Starch, 3 Other Carbohydrate, 2-1/2 Fat.
CARBOHYDRATE CHOICES: 5.

tips&ideas _____

Use a fork as a tool to lift the waffle from the waffle maker. It will help prevent the waffle from breaking, and you won't burn your fingers.

ham and broccoli bake with parmesan streusel

PREP TIME: 20 minutes • START TO FINISH: 1 hour 30 minutes • MAKES: 12 servings

2 cups chopped fully cooked ham
2 cups fresh broccoli florets
3 cups frozen O'Brien potatoes (from 28-oz bag), thawed
2 cups shredded Cheddar cheese (8 oz)
8 eggs
1 cup milk
1 container (8 oz) sour cream
1 teaspoon salt
1/4 teaspoon pepper
3/4 cup Gold Medal® all-purpose flour
1/4 cup grated Parmesan cheese
1/4 cup butter or margarine, softened
2 tablespoons chopped fresh parsley

tips&ideas

Remember this recipe when you have holiday ham left over. Serve with fresh sliced pears or apples.

① Heat oven to 350°F. In ungreased 13x9-inch (3-quart) glass baking dish, mix ham, broccoli, potatoes and Cheddar cheese.

② In large bowl, beat eggs, milk, sour cream, salt and pepper with wire whisk. Pour egg mixture over ham mixture. (If desired, cover and refrigerate casserole at this point up to 8 hours or overnight.)

③ Bake uncovered 45 to 50 minutes or until center is almost set.

④ Meanwhile, in small bowl, stir remaining ingredients with fork until crumbly. Sprinkle crumb mixture on ungreased cookie sheet. Bake on lower oven rack for last 20 minutes of casserole bake time, stirring once. Sprinkle over casserole before serving.

High Altitude (3500-6500 ft): Cut broccoli florets into 1/2- to 1-inch pieces. Bake 50 to 55 minutes.

1 SERVING: Calories 340; Total Fat 22g (Saturated Fat 11g, Trans Fat 0.5g); Cholesterol 200mg; Sodium 660mg; Total Carbohydrate 19g (Dietary Fiber 2g); Protein 18g. EXCHANGES: 1-1/2 Starch, 2 Medium-Fat Meat, 2 Fat. CARBOHYDRATE CHOICES: 1.

ham and swiss brunch bake

PREP TIME: 25 minutes • START TO FINISH: 2 hours • MAKES: 10 servings

1 loaf (1 lb) French bread, cut into
  1/2-inch slices
2 tablespoons Dijon mustard
8 oz thinly sliced cooked ham
8 oz thinly sliced Swiss cheese
4 eggs
2 cups milk
1/4 cup grated Parmesan cheese
1/4 cup Progresso® plain bread crumbs
2 tablespoons chopped fresh parsley
3 tablespoons butter or margarine,
  melted

① In ungreased 13x9-inch (3-quart) glass baking dish, arrange half of the bread slices, overlapping as needed. Brush bread in dish with mustard. Top evenly with ham and Swiss cheese, overlapping as needed. Top with remaining bread slices, arranging them over first layer of bread slices to make sandwiches.

② In medium bowl, beat eggs and milk with wire whisk until well blended. Carefully pour over sandwiches. Cover and refrigerate at least 1 hour but no longer than 12 hours.

③ Meanwhile, in small bowl, mix Parmesan cheese, bread crumbs, parsley and butter.

④ Heat oven to 375°F. Sprinkle crumb topping over casserole. Bake uncovered 30 to 35 minutes or until sandwiches are puffed and golden brown.

High Altitude (3500-6500 ft): Heat oven to 400°F. Reserve crumb topping. Cover and bake 15 minutes. Sprinkle crumb topping over casserole. Bake uncovered 20 minutes longer.

1 SERVING: Calories 350; Total Fat 17g (Saturated Fat 8g, Trans Fat 0.5g); Cholesterol 135mg; Sodium 810mg; Total Carbohydrate 29g (Dietary Fiber 1g); Protein 21g. EXCHANGES: 2 Starch, 2 Medium-Fat Meat, 1 Fat. CARBOHYDRATE CHOICES: 2.

overnight filled french toast with raspberry sauce

PREP TIME: 25 minutes • START TO FINISH: 9 hours 5 minutes • MAKES: 6 servings

FRENCH TOAST

12 slices French bread, 1-1/2 inches thick
2 packages (3 oz each) cream cheese, softened
2 tablespoons sugar
2 tablespoons orange marmalade
1/2 cup dried cranberries
8 eggs
2 cups milk
1/4 cup sugar
1/4 teaspoon salt
3 tablespoons butter or margarine, melted

RASPBERRY SAUCE

1 package (10 oz) frozen sweetened raspberries, thawed
2 teaspoons cornstarch
2 tablespoons sugar
2 tablespoons orange marmalade

① Spray 13x9-inch glass baking dish with cooking spray. Cut almost through each bread slice, cutting from top crust to—but not through—bottom crust. In small bowl, stir together cream cheese, 2 tablespoons sugar, 2 tablespoons marmalade and the cranberries. Open bread slices enough to spread 1 heaping tablespoon cheese mixture evenly on 1 cut surface of each slice. Press bread slices together. Place in baking dish.

② In medium bowl, beat eggs, milk, 1/4 cup sugar and the salt with wire whisk until well blended. Pour over bread; turn slices carefully to coat. Cover and refrigerate at least 8 hours or overnight.

③ Heat oven to 425°F. Drizzle melted butter over bread. Bake uncovered 20 to 25 minutes or until golden brown.

④ Meanwhile, drain juice from raspberries into 1-cup glass measuring cup; add enough water to measure 3/4 cup. In 1-quart saucepan, stir together juice mixture, cornstarch, 2 tablespoons sugar and 2 tablespoons marmalade. Heat to boiling, stirring occasionally; remove from heat. Cool 15 minutes. Stir in raspberries. Serve sauce with French toast.

High Altitude (3500-6500 ft): No change.

1 SERVING: Calories 790; Total Fat 29g (Saturated Fat 13g, Trans Fat 1-1/2g); Cholesterol 335mg; Sodium 1090mg; Total Carbohydrate 107g; (Dietary Fiber 6g), Protein 25g.
EXCHANGES: 3 Starch, 1 Fruit, 3 Other Carbohydrate; 3 Fat.
CARBOHYDRATE CHOICES: 7.

tips&ideas

This is an easy make-ahead dish. Assemble the French toast and make the sauce the night before and refrigerate. In the morning, bake the French toast and reheat the sauce.

potato, egg and sausage frittata

PREP TIME: 30 minutes • START TO FINISH: 30 minutes • MAKES: 4 servings

4 eggs or 8 egg whites
1/4 cup fat-free (skim) milk
1 teaspoon olive oil
2 cups frozen country-style shredded hash brown potatoes (from 30-oz bag)
4 frozen soy-protein breakfast sausage links (from 8-oz box), cut into eighths
1/4 teaspoon salt
1/8 teaspoon dried basil leaves
1/8 teaspoon dried oregano leaves
1-1/2 cups chopped plum (Roma) tomatoes (4 medium)
1/2 cup shredded mozzarella and Asiago cheese blend with garlic (2 oz)
Freshly ground pepper, if desired

① In small bowl, beat eggs and milk with fork or wire whisk until well blended; set aside.

② Coat 10-inch nonstick skillet with oil; heat over medium heat. Cook potatoes and breakfast links in oil 6 to 8 minutes, stirring occasionally, until potatoes are golden brown.

③ Pour egg mixture over potato mixture. Cook uncovered over medium-low heat about 5 minutes; as mixture begins to set on bottom and side, gently lift cooked portions with spatula so that thin, uncooked portion can flow to bottom. Cook until eggs are thickened throughout but still moist; avoid constant stirring.

④ Sprinkle with salt, basil, oregano, tomatoes and cheese. Reduce heat to low; cover and cook about 5 minutes or until center is set and cheese is melted. Sprinkle with pepper.

High Altitude (3500-6500 ft): No change.

1 SERVING: Calories 280; Total Fat 12g (Saturated Fat 4.5g, Trans Fat 0g); Cholesterol 220mg; Sodium 590mg; Total Carbohydrate 26g (Dietary Fiber 3g); Protein 17g. EXCHANGES: 1-1/2 Starch, 2 Medium-Fat Meat. CARBOHYDRATE CHOICES: 2.

tips&ideas

If you haven't tried the newest soy products lately, you're in for a pleasant surprise. Soy sausage is a tasty alternative to higher-fat regular sausage and it's an easy addition to this frittata.

banana cream waffles

PREP TIME: 35 minutes • START TO FINISH: 35 minutes • MAKES: 8 servings

1 cup whipping (heavy) cream
1 box (4-serving size) vanilla pudding and pie filling mix (not instant)
2 cups milk
2 ripe medium bananas, sliced
2 cups Gold Medal® all-purpose flour
1 tablespoon sugar
4 teaspoons baking powder
1/4 teaspoon salt
1/3 cup butter or margarine, melted
1-1/2 cups milk
2 very ripe medium bananas, mashed (3/4 cup)
2 eggs, beaten

① In chilled small bowl, beat whipping cream with electric mixer on high speed until soft peaks form. Refrigerate until serving time.

② In 2-quart saucepan, stir pudding mix and 2 cups milk with wire whisk. Cook over medium heat about 10 minutes, stirring constantly, until mixture boils and thickens slightly; remove from heat. Stir in sliced bananas. Cover to keep warm.

③ Heat waffle maker. If necessary, brush with vegetable oil before batter for each waffle is added (or spray with cooking spray before heating). In large bowl, mix flour, sugar, baking powder and salt. Stir in remaining ingredients just until moistened.

④ Pour about 1/2 cup batter from cup or pitcher onto center of hot waffle maker. (Check manufacturer's directions for recommended amount of batter.) Close lid of waffle maker.

⑤ Bake about 5 minutes or until steaming stops. Carefully remove waffle. Repeat with remaining batter. Serve each waffle topped with about 1/3 cup banana mixture and 2 tablespoons whipped cream.

High Altitude (3500-6500 ft): Decrease baking powder to 1-1/2 teaspoons.

1 SERVING: Calories 450; Total Fat 23g (Saturated Fat 12g, Trans Fat 1g); Cholesterol 125mg; Sodium 510mg; Total Carbohydrate 54g (Dietary Fiber 2g); Protein 10g. EXCHANGES: 3 Starch, 1/2 Fruit, 4 Fat. CARBOHYDRATE CHOICES: 3-1/2.

tips&ideas

For a speedy dessert, drizzle hot caramel sauce over the banana and pudding mixture, before adding the whipped cream.

smoked salmon and cream cheese quiche

PREP TIME: 15 minutes • START TO FINISH: 2 hours 10 minutes • MAKES: 6 servings

① Heat oven to 425°F. In medium bowl, mix flour and 1/2 teaspoon salt. Cut in shortening, using pastry blender (or pulling 2 table knives through ingredients in opposite directions), until particles are size of small peas. Sprinkle with cold water, 1 tablespoon at a time, tossing with fork until all flour is moistened and pastry almost leaves side of bowl (1 to 2 teaspoons more water can be added if necessary).

② Gather pastry into a ball. On lightly floured surface, shape pastry into flattened round. Wrap flattened round in plastic wrap; refrigerate about 45 minutes or until dough is firm and cold, yet pliable.

③ With floured rolling pin, roll pastry into circle 2 inches larger than upside-down 9-inch glass pie plate. Fold pastry into fourths; place in pie plate. Unfold and ease into plate, pressing firmly against bottom and side. Carefully trim overhanging edge of pastry 1 inch from rim of plate. Fold and roll pastry under, even with plate; flute. Prick bottom and side of pastry thoroughly with fork. Bake 15 to 20 minutes or until light brown. Pat down center if necessary.

④ Reduce oven temperature to 325°F. Spread salmon in bottom of pastry. Top with cream cheese and green onions. In large bowl, beat eggs, half-and-half, 1/2 teaspoon salt and the pepper with wire whisk until smooth. Pour over salmon mixture.

⑤ Bake uncovered 35 to 40 minutes or until knife inserted in center comes out clean. Let stand 10 minutes before cutting.

High Altitude (3500-6500 ft): In Step 4, reduce temperature to 350°F. In Step 5, bake uncovered 50 to 55 minutes.

1 cup Gold Medal® all-purpose flour
1/2 teaspoon salt
1/3 cup plus 1 tablespoon shortening
2 to 3 tablespoons cold water
1/2 lb smoked salmon, skin and bones removed, flaked or chopped
1 package (3 oz) cream cheese, cut into 1/2-inch cubes
4 medium green onions, sliced (1/4 cup)
6 eggs, beaten
1-1/2 cups half-and-half
1/2 teaspoon salt
1/8 teaspoon pepper

1 SERVING: Calories 450; Total Fat 33g (Saturated Fat 13g, Trans Fat 2.5g); Cholesterol 260mg; Sodium 820mg; Total Carbohydrate 20g (Dietary Fiber 0g); Protein 18g. EXCHANGES: 1-1/2 Starch, 2 Lean Meat, 5 Fat. CARBOHYDRATE CHOICES: 1.

french toast with gingered applesauce

PREP TIME: 15 minutes • START TO FINISH: 25 minutes • MAKES: 4 servings

1/2 to 1 teaspoon grated gingerroot
　　or 1/8 teaspoon ground ginger

1/2 cup natural applesauce

1/4 cup sugar-free maple-flavored syrup

2 eggs plus 1 egg white or 3/4 cup fat-free,
　　cholesterol-free egg product

3/4 cup fat-free (skim) milk

1 teaspoon vanilla

1/4 teaspoon salt

8 slices sandwich bread

① Stir together gingerroot, applesauce and syrup in small microwavable bowl. Microwave uncovered on Medium (50%) about 1 minute or until very warm; set aside.

② Beat eggs and egg white, milk, vanilla and salt in small bowl with fork or wire whisk until well mixed; pour into shallow bowl.

③ Spray griddle or 10-inch skillet with cooking spray; heat griddle to 375° or heat skillet over medium heat. Dip bread into egg mixture, coating both sides. Cook about 2 minutes on each side or until golden brown. Serve with applesauce mixture.

High Altitude (3500-6500 ft): No change.

1 SERVING: Calories 230; Total Fat 4.5g (Saturated Fat 1g, Trans Fat 0g); Cholesterol 105mg; Sodium 470mg; Total Carbohydrate 39g (Dietary Fiber 2g); Protein 8g. EXCHANGES: 2 Starch, 1 Fat. CARBOHYDRATE CHOICES: 2-1/2.

tips&ideas

For a great start to the day, sizzle a couple of reduced-fat breakfast sausage links while the French toast is cooking, and serve with herbal tea or coffee.

basil breakfast strata

PREP TIME: 15 minutes • **START TO FINISH:** 9 hours • **MAKES:** 12 servings

6 eggs
3-1/2 cups milk
1 teaspoon salt
1/2 teaspoon pepper
8 cups cubed (1 inch) French bread
2 cups shredded mozzarella cheese (8 oz)
1/4 cup basil pesto
1/2 cup grated Parmesan cheese (2 oz)

① Spray 13x9-inch (3-quart) glass baking dish with cooking spray. In large bowl, beat eggs with wire whisk until foamy. Beat in milk until blended; beat in salt and pepper. Set aside.

② Place bread cubes in baking dish. Sprinkle with mozzarella cheese. Pour egg mixture over top, pressing lightly to moisten bread. Using spoon, swirl pesto through mixture. Sprinkle Parmesan cheese over top. Cover with plastic wrap; refrigerate at least 8 hours but no longer than 24 hours.

③ Heat oven to 350°F. Remove plastic wrap; bake uncovered 40 to 45 minutes or until strata is puffed and knife inserted in center comes out clean. Let stand 5 minutes before serving. Cut into squares.

High Altitude (3500-6500 ft): No change.

1 SERVING: Calories 240; Total Fat 13g (Saturated Fat 6g, Trans Fat 0g); Cholesterol 125mg; Sodium 600mg; Total Carbohydrate 16g (Dietary Fiber 0g); Protein 15g. EXCHANGES: 1 Starch, 1-1/2 Medium-Fat Meat, 1 Fat. CARBOHYDRATE CHOICES: 1.

scrambled egg biscuit cups

PREP TIME: 30 minutes • **START TO FINISH:** 30 minutes • **MAKES:** 12 biscuit cups

2 cups Original Bisquick® mix
1/3 cup shredded Cheddar cheese (1-1/2 oz)
3/4 cup milk
8 eggs
1/8 teaspoon pepper
1 tablespoon butter or margarine, softened
1/2 cup Parmesan and mozzarella cheese pasta
    sauce (from 1-lb jar)
3 tablespoons cooked real bacon bits or pieces
    (from 3-oz package)
1 tablespoon chopped fresh chives
Additional cooked real bacon bits or pieces

① Heat oven to 425°F. Spray bottoms only of 12 regular-size muffin cups with cooking spray. In medium bowl, combine Bisquick mix, cheese and 1/2 cup of the milk until soft dough forms.

② Place dough on surface sprinkled with Bisquick mix. Shape into a ball; knead 4 or 5 times. Shape into 10-inch-long roll. Cut roll into 12 pieces. Press each piece in bottom and up side of muffin cup, forming edge at rim.

③ Bake 8 to 10 minutes or until golden brown. Remove from oven. With back of spoon, press puffed crust in each cup to make indentation.

④ In large bowl, beat eggs, remaining 1/4 cup milk and the pepper until well blended. In 10-inch nonstick skillet, melt butter over medium heat. Add egg mixture; cook 3 to 4 minutes, stirring occasionally, until firm but still moist. Fold in pasta sauce and bacon until blended.

⑤ To remove biscuit cups from pan, run knife around edge of cups. Spoon egg mixture into biscuit cups. Sprinkle chives and additional bacon bits over tops.

High Altitude (3500-6500 ft): Bake 10 to 12 minutes.

1 BISCUIT CUP: Calories 180; Total Fat 9g (Saturated Fat 3.5g, Trans Fat 1g); Cholesterol 150mg; Sodium 420mg; Total Carbohydrate 15g (Dietary Fiber 0g); Protein 8g. EXCHANGES: 1 Starch, 1 Medium-Fat Meat, 1/2 Fat. CARBOHYDRATE CHOICES: 1.

tips&ideas

The biscuit cups can be baked the day before and stored in an airtight container at room temperature. Just fill with scrambled eggs and serve the next morning.

ham with tropical fruit sauce

PREP TIME: 20 minutes • START TO FINISH: 8 hours 20 minutes • MAKES: 12 servings

1 fully cooked smoked boneless ham (4-1/2 lb)
1/4 teaspoon pepper
1 jar (24 oz) mango in extra-light syrup, drained
1 jar (12 oz) pineapple preserves
1 jalapeño chile, seeded, chopped
2 tablespoons white wine vinegar
1/4 cup chopped fresh cilantro
1 can (20 oz) sliced pineapple, drained, each cut into 6 pieces

① Spray inside of 4- to 5-quart slow cooker with cooking spray. Place ham in slow cooker; sprinkle with pepper.

② In blender, place mango, preserves, chile and vinegar. Cover; blend on high speed 30 seconds; pour over ham.

③ Cover slow cooker; cook on Low heat setting for 6 to 8 hours.

④ Remove ham from cooker; place on serving platter. Sprinkle ham with 1 tablespoon of the cilantro. Stir remaining 3 tablespoons cilantro and the pineapple into sauce in cooker. Serve sauce with ham.

High Altitude (3500-6500 ft): No change.

1 SERVING: Calories 400; Total Fat 13g (Saturated Fat 4.5g, Trans Fat 0g); Cholesterol 85mg; Sodium 2180mg; Total Carbohydrate 37g (Dietary Fiber 2g); Protein 33g. EXCHANGES: 1 Fruit, 1-1/2 Other Carbohydrate, 4-1/2 Lean Meat. CARBOHYDRATE CHOICES: 2-1/2.

tips&ideas

Freeze leftovers in a freezer-friendly container for up to 4 months. To thaw them, place the container in the fridge for about 8 hours, or thaw in the microwave.

sausage 'n apple cheddar biscuit bake

PREP TIME: 20 minutes • START TO FINISH: 60 minutes • MAKES: 12 servings

1 package (1 lb) bulk pork sausage

4 medium cooking apples, coarsely chopped (4 cups)

1 large onion, chopped (1 cup)

6 eggs

1/2 teaspoon salt

2-1/4 cups Gold Medal® all-purpose flour

2-1/2 teaspoons baking powder

2 teaspoons sugar

3/4 teaspoon baking soda

1 teaspoon salt

6 tablespoons firm butter or margarine, cut into 1/2-inch cubes

1-1/2 cups shredded Cheddar cheese (6 oz)

2 medium green onions, finely chopped (2 tablespoons)

1 cup buttermilk

1 SERVING: Calories 340; Total Fat 19g (Saturated Fat 9g, Trans Fat 0g); Cholesterol 150mg; Sodium 880mg; Total Carbohydrate 28g (Dietary Fiber 2g); Protein 14g. EXCHANGES: 1-1/2 Starch, 1/2 Other Carbohydrate, 1-1/2 Medium-Fat Meat, 2 Fat. CARBOHYDRATE CHOICES: 2.

tips & ideas

This tasty breakfast casserole can be a meal in itself. Just serve with fresh fruit juice.

① Heat oven to 425°F. Spray bottom and sides of 13x9-inch (3-quart) glass baking dish with cooking spray or grease with shortening. In 12-inch skillet, cook sausage, apples and onion over medium-high heat 8 to 10 minutes, stirring frequently, until sausage is no longer pink; drain if necessary. Spoon into baking dish.

② In medium bowl, beat eggs and 1/2 teaspoon salt with wire whisk or fork until well mixed. Pour eggs over sausage mixture.

③ In large bowl, mix flour, baking powder, sugar, baking soda and 1 teaspoon salt. Cut in butter, using pastry blender (or pulling 2 table knives through ingredients in opposite directions), until mixture looks like coarse crumbs. Stir in cheese and green onions. Add buttermilk; stir just until combined. Drop dough by rounded tablespoonfuls evenly onto sausage mixture.

④ Bake uncovered 20 to 30 minutes or until biscuits are deep golden brown and done in the middle. Let stand 10 minutes before serving.

High Altitude (3500-6500 ft): Use 1-1/2 teaspoons baking powder.

p. 223

p. 217

gifts from your kitchen

Whip up a fresh batch of homemade goodness to share with family and friends to show how much you care.

salty sweet peanutty treat

PREP TIME: 30 minutes • **START TO FINISH:** 3 hours 20 minutes • **MAKES:** 32 bars

① Heat oven to 350°F. Spray bottom and sides of 13x9-inch pan with cooking spray. In large bowl, stir cookie base ingredients until soft dough forms. Spread dough in bottom of pan. Bake 10 minutes.

② Meanwhile, in 2-quart saucepan, heat filling ingredients over medium-low heat 5 to 10 minutes, stirring constantly, until caramels are melted. Remove from heat.

③ As soon as pan is removed from oven, press pretzels firmly into partially baked base, slightly overlapping pretzels. Sprinkle chopped peanuts evenly over pretzels. Pour caramel filling over top; spread evenly.

④ Bake 20 minutes longer or until caramel filling bubbles. Cool completely, about 2 hours.

⑤ In small microwaveable bowl, microwave chocolate chips uncovered on High 1 to 2 minutes or until melted. Dip fork into melted chocolate; drizzle chocolate over bars. Refrigerate 30 minutes or until chocolate is set. For bars, cut into 8 rows by 4 rows. Store covered at room temperature.

High Altitude (3500-6500 ft): No change.

1 BAR: Calories 250; Total Fat 12g (Saturated Fat 5g, Trans Fat 0g); Cholesterol 20mg; Sodium 190mg; Total Carbohydrate 31g (Dietary Fiber 0g); Protein 4g. EXCHANGES: 2 Other Carbohydrate, 1/2 High-Fat Meat, 1-1/2 Fat. CARBOHYDRATE CHOICES: 2.

COOKIE BASE
- 1 pouch (1 lb 1.5 oz) Betty Crocker® chocolate chip cookie mix
- 1/2 cup butter or margarine, softened
- 1 egg

FILLING
- 24 caramels, unwrapped
- 2 tablespoons butter or margarine
- 1 can (14 oz) sweetened condensed milk (not evaporated)

TOPPING
- 60 small pretzel twists (2 cups)
- 1-1/2 cups dry-roasted salted peanuts, chopped
- 1 cup semisweet chocolate chips (6 oz)

tips&ideas

After drizzling with chocolate, chilling the bars for 30 minutes sets the chocolate so cutting and serving is a snap.

cranberry-pistachio biscotti

PREP TIME: 30 minutes • **START TO FINISH:** 3 hours 30 minutes • **MAKES:** 40 cookies

1 pouch (1 lb 1.5 oz) Betty Crocker® sugar cookie mix

1 box (4-serving size) pistachio instant pudding and pie filling mix

1/4 cup Gold Medal® all-purpose flour

1/2 cup butter or margarine, melted

2 eggs

1/2 cup dry-roasted salted pistachio nuts, finely chopped

1/2 cup sweetened dried cranberries

2 tablespoons powdered sugar

(1) Heat oven to 375°F. In large bowl, stir together cookie mix, pudding mix and flour. Stir in melted butter and eggs until soft dough forms. Stir in pistachios and cranberries. Divide dough in half.

(2) On each of 2 ungreased cookie sheets, shape half of dough into 15x2-inch log.

(3) Bake 18 to 20 minutes or until golden brown. Cool on cookie sheets 20 minutes. Reduce oven temperature to 250°F. Place logs on cutting board. Cut crosswise into 3/4-inch slices. Place slices cut sides down on ungreased cookie sheets.

(4) Bake 40 minutes, turning once. Immediately remove from cookie sheets to cooling racks. Cool 10 minutes. With small, fine strainer, lightly sprinkle powdered sugar over tops of cookies. Store loosely covered.

High Altitude (3500-6500 ft): Increase flour to 1/2 cup.

1 COOKIE: Calories 100; Total Fat 4.5g (Saturated Fat 2g, Trans Fat 0.5g); Cholesterol 15mg; Sodium 90mg; Total Carbohydrate 15g (Dietary Fiber 0g); Protein 1g. EXCHANGES: 1/2 Starch, 1/2 Other Carbohydrate, 1 Fat. CARBOHYDRATE CHOICES: 1.

white candy fantasy clusters

PREP TIME: 10 minutes • **START TO FINISH:** 45 minutes • **MAKES:** 24 clusters

4 cups Rice Chex® cereal
2 cups pretzel sticks, coarsely broken
1 cup cashews, coarsely chopped
1/2 package (16-oz size) vanilla-flavored candy coating (almond bark)
1/2 cup semisweet chocolate chips

① Spray 13x9-inch pan with cooking spray. In large bowl, mix cereal, pretzels and cashews.

② In 2-quart saucepan, melt candy coating over low heat, stirring constantly. Pour over cereal mixture, stirring until evenly coated. Press in pan; cool slightly.

③ In microwavable bowl, microwave chocolate chips uncovered on High about 1 minute; stir until smooth. Drizzle chocolate over snack. Let stand about 30 minutes or until chocolate is set. Break into clusters. Store in airtight container.

High Altitude (3500-6500 ft): No change.

1 CLUSTER: Calories 130; Total Fat 7g (Saturated Fat 3g, Trans Fat 0g); Cholesterol 0mg; Sodium 110mg; Total Carbohydrate 16g (Dietary Fiber 0g); Protein 2g. EXCHANGES: 1/2 Starch, 1/2 Other Carbohydrate, 1-1/2 Fat. CARBOHYDRATE CHOICES: 1.

tips&ideas

Fill cellophane bags with this extra-special mix, and tie with holiday ribbons for gift giving or add pretty tissue paper to a simple tin.

chili and garlic snack mix (gluten free)

PREP TIME: 10 minutes • START TO FINISH: 35 minutes • MAKES: 32 servings (1/2 cup each)

8 cups Rice Chex® cereal (gluten free)
1 bag (3 oz) fat-free butter-flavor microwave popcorn, popped
1/4 cup dry-roasted peanuts
3 tablespoons canola or vegetable oil
1/3 cup grated Parmesan cheese
2 teaspoons chili powder
2 teaspoons garlic powder

① Heat oven to 300°F. In very large bowl, mix cereal, popcorn and peanuts. Drizzle with oil; toss until evenly coated.

② In small bowl, mix remaining ingredients; sprinkle over cereal mixture. Toss until evenly coated. Spread cereal mixture in ungreased large roasting pan.

③ Bake uncovered 15 minutes, stirring once. Spread on waxed paper to cool, about 10 minutes. Store in airtight container.

High Altitude (3500-6500 ft): No change.

1 SERVING: Calories 60; Total Fat 2.5g (Saturated Fat 0g, Trans Fat 0g); Cholesterol 0mg; Sodium 110mg; Total Carbohydrate 8g (Dietary Fiber 0g); Protein 1g. EXCHANGES:1/2 Starch, 1/2 Fat. CARBOHYDRATE CHOICES: 1/2.

tips&ideas

Cooking gluten free? Always read labels to make sure that each recipe ingredient is gluten free. Products and ingredient sources can change.

reindeer feed (gluten free)

PREP TIME: 10 minutes • **START TO FINISH:** 30 minutes • **MAKES:** 20 servings (1/2 cup each)

6 cups Rice Chex® or Chocolate Chex® cereal
1 bag (12 oz) white vanilla baking chips (2 cups)
1/3 cup coarsely crushed peppermint candy canes
(14 miniature, unwrapped)

① Line cookie sheet with foil or waxed paper.
Place cereal in large bowl.

② In microwavable bowl, microwave white
vanilla baking chips uncovered on High about 1
minute 30 seconds, stirring every 30 seconds,
until chips can be stirred smooth. Stir in half
the crushed peppermint candy.

③ Pour over cereal; toss to evenly coat. Spread
mixture in single layer on cookie sheet.
Immediately sprinkle with remaining candy. Let
stand until set, about 20 minutes. Gently break
up coated cereal. Store in airtight container.

High Altitude (3500-6500 ft): No change.

1 SERVING (1/2 CUP): Calories 130; Total Fat 4.5g
(Saturated Fat 4g, Trans Fat 0g); Cholesterol 0mg; Sodium
110mg; Total Carbohydrate 20g (Dietary Fiber 0g); Protein
1g. EXCHANGES: 1/2 Starch, 1 Other Carbohydrate, 1 Fat.
CARBOHYDRATE CHOICES: 1.

tips&ideas

*If cooking gluten free is essential
at your house, always check product
labels to make certain that each
recipe ingredient is gluten free.
Products and ingredient sources
can change.*

peppermint cookie bark

PREP TIME: 20 minutes • **START TO FINISH:** 1 hour 15 minutes • **MAKES:** About 36 pieces

12 hard round peppermint candies, unwrapped
1 pouch (1 lb 1.5 oz) Betty Crocker® chocolate chip cookie mix
1/4 cup Gold Medal® all-purpose flour
1/3 cup butter or margarine, softened
1 egg
3/4 cup white vanilla baking chips
2 teaspoons vegetable oil

1 Heat oven to 375°F. Grease 15x10-inch pan with sides with shortening or cooking spray. In resealable food-storage plastic bag, place mints. With rolling pin or flat side of meat mallet, coarsely crush mints. Place fine strainer over large bowl. Pour crushed mints into strainer and shake lightly so tiny pieces fall into bowl (reserve larger pieces of mints for garnish).

2 In large bowl with tiny mint pieces, stir cookie mix, flour, butter and egg until stiff dough forms. Press in bottom of pan.

3 Bake 13 to 15 minutes or until golden brown. Cool completely in pan, about 30 minutes.

4 In small microwavable bowl, microwave baking chips and oil uncovered on High 30 to 60 seconds, stirring every 15 seconds, until chips are melted and mixture is smooth.

5 With fork, drizzle half of melted chips over cooled bars. Sprinkle with reserved crushed mints. Drizzle with remaining melted chips. Let stand about 10 minutes or until set. Break into irregular 2- to 3-inch pieces. Store between sheets of waxed paper in tightly covered container.

High Altitude (3500-6500 ft): No change.

1 PIECE: Calories 110; Total Fat 5g (Saturated Fat 3g, Trans Fat 0g); Cholesterol 10mg; Sodium 65mg; Total Carbohydrate 16g (Dietary Fiber 0g); Protein 1g. EXCHANGES: 1 Other Carbohydrate, 1 Fat. CARBOHYDRATE CHOICES: 1.

tips&ideas

Wrapped hard round peppermint candies come in red and white or green and white. Use either one to make this delicious cookie bark.

chocolate-covered caramel corn

PREP TIME: 20 minutes • **START TO FINISH:** 3 hours 50 minutes • **MAKES:** 18 servings (1 cup each)

1. Heat oven to 200°F. Remove any unpopped kernels from popcorn. In very large roasting pan or very large bowl, place popcorn and nuts, or divide popcorn and nuts between 2 ungreased 13x9-inch pans.

2. In 2-quart saucepan, melt butter over medium heat. Stir in brown sugar, corn syrup and salt. Heat to boiling, stirring occasionally. Continue cooking 5 minutes without stirring. Remove from heat. Stir in baking soda until foamy. Pour sugar mixture over popcorn mixture; toss until evenly coated. If using bowl, transfer mixture to 2 ungreased 13x9-inch pans.

3. Bake 1 hour, stirring every 15 minutes. Spread on foil or cooking parchment paper. Cool completely, about 30 minutes.

4. In medium bowl, place 3 cups popcorn mixture. In 1-quart saucepan, melt chocolate chips over low heat, stirring constantly. Drizzle chocolate evenly over 3 cups popcorn mixture; toss gently to thoroughly coat popcorn. Spread in single layer on foil or cooking parchment paper. Cool about 2 hours or until chocolate is firm.

5. Add chocolate-covered popcorn mixture to remaining popcorn mixture; toss gently to combine. Store tightly covered.

*EDITOR'S NOTE: Omit salt if using salted microwave popcorn or bags of popped popcorn containing salt.

High Altitude (3500-6500 ft): No change.

1 CUP: Calories 330; Total Fat 22g (Saturated Fat 5g, Trans Fat 0g); Cholesterol 15mg; Sodium 150mg; Total Carbohydrate 27g (Dietary Fiber 4g); Protein 6g. EXCHANGES: 1 Starch, 1 Other Carbohydrate, 1/2 High-Fat Meat, 3-1/2 Fat. CARBOHYDRATE CHOICES: 2.

12 cups popped popcorn

3 cups unblanched whole almonds, pecan halves or walnut halves

1/2 cup butter or margarine

1 cup packed brown sugar

1/4 cup light corn syrup

1/2 teaspoon salt*

1/2 teaspoon baking soda

1/2 cup semisweet chocolate chips, milk chocolate chips or white vanilla baking chips

curried snack mix

PREP TIME: 15 minutes • START TO FINISH: 1 hour 25 minutes • MAKES: 24 servings (1/2 cup each)

3 cups Corn Chex® cereal
3 cups Cheerios® cereal
3 cups small pretzel twists
2 cups salted cashew pieces
1 cup golden raisins
1 cup sweetened dried cranberries
1/2 cup butter or margarine, melted
2 tablespoons curry powder
1 tablespoon garlic salt

1 Heat oven to 250°F. In 15x10x1-inch pan or large roaster, mix cereals, pretzels, cashews, raisins and cranberries.

2 In small bowl, mix remaining ingredients. Pour over cereal mix; stir to coat well.

3 Bake 1 hour, stirring every 15 minutes, until crispy and well coated with seasoning. Spread on waxed paper or cooking parchment paper to cool. Cool completely, about 10 minutes.

High Altitude (3500-6500 ft): No change.

1/2 CUP: Calories 170; Total Fat 10g (Saturated Fat 3g, Trans Fat 0g); Cholesterol 10mg; Sodium 340mg; Total Carbohydrate 18g (Dietary Fiber 1g); Protein 3g. EXCHANGES: 1 Starch, 2 Fat. CARBOHYDRATE CHOICES: 1.

ginger-almond biscotti

PREP TIME: 30 minutes • **START TO FINISH:** 1 hour 25 minutes • **MAKES:** 34 cookies

1/2 cup butter or margarine, melted
  1 teaspoon grated orange peel
1/4 cup fresh orange juice
  2 eggs
  1 pouch (1 lb 1.5 oz) Betty Crocker® sugar cookie mix
  1 cup Gold Medal® all-purpose flour
1/2 cup slivered almonds
1/2 cup white vanilla baking chips
1/4 cup finely chopped crystallized ginger

1 Heat oven to 350°F. In large bowl, beat melted butter, orange peel, orange juice and eggs with wire whisk. Stir in remaining ingredients until soft dough forms.

2 Divide dough in half. Shape each half into 12x2-inch roll. On ungreased cookie sheet, place rolls 5 inches apart.

3 Bake 25 to 30 minutes or until edges are golden brown. Cool on cookie sheet 10 minutes. Place rolls on cutting board. Cut crosswise into 3/4-inch slices. Place slices cut sides down on ungreased cookie sheets.

4 Bake 15 minutes. Immediately remove from cookie sheets to cooling racks. Cool completely. Store loosely covered.

High Altitude (3500-6500 ft): Increase flour in dough to 1-1/4 cups, and add up to 1/4 cup additional flour as needed when shaping dough into rolls.

1 COOKIE: Calories 140; Total Fat 6g (Saturated Fat 3g, Trans Fat 0.5g); Cholesterol 20mg; Sodium 65mg; Total Carbohydrate 18g (Dietary Fiber 0g); Protein 2g. EXCHANGES: 1/2 Starch, 1/2 Other Carbohydrate, 1-1/2 Fat. CARBOHYDRATE CHOICES: 1.

easy butterscotch-almond pralines

PREP TIME: 25 minutes • **START TO FINISH:** 55 minutes • **MAKES:** 2 dozen candies

1/2 cup packed brown sugar
1 box (4-serving size) butterscotch-flavored pudding and pie filling mix (not instant)
1 cup granulated sugar
1/2 cup half-and-half
1 tablespoon butter or margarine
1 cup blanched whole almonds, toasted if desired
1/4 cup boiling water

① Line cookie sheet with foil. In 2-quart saucepan, stir all ingredients except boiling water with wooden spoon. Heat over medium heat, stirring constantly, until boiling rapidly. Boil and stir 3 minutes. Place boiling water in measuring cup. Remove candy from heat and continue stirring vigorously 4 to 5 minutes or until thick but still shiny.

② Working quickly, drop praline mixture by tablespoonfuls onto cookie sheet, flattening into patty shape with back of wooden spoon if needed. If mixture stiffens too much to drop from a spoon, quickly stir in hot water, 1/4 teaspoon at a time, until smooth. Cool completely, about 30 minutes. Store in tightly covered container.

High Altitude (3500-6500 ft): No change.

1 CANDY: Calories 80; Total Fat 1g (Saturated Fat 0.5g, Trans Fat 0g); Cholesterol 0mg; Sodium 30mg; Total Carbohydrate 16g (Dietary Fiber 0g); Protein 0g. EXCHANGES: 1 Other Carbohydrate. CARBOHYDRATE CHOICES: 1.

tips&ideas

Fill an oversized coffee mug with these yummy candies and a packet of chicory coffee for a gift with traditional Louisiana style.

banana-chocolate bread

PREP TIME: 15 minutes • **START TO FINISH:** 3 hours 25 minutes • **MAKES:** 1 loaf (16 slices)

1 cup sugar
1/2 cup butter or margarine, softened
2 eggs
2 tablespoons buttermilk
1-1/2 cups sliced bananas (3 to 4 medium), mashed
2 cups Gold Medal® all-purpose flour
1/2 cup baking cocoa
1/2 cup miniature semisweet chocolate chips
1-1/2 teaspoons baking powder
1/2 teaspoon baking soda
1/2 teaspoon salt
1/4 cup miniature semisweet chocolate chips
1 teaspoon vegetable oil

① Heat oven to 350°F. Grease bottom only of 9x5-inch loaf pan with shortening; lightly flour (or spray bottom of pan with cooking spray; do not flour).

② In large bowl, beat sugar and butter with electric mixer on medium speed until creamy. Beat in eggs. Beat in buttermilk and bananas. Stir in remaining ingredients except 1/4 cup chocolate chips and 1 teaspoon oil until dry ingredients are moistened. Spread in pan.

③ Bake 50 to 60 minutes or until toothpick inserted in center of bread comes out clean. Cool in pan 10 minutes; remove from pan to wire rack. Cool completely, about 2 hours.

④ In small microwavable bowl, mix 1/4 cup chocolate chips and 1 teaspoon oil. Microwave uncovered on High 1 minute; stir until melted. Drizzle chocolate over loaf.

High Altitude (3500-6500 ft): No change.

1 SLICE: Calories 250; Total Fat 10g (Saturated Fat 5g, Trans Fat 0g); Cholesterol 40mg; Sodium 210mg; Total Carbohydrate 36g (Dietary Fiber 2g); Protein 4g. EXCHANGES: 1 Starch, 1-1/2 Other Carbohydrate, 2 Fat. CARBOHYDRATE CHOICES: 2-1/2.

tips&ideas

For an extra burst of mouthwatering flavor, stir 1/2 cup of peanut butter or butterscotch chips into the batter.

holiday cookie ornaments

PREP TIME: 1 hour 15 minutes • **START TO FINISH:** 2 hours 15 minutes • **MAKES:** About 3 dozen cookies

1 pouch Betty Crocker® sugar cookie mix
1/3 cup butter or margarine, melted
2 tablespoons Gold Medal® all-purpose flour
1 egg
36 small candy canes
2 containers (1 lb each) Betty Crocker® Rich & Creamy creamy white or vanilla frosting

① Heat oven to 375°F. Line cookie sheets with cooking parchment paper. In medium bowl, stir cookie mix, butter, flour and egg until soft dough forms.

② On floured surface, roll dough until about 1/8 inch thick. Cut with 3- to 3-1/2-inch cookie cutters. Place cutouts 1 inch apart on cookie sheets.

③ Bake 5 minutes. Meanwhile, break off top of each candy cane to create loop for hanging cookies. To evenly break candy canes, cut with scissors while still in wrapper, then unwrap and use. Remove cookies from oven; press 1 candy piece on top of each cookie to make a loop. Bake 1 to 2 minutes longer or until edges are set. Cool on cookie sheets 2 minutes. Remove from cookie sheets to cooling rack. Cool completely, about 20 minutes.

④ Line cookie sheet with parchment paper. Place 1 container of frosting at a time in 2-cup glass measuring cup. Microwave on High 45 to 60 seconds, stirring every 15 seconds, until melted. Dip each cookie in frosting, allowing excess to drip off. Place cookies on parchment paper. Decorate as desired. Let stand about 1 hour until frosting is set.

High Altitude (3500-6500 ft): No change.

1 COOKIE: Calories 200; Total Fat 9g (Saturated Fat 3.5g, Trans Fat 2.5g); Cholesterol 10mg; Sodium 110mg; Total Carbohydrate 29g (Dietary Fiber 0g); Protein 0g. EXCHANGES: 2 Other Carbohydrate, 2 Fat. CARBOHYDRATE CHOICES: 2.

tips&ideas

The 1/8-inch rolled thickness of these cookies is important for the candy holder to stay connected. The recipe calls for using cooking parchment paper. If you are out of that product, use non-stick foil.

crunchy cranberry-almond snack

PREP TIME: 10 minutes • **START TO FINISH:** 45 minutes • **MAKES:** 6 servings (2/3 cup each)

2-1/2 cups Total® Cranberry Crunch cereal
  1/2 cup old-fashioned or quick-cooking oats
  1/2 cup sweetened dried cranberries
  1/2 cup sliced almonds
  1/3 cup frozen apple juice concentrate, thawed

① Heat oven to 300°F. Spray 15x10x1-inch pan with cooking spray.

② In large bowl, mix all ingredients until well blended. Spread evenly in pan.

③ Bake 25 to 30 minutes, stirring halfway through bake time, until almonds are lightly browned. Cool 10 minutes. Serve with yogurt or milk.

High Altitude (3500-6500 ft): No change.

1 SERVING: Calories 200; Total Fat 5g (Saturated Fat 0g, Trans Fat 0g); Cholesterol 0mg; Sodium 100mg; Total Carbohydrate 35g (Dietary Fiber 3g); Protein 4g. EXCHANGES: 1 Starch, 1-1/2 Other Carbohydrate, 1 Fat. CARBOHYDRATE CHOICES: 2.

sun-dried tomato spread

PREP TIME: 15 minutes • **START TO FINISH:** 15 minutes • **MAKES:** 18 servings (1 tablespoon spread and 3 crackers each)

1 package (8 oz) cream cheese
4 medium green onions, chopped (1/4 cup)
1/4 cup chopped drained oil-packed sun-dried tomatoes
1/4 teaspoon dried basil leaves
1/4 teaspoon salt
1/8 teaspoon freshly cracked pepper
8 oz assorted crackers

① In food processor, place all ingredients except crackers. Cover and process, using quick on-and-off motions, until well blended.

② Place spread in serving bowl. Serve immediately or cover and refrigerate until serving. Remove from refrigerator 30 minutes before serving. Serve with crackers.

High Altitude (3500-6500 ft): No change.

1 SERVING: Calories 110; Total Fat 6g (Saturated Fat 3.5g, Trans Fat 0.5g); Cholesterol 15mg; Sodium 160mg; Total Carbohydrate 10g (Dietary Fiber 0g); Protein 2g. EXCHANGES: 1/2 Starch, 1 Fat. CARBOHYDRATE CHOICES: 1/2.

chocolate chip pumpkin bread

PREP TIME: 15 minutes • **START TO FINISH:** 3 hours 10 minutes • **MAKES:** 2 loaves (16 slices each)

4 cups Gold Medal® all-purpose flour
2 teaspoons baking soda
1 teaspoon salt
1 teaspoon ground cinnamon
1/2 teaspoon ground nutmeg
2 cups sugar
3/4 cup butter or margarine, softened
4 eggs
1/2 cup water
1 can (15 oz) pumpkin (not pumpkin pie mix)
1 cup plus 2 tablespoons miniature semisweet chocolate chips
2 tablespoons chopped pecans
2 teaspoons sugar

tips&ideas

Greasing only the bottoms of the pans ensures your loaves will have gently rounded tops without any "lipping" at the edges.

① Heat oven to 350°F. Grease bottom only of two 8x4-inch loaf pans with shortening; lightly flour (or spray bottoms of pans with cooking spray; do not flour).

② In medium bowl, stir flour, baking soda, salt, cinnamon and nutmeg until mixed; set aside.

③ In large bowl, beat 2 cups sugar and the butter with electric mixer on medium speed 1 to 2 minutes or until creamy. Add eggs, one at a time, beating well after each addition. Beat in water and pumpkin on low speed. Add flour mixture; beat on low speed about 1 minute or until moistened. Stir in 1 cup of the chocolate chips. Spread evenly in pans. Sprinkle tops with remaining 2 tablespoons chocolate chips, the pecans and 2 teaspoons sugar.

④ Bake 1 hour 5 minutes to 1 hour 15 minutes or until toothpick inserted in center comes out clean. Cool in pans 10 minutes; remove from pans to cooling rack. Cool completely, about 1-1/2 hours.

High Altitude (3500-6500 ft): Bake 1 hour 10 minutes to 1 hour 20 minutes.

1 SLICE: Calories 200; Total Fat 7g (Saturated Fat 3.5g, Trans Fat 0g); Cholesterol 40mg; Sodium 190mg; Total Carbohydrate 30g (Dietary Fiber 1g); Protein 3g. EXCHANGES: 1 Starch, 1 Other Carbohydrate, 1 Fat. CARBOHYDRATE CHOICES: 2.

cranberry-apple-nut bread

PREP TIME: 15 minutes • **START TO FINISH:** 2 hours 50 minutes • **MAKES:** 1 loaf (12 slices)

3/4 cup sugar
1/2 cup vegetable oil
1 egg
1 cup shredded peeled apple (about 1 medium)
1-1/2 cups Gold Medal® all-purpose flour
1/2 teaspoon baking soda
1/2 teaspoon baking powder
1/2 teaspoon salt
3/4 cup chopped walnuts
1/2 cup dried cranberries
1 tablespoon sugar
1/2 teaspoon ground cinnamon

① Heat oven to 350°F. Grease bottom only of 8x4- or 9x5-inch loaf pan with shortening.

② In large bowl, mix 3/4 cup sugar, the oil and egg. Stir in apple, flour, baking soda, baking powder and salt. Stir in walnuts and cranberries. Pour batter into pan. In small bowl, mix 1 tablespoon sugar and the cinnamon; sprinkle over batter.

③ Bake 45 to 55 minutes or until toothpick inserted in center comes out clean. Cool 10 minutes. Loosen sides of loaf from pan; remove from pan to cooling rack. Cool completely, about 1-1/2 hours.

High Altitude (3500-6500 ft): No change.

1 SLICE: Calories 270; Total Fat 15g (Saturated Fat 2g, Trans Fat 0g); Cholesterol 20mg; Sodium 180mg; Total Carbohydrate 32g (Dietary Fiber 1g); Protein 3g. EXCHANGES: 1 Starch, 1 Fruit, 3 Fat. CARBOHYDRATE CHOICES: 2.

tips&ideas

To easily shred the apple, use a medium-sized grater. Health Twist: For added fiber, leave the peel on the apple.

sugar 'n spice snack

PREP TIME: 15 minutes • **START TO FINISH:** 2 hours 5 minutes • **MAKES:** 21 servings (1/2 cup each)

2 cups Corn Chex® cereal
2 cups Rice Chex® cereal
2 cups Apple Cinnamon Cheerios® cereal
3 cups original-flavor Bugles® corn snacks
1-1/2 cups dry-roasted peanuts
2 egg whites
2 tablespoons orange juice or water
1 cup sugar
1 teaspoon ground cinnamon

① Heat oven to 300°F. Spray with cooking spray or grease 15x10x1-inch pan. Mix cereals, corn snacks and peanuts in very large bowl; set aside. Beat egg whites, orange juice, sugar and cinnamon, using a wire whisk or hand beater, until foamy. Pour over cereal mixture, stirring until evenly coated. Spread in pan.

② Bake 45 to 50 minutes, stirring about every 15 minutes, until light brown and crisp. Cool completely, about 1 hour. Store in airtight container.

High Altitude (3500-6500 ft): No change.

1 SERVING: Calories 160; Total Fat 6g (Saturated Fat 1.5g, Trans Fat 0g); Cholesterol 0mg; Sodium 190mg; Total Carbohydrate 21g (Dietary Fiber 1g); Protein 4g. EXCHANGES: 1 Starch, 1/2 Other Carbohydrate, 1 Fat. CARBOHYDRATE CHOICES: 1-1/2.

p. 267

p. 263

joyful cookies & bars

If it's Christmastime, there must be cookies. Whether you're serving guests or St. Nick himself, you're set.

lemon linzer bars

PREP TIME: 20 minutes • START TO FINISH: 5 hours 15 minutes • MAKES: 24 bars

COOKIE BASE

1 pouch (1 lb 1.5 oz) Betty Crocker® sugar cookie mix

1/3 cup butter or margarine, softened

2 oz cream cheese, softened

4-1/2 teaspoons frozen (thawed) lemonade concentrate

3/4 teaspoon almond extract

1 egg

FILLING

2/3 cup seedless raspberry jam

1 package (8 oz) cream cheese, softened

1/2 cup lemon curd (from 10- to 12-oz jar)

2 cups frozen (thawed) whipped topping or 2 cups sweetened whipped cream

TOPPING

1/3 cup sliced almonds, toasted

24 fresh or frozen (thawed and drained) raspberries

① Heat oven to 350°F. Spray bottom and sides of 13x9-inch pan with cooking spray. In large bowl, stir cookie base ingredients until soft dough forms. Spread dough in bottom of pan.

② Bake 20 to 23 minutes or until golden brown. Cool completely, about 30 minutes.

③ Spread raspberry jam over cooled base. In large bowl, beat cream cheese and lemon curd with electric mixer on medium speed until smooth. Fold in whipped topping. Drop lemon mixture by teaspoonfuls over jam layer; spread gently and evenly over jam.

④ Sprinkle toasted almonds over top. Refrigerate at least 4 hours or overnight. For bars, cut into 6 rows by 4 rows. To serve, top each bar with 1 raspberry, gently pressing into lemon mixture. Store covered in refrigerator.

High Altitude (3500-6500 ft): Bake 22 to 25 minutes.

1 BAR: Calories 230; Total Fat 11g (Saturated Fat 6g, Trans Fat 1g); Cholesterol 35mg; Sodium 115mg; Total Carbohydrate 30g (Dietary Fiber 0g); Protein 2g. EXCHANGES: 2 Other Carbohydrate, 1/2 High-Fat Meat, 1-1/2 Fat. CARBOHYDRATE CHOICES: 2.

almond crescents

PREP TIME: 1 hour • START TO FINISH: 1 hour 30 minutes • MAKES: 5 dozen cookies

1 pouch (1 lb 1.5 oz) Betty Crocker®
   sugar cookie mix
1/2 cup cornstarch
1/2 cup ground blanched almonds
1/2 cup butter or margarine, melted
1 teaspoon almond extract
1 egg
1 cup powdered sugar

① Heat oven to 375°F. In large bowl, stir cookie
mix, cornstarch, ground almonds, melted
butter, almond extract and egg until soft
dough forms.

② Shape dough by rounded teaspoonfuls into
2-1/2 inch strips. On ungreased cookie sheets,
taper ends of strips and form crescent shapes.

③ Bake 9 to 10 minutes or until set. Cool 1
minute; remove from cookie sheets to cooling
racks. Cool completely, about 30 minutes. Roll
in powdered sugar.

VARIATION: Try ground pecans in place of
almonds for a different flavor.

High Altitude (3500-6500 ft): No change.

1 COOKIE: Calories 70; Total Fat 3g (Saturated Fat 1g, Trans
Fat 0g); Cholesterol 10mg; Sodium 30mg; Total Carbohydrate
10g (Dietary Fiber 0g); Protein 0g. EXCHANGES: 1 Other
Carbohydrate, 1/2 Fat. CARBOHYDRATE CHOICES: 1/2.

tips&ideas

*This crescent-shaped rich butter cookie is sometimes called a Mexican
Wedding Cake.*

elegant almond bars

PREP TIME: 25 minutes • **START TO FINISH:** 2 hours 30 minutes • **MAKES:** 32 bars

TOPPING

> 2 oz white chocolate baking bar, coarsely chopped (1/3 cup)
> 2 tablespoons shortening
> 1/4 cup sliced almonds

① Heat oven to 350°F. In large bowl, stir cookie base ingredients until soft dough forms. Spread in ungreased 13x9-inch pan. Bake 15 to 18 minutes or until light golden brown.

② Meanwhile, in large bowl, beat almond paste, sugar and 1/4 cup melted butter with electric mixer on low speed until blended. Add 2 eggs; beat until well blended (mixture may be slightly lumpy).

③ Spread almond paste mixture over partially baked base. Sprinkle with 1/2 cup almonds. Bake 15 to 20 minutes longer or until filling is set (filling will puff up during baking). Cool completely, about 1 hour.

④ In 1-quart heavy saucepan, melt white chocolate and shortening over low heat, stirring constantly, until smooth. Pour and spread over cooled bars. Sprinkle with 1/4 cup almonds. Let stand about 30 minutes or until topping is set. For bars, cut into 8 rows by 4 rows. Store covered at room temperature.

High Altitude (3500-6500 ft): In Step 1, bake 18 to 21 minutes. In Step 3, bake 17 to 22 minutes.

1 BAR: Calories 180; Total Fat 10g (Saturated Fat 4g, Trans Fat 1g); Cholesterol 30mg; Sodium 75mg; Total Carbohydrate 19g (Dietary Fiber 0g); Protein 3g. EXCHANGES: 1-1/2 Other Carbohydrate, 1/2 High-Fat Meat, 1 Fat. CARBOHYDRATE CHOICES: 1.

COOKIE BASE

> 1 pouch (1 lb 1.5 oz) Betty Crocker® sugar cookie mix
> 1/2 cup butter or margarine, melted
> 1/2 teaspoon almond extract
> 1 egg

FILLING

> 1 can (8 oz) or 1 package (7 oz) almond paste, crumbled into 1/2-inch pieces
> 1/4 cup sugar
> 1/4 cup butter or margarine, melted
> 2 eggs
> 1/2 cup sliced almonds

tips&ideas

The glaze can also be prepared in the microwave. In small microwavable bowl, microwave white chocolate and shortening 1 to 1-1/2 minutes, stirring every 30 seconds, until melted and smooth.

starlight sugar cookies

PREP TIME: 1 hour 15 minutes • **START TO FINISH:** 1 hour 30 minutes • **MAKES:** about 2 dozen cookies

1 pouch (1 lb 1.5 oz) Betty Crocker® sugar cookie mix
1/3 cup butter or margarine, melted
2 tablespoons Gold Medal® all-purpose flour
1 egg
1 container (1 lb) Betty Crocker® Rich & Creamy creamy white frosting
Betty Crocker® decorating icing (assorted colors)
Betty Crocker® decorating decors and colored sugars (assorted colors)

① Heat oven to 375°F. In medium bowl, stir cookie mix, melted butter, flour and egg until soft dough forms.

② On floured surface, roll out dough to about 1/4-inch thickness. Cut with cookie cutters. On ungreased cookie sheets, place 1 inch apart.

③ Bake 7 to 9 minutes or until edges are light golden brown. Cool 1 minute; remove from cookie sheets. Cool completely, about 15 minutes.

④ Spread frosting on cooled cookies. Decorate as desired with icing, decors and sugars.

VARIATION: For a slightly different look, tint the white frosting yellow with a few drops of food color.

High Altitude (3500-6500 ft): No change.

1 COOKIE (undecorated): Calories 200; Total Fat 9g (Saturated Fat 3.5g, Trans Fat 2g); Cholesterol 15mg; Sodium 115mg; Total Carbohydrate 28g (Dietary Fiber 0g); Protein 1g. EXCHANGES: 2 Other Carbohydrate, 2 Fat. CARBOHYDRATE CHOICES: 2.

tips&ideas

This is a great recipe to involve your kids. Have assorted sprinkles and decorations ready and let them create their own masterpieces.

ultimate chocolate-cappuccino cookie cups

PREP TIME: 45 minutes • START TO FINISH: 1 hour 15 minutes • MAKES: about 3 dozen cookies

2 tablespoons cappuccino-flavored instant coffee mix

1 tablespoon water

1 pouch (1 lb 1.5 oz) Betty Crocker® double chocolate chunk or chocolate chip cookie mix

3 tablespoons vegetable oil

1 egg

1 container (1 lb) Betty Crocker® Rich & Creamy chocolate frosting

1 teaspoon coffee-flavored liqueur

1 cup frozen (thawed) whipped topping

36 chocolate-covered espresso beans

① Heat oven to 375°F. Line 36 miniature muffin cups with paper baking cups, or spray with cooking spray. In large bowl, dissolve coffee mix in water. Add cookie mix, oil and egg; stir until soft dough forms.

② Shape dough into 36 (1-inch) balls; place in muffin cups.

③ Bake cookies 8 to 9 minutes or until set. Immediately make indentation in center of each cookie with end of wooden spoon to form a cup. Cool 30 minutes. Remove from pan.

④ In small bowl, stir frosting and liqueur until well blended. Gently stir in whipped topping. Spoon frosting mixture into decorating bag with star tip. Pipe frosting into each cookie cup. Top each with espresso bean. Store covered in the refrigerator.

High Altitude (3500-6500 ft): Spray paper baking cups or muffin cups with cooking spray. Bake 9 to 10 minutes.

1 COOKIE: Calories 170; Total Fat 7g (Saturated Fat 2.5g, Trans Fat 1g); Cholesterol 5mg; Sodium 85mg; Total Carbohydrate 27g (Dietary Fiber 0g); Protein 0g. EXCHANGES: 2 Other Carbohydrate, 1-1/2 Fat. CARBOHYDRATE CHOICES: 2.

tiny snowmen cookies

PREP TIME: 1 hour • **START TO FINISH:** 1 hour 30 minutes • **MAKES:** 28 cookies

1-1/2 cups butter, softened (do not use margarine)
   3/4 cup powdered sugar
     2 teaspoons vanilla
     3 cups Gold Medal® all-purpose flour
   1/2 teaspoon salt
   1/2 cup granulated sugar, white decorating sugar or
        white edible glitter
Assorted candies for decoration
Betty Crocker® Rich & Creamy ready-to-spread frosting
(any flavor), if desired
Betty Crocker® decorating gels (any colors), if desired

① Heat oven to 400°F (if using dark or nonstick cookie sheet, heat oven to 375°F). In large bowl, beat butter, powdered sugar and the vanilla with electric mixer on medium speed until smooth. Beat in flour and salt.

② Make 28 balls that are 1-1/4 inches in diameter. Make 28 balls that are 1 inch in diameter. Make 28 balls that are 3/4 inch in diameter. Roll each ball in granulated sugar. On ungreased cookie sheet, for each snowman, place 1 ball of each size (small, medium, large) in a row with sides touching, pressing together slightly. Place snowmen 1 inch apart.

③ Bake 9 to 12 minutes or until edges are light brown. Cool on cookie sheet 2 minutes; remove from cookie sheet to wire rack. Cool completely, about 30 minutes. Decorate as desired with candies (attach to cookies with small amount of frosting) and decorating gels.

High Altitude (3500-6500 ft): No change.

1 COOKIE: Calories 180; Total Fat 11g (Saturated Fat 5g); Cholesterol 25mg; Sodium 100mg; Total Carbohydrate 19g (Dietary Fiber 0g); Protein 2g. EXCHANGES: nc.

lime crescents

PREP TIME: 1 hour 15 minutes • START TO FINISH: 1 hour 15 minutes • MAKES: about 4 dozen cookies

COOKIES

1 cup butter or margarine, softened
1/2 cup powdered sugar
1 teaspoon lime juice
2-1/4 cups Gold Medal® all-purpose flour
1/4 teaspoon salt
2 teaspoons grated lime peel

ICING

1 cup powdered sugar
1 teaspoon grated lime peel

① Heat oven to 400°F (if using dark or nonstick cookie sheet, heat oven to 375°F). In medium bowl, beat butter, 1/2 cup powdered sugar and the lime juice with electric mixer on medium speed until smooth. Beat in flour, salt and 2 teaspoons lime peel.

② Gently shape dough by level measuring tablespoonfuls into crescent shapes, about 2 inches long. On ungreased cookie sheet, place crescents 1 inch apart.

③ Bake about 6 to 10 minutes or until edges begin to brown.

④ Meanwhile, in small bowl, stir 1 cup powdered sugar and 1 teaspoon lime peel with fork. Roll warm cookies in sugar mixture; place on wire rack. Roll in sugar again.

VARIATION: For orange-flavored crescents, substitute orange juice and orange peel for the lime juice and lime peel.

High Altitude (3500-6500 ft): No change.

1 COOKIE: Calories 70; Total Fat 4g (Saturated Fat 2g, Trans Fat 0g); Cholesterol 10mg; Sodium 40mg; Total Carbohydrate 8g (Dietary Fiber 0g); Protein 0g. EXCHANGES: 1/2 Starch, 1/2 Fat. CARBOHYDRATE CHOICES: 1/2.

tips & ideas

To ensure even baking, bake one sheet of cookies at a time and place the cookie sheet on the middle rack of your oven.

easy spritz cookies

PREP TIME: 45 minutes • **START TO FINISH:** 45 minutes • **MAKES:** 4 dozen cookies

1 pouch (1 lb 1.5 oz) Betty Crocker® sugar cookie mix
1/2 cup Gold Medal® all-purpose flour
1/2 cup butter, melted*
1 teaspoon almond extract
1 egg
Betty Crocker® decorating decors and colored sugars, if desired
Coarse white sugar

① Heat oven to 375°F. In large bowl, stir cookie mix, flour, melted butter, extract and egg until soft dough forms.

② Fit desired template in cookie press; fill cookie press with dough. Force dough through template onto ungreased cookie sheets. Sprinkle with decors or sugars.

③ Bake 6 to 8 minutes or until set but not brown. Cool 1 minute; remove from cookie sheets to cooling racks.

*EDITOR'S NOTE: We recommend not using margarine or vegetable oil spreads for this recipe.

High Altitude (3500-6500 ft): No change.

1 COOKIE: Calories 70; Total Fat 3g (Saturated Fat 1g, Trans Fat 0g); Cholesterol 10mg; Sodium 40mg; Total Carbohydrate 10g (Dietary Fiber 0g); Protein 0g. EXCHANGES: 1 Other Carbohydrate, 1/2 Fat. CARBOHYDRATE CHOICES: 1/2.

tips&ideas

To drizzle cookies with white icing: combine 1/2 cup powdered sugar, 1-1/2 teaspoons milk and 1/4 teaspoon rum extract.

raspberry thumbprint cookies

PREP TIME: 50 minutes • START TO FINISH: 50 minutes • MAKES: 5-1/2 dozen cookies

1 pouch (1 lb 1.5 oz) Betty Crocker®
   sugar cookie mix
1/2 cup butter or margarine, melted
1 egg
3 tablespoons Gold Medal® all-purpose flour
1/3 cup seedless raspberry jam
1 cup white vanilla baking chips

1 Heat oven to 375°F. In large bowl, stir cookie mix, melted butter, egg and flour until soft dough forms.

2 Shape dough into 3/4-inch balls. On ungreased cookie sheets, place balls 2 inches apart. Using the thumb or handle of a wooden spoon, make an indentation in center of each cookie. Spoon about 1/4 teaspoon jam into each indentation.

3 Bake 8 to 10 minutes or until edges are light golden brown. Cool 5 minutes; remove from cookie sheets to cooling racks.

4 In small microwavable bowl, microwave white vanilla baking chips uncovered on High 1 to 2 minutes or until chips are melted; stir until smooth. Spoon melted chips into small resealable food-storage plastic bag; cut small hole in corner of bag. Squeeze bag gently to drizzle melted chips over cookies.

High Altitude (3500-6500 ft): Decrease butter to 1/3 cup; increase flour to 1/4 cup. Bake 8 to 10 minutes.

1 COOKIE: Calories 70; Total Fat 3.5g (Saturated Fat 1.5g, Trans Fat 0g); Cholesterol 5mg; Sodium 35mg; Total Carbohydrate 10g (Dietary Fiber 0g); Protein 0g. EXCHANGES: 1 Other Carbohydrate, 1/2 Fat. CARBOHYDRATE CHOICES: 1/2.

irish cream-coffee bars

PREP TIME: 25 minutes • **START TO FINISH:** 2 hours 35 minutes • **MAKES:** 25 bars

BARS
- 1 pouch (1 lb 1.5 oz) Betty Crocker® sugar cookie mix
- 1/2 cup chopped pecans
- 1/2 cup cold butter
- 1 egg
- 1 can (14 oz) sweetened condensed milk (not evaporated)
- 2 tablespoons Irish cream liqueur
- 1 teaspoon instant coffee granules or crystals

TOPPING
- 1 cup whipping (heavy) cream
- 3 tablespoons packed brown sugar
- 1 tablespoon Irish cream liqueur
- 1 teaspoon vanilla
- 1/8 teaspoon ground cinnamon
- 25 cinnamon sticks (2 inch)

① Heat oven to 350°F. Spray bottom and sides of 8-inch square pan with cooking spray. In large bowl, place cookie mix and pecans. Cut in butter, using pastry blender or fork, until mixture looks like coarse crumbs. With fork, stir in egg. Press half of cookie mixture in bottom of pan. Bake 15 to 18 minutes or until golden brown. Reserve remaining cookie mixture.

② Meanwhile, in small bowl, stir milk, 2 tablespoons liqueur and the coffee granules until well blended. Pour evenly over warm crust. Sprinkle reserved cookie mixture over top. Bake 25 to 30 minutes longer or until golden brown. Cool for 30 minutes at room temperature. Refrigerate 1 hour to cool completely. Let stand 10 minutes before cutting into bars (5 rows by 5 rows). Store bars covered at room temperature.

③ Just before serving, in small bowl, beat whipping cream, brown sugar, 1 tablespoon liqueur and the vanilla with electric mixer on high speed until soft peaks form. Top each bar with dollop of whipped cream; sprinkle with ground cinnamon. Insert cinnamon stick into each dollop of whipped cream.

High Altitude (3500-6500 ft): No change.

1 BAR: Calories 220; Total Fat 12g (Saturated Fat 6g, Trans Fat 1g); Cholesterol 35mg; Sodium 110mg; Total Carbohydrate 26g (Dietary Fiber 0g); Protein 2g. EXCHANGES: 1 Starch, 1/2 Other Carbohydrate, 2-1/2 Fat. CARBOHYDRATE CHOICES: 2.

tips&ideas

Try using hazelnuts—they make a good stand-in for the pecans.

crisp peanut butter chews

PREP TIME: 25 minutes • **START TO FINISH:** 55 minutes • **MAKES:** 6 dozen cookies

1-1/2 cups light corn syrup
1 cup creamy peanut butter
1 pouch (1 lb 1.5 oz) Betty Crocker® peanut butter cookie mix
7 cups crisp rice cereal
1 cup salted peanuts

① Line 2 large cookie sheets with waxed paper or foil. In 5-quart heavy Dutch oven, heat corn syrup to boiling over medium heat, stirring occasionally. Stir in peanut butter until melted. Stir in cookie mix until well blended. Cook 2 minutes, stirring constantly. (Candy thermometer should read 160°F.)

② Immediately remove from heat. With wooden spoon or rubber spatula, gently fold in cereal and peanuts until well coated.

③ Drop by rounded tablespoonfuls onto cookie sheets. Flatten each cookie slightly with fingertips. Cool completely, about 30 minutes. Store covered at room temperature.

High Altitude (3500-6500 ft): No change.

1 COOKIE: Calories 100; Total Fat 4g (Saturated Fat 1g, Trans Fat 0g); Cholesterol 0mg; Sodium 85mg; Total Carbohydrate 14g (Dietary Fiber 0g); Protein 2g. EXCHANGES: 1 Other Carbohydrate, 1/2 High-Fat Meat. CARBOHYDRATE CHOICES: 1.

cranberry-apricot bars

PREP TIME: 20 minutes • **START TO FINISH:** 1 hour 40 minutes • **MAKES:** 16 bars

CRUST
1-1/4 cups Gold Medal® all-purpose flour
1/2 cup butter or margarine, softened
1/4 cup sugar

FILLING
1/2 cup chopped dried apricots
1/2 cup sweetened dried cranberries
1/4 cup sugar
1 tablespoon cornstarch
1/4 cup honey
3 tablespoons orange juice

① Heat oven to 350°F. Line 8-inch square pan with foil; spray foil with cooking spray. In large bowl, beat crust ingredients with electric mixer on low speed until mixture looks like coarse crumbs. Press in pan.

② Bake 28 to 30 minutes or until light golden brown. Meanwhile, in medium bowl, mix the filling ingredients.

③ Remove partially baked crust from oven. Reduce oven temperature to 325°F. Spread filling evenly over crust.

④ Bake 8 to 10 minutes longer or until mixture is set and appears glossy. Cool completely, about 45 minutes. For bars, cut into 4 rows by 4 rows.

High Altitude (3500-6500 ft): Decrease sugar in filling to 2 tablespoons. In Step 2, bake 30 to 32 minutes. In Step 3, do not reduce temperature. In Step 4, bake at 350°F for 10 to 12 minutes.

1 BAR: Calories 160; Total Fat 6g (Saturated Fat 3.5g, Trans Fat 0g); Cholesterol 15mg; Sodium 40mg; Total Carbohydrate 24g (Dietary Fiber 0g); Protein 1g. EXCHANGES: 1/2 Starch, 1 Other Carbohydrate, 1 Fat. CARBOHYDRATE CHOICES: 1-1/2.

caribbean lime coolers

PREP TIME: 1 hour • START TO FINISH: 1 hour 30 minutes • MAKES: 2-1/2 dozen cookies

1 pouch (1 lb 1.5 oz) Betty Crocker®
    sugar cookie mix
1/2 cup coconut
1 tablespoon grated lime peel (about 1 lime)
3 tablespoons lime juice
6 tablespoons butter or margarine, melted
1 egg
1/4 cup powdered sugar

① Heat oven to 350°F. In large bowl, stir cookie mix, coconut, lime peel, lime juice, butter and egg until soft dough forms.

② On ungreased cookie sheets, drop dough by level tablespoonfuls 2 inches apart.

③ Bake 9 to 13 minutes or until edges are light golden brown. Cool 1 minute; remove from cookie sheets to cooling racks. Cool completely, about 15 minutes.

④ With small strainer, sift powdered sugar over cooled cookies. Store the cookies covered at room temperature.

High Altitude (3500-6500 ft): Bake 13 to 17 minutes.

1 COOKIE: Calories 100; Total Fat 4.5g (Saturated Fat 2.5g, Trans Fat 0.5g); Cholesterol 15mg; Sodium 60mg; Total Carbohydrate 15g (Dietary Fiber 0g); Protein 0g.
EXCHANGES: 1 Other Carbohydrate, 1 Fat.
CARBOHYDRATE CHOICES: 1.

easy stained glass holiday cookies

PREP TIME: 30 minutes • **START TO FINISH:** 1 hour 10 minutes • **MAKES:** 2 dozen cookies

1 pouch (1 lb 1.5 oz) Betty Crocker®
  sugar cookie mix
1/3 cup butter or margarine, melted
1 egg
2 tablespoons Gold Medal® all-purpose flour
Betty Crocker® red and green decorating gels
(from 0.68-oz tubes)

① Heat oven to 375°F. In medium bowl, stir the cookie mix, butter, egg and flour until dough forms.

② Roll dough on floured surface until about 1/4 inch thick. Cut with 3 to 3-1/2-inch cookie cutters. On ungreased cookie sheets, place cutouts 1 inch apart. Decorate unbaked cookies with gels.

③ Bake 7 to 9 minutes or until light golden brown around edges. Cool 1 minute before removing from cookie sheets to cooling racks. Cool completely, about 20 minutes.

High Altitude (3500-6500 ft): No change.

1 COOKIE: Calories 110; Total Fat 4.5g (Saturated Fat 2g, Trans Fat 1g); Cholesterol 15mg; Sodium 70mg; Total Carbohydrate 17g (Dietary Fiber 0g); Protein 1g. EXCHANGES: 1/2 Starch, 1/2 Other Carbohydrate, 1 Fat. CARBOHYDRATE CHOICES: 1.

tips&ideas

Carefully cut cookie dough with a cutter dipped in flour or powdered sugar (unsweetened baking cocoa for chocolate dough). Cut dough as close together as possible on rolled dough to avoid re-rolling as re-rolled dough will be a little tougher.

apple streusel cheesecake bars

PREP TIME: 20 minutes • **START TO FINISH:** 3 hours 40 minutes • **MAKES:** 24 bars

1 pouch (1 lb 1.5 oz) Betty Crocker® oatmeal
   cookie mix
1/2 cup firm butter or margarine
2 packages (8 oz each) cream cheese, softened
1/2 cup sugar
2 tablespoons Gold Medal® all-purpose flour
1 teaspoon vanilla
1 egg
1 can (21 oz) apple pie filling
1/2 teaspoon ground cinnamon
1/4 cup chopped walnuts

1 Heat oven to 350°F. Spray bottom and sides of 13x9-inch pan with cooking spray. Place cookie mix in large bowl. With pastry blender or fork, cut in butter until mixture is crumbly and coarse. Reserve 1-1/2 cups crumb mixture; press remaining crumbs in bottom of pan. Bake 10 minutes.

2 Meanwhile, in large bowl, beat cream cheese, sugar, flour, vanilla and egg with electric mixer on medium speed until smooth.

3 Spread cream cheese mixture evenly over partially baked crust. In medium bowl, mix pie filling and cinnamon. Spoon evenly over cream cheese mixture. Sprinkle reserved crumbs over top. Sprinkle with walnuts.

4 Bake 35 to 40 minutes longer or until light golden brown. Cool for about 30 minutes. Refrigerate to chill, about 2 hours. For bars, cut into 6 rows by 4 rows. Store covered in the refrigerator.

High Altitude (3500-6500 ft): Bake 40 to 45 minutes.

1 BAR: Calories 240; Total Fat 13g (Saturated Fat 7g, Trans Fat 0g); Cholesterol 40mg; Sodium 170mg; Total Carbohydrate 29g (Dietary Fiber 0g); Protein 4g. EXCHANGES: 2 Other Carbohydrate, 1/2 High-Fat Meat, 1-1/2 Fat. CARBOHYDRATE CHOICES: 2.

peanut butter reindeer cookies

PREP TIME: 50 minutes • **START TO FINISH:** 1 hour 20 minutes • **MAKES:** about 4 dozen cookies

1/2 cup creamy peanut butter
1/2 cup butter or margarine, softened
1/2 cup granulated sugar
1/2 cup packed brown sugar
1 egg
1-1/3 cups Gold Medal® all-purpose flour
1 teaspoon baking powder
96 small round pretzel twists
1/4 cup semisweet chocolate chips (96 chips)
1 tablespoon green hard candy pieces or green candy-coated chocolate pieces (48 pieces)

① Heat oven to 375°F (if using dark or nonstick cookie sheet, heat oven to 350°F). In large bowl, beat peanut butter, butter, granulated sugar and brown sugar with electric mixer on medium speed until light and fluffy. Beat in egg. Stir in flour and baking powder.

② For each cookie, shape 1-inch ball of dough into triangle shape about 1-1/2 inches long. On ungreased cookie sheet, place 2 pretzel twists about 1 inch apart to look like antlers; press top of dough triangle gently into pretzels. Repeat with remaining dough and pretzels.

③ Bake 5 to 10 minutes or until edges just begin to brown. Immediately press 2 chocolate chips for eyes and 1 green candy for nose onto each cookie. Let stand 2 minutes; remove from cookie sheet to wire rack. Cool completely, about 30 minutes.

High Altitude (3500-6500 ft): Bake 6 to 10 minutes.

1 COOKIE: Calories 80; Total Fat 4g (Saturated Fat 1.5g, Trans Fat 0g); Cholesterol 10mg; Sodium 80mg; Total Carbohydrate 10g (Dietary Fiber 0g); Protein 1g. EXCHANGES: 1/2 Starch, 1 Fat. CARBOHYDRATE CHOICES: 1/2.

tips&ideas

Welcome the kids home from school with a plateful of these cheery reindeer cookies. They'll be smiling until dinnertime!

finger-paint holiday wreath cookies

PREP TIME: 1 hour • **START TO FINISH:** 3 hours • **MAKES:** about 1-1/2 dozen cookies

1/4 cup shortening
1/4 cup butter or margarine, softened
1/2 cup sugar
1 egg
1 teaspoon vanilla
1-3/4 cups Gold Medal® all-purpose flour
1/4 teaspoon baking soda
1 tub (1 lb) Betty Crocker® Rich & Creamy vanilla frosting
1/4 teaspoon green food color
1/4 teaspoon red food color
1/4 cup red cinnamon candies

① In medium bowl, beat shortening, butter and sugar with electric mixer on medium speed until well blended. Beat in egg and vanilla until smooth. Beat in flour and baking soda, scraping bowl occasionally, until well blended.

② Shape dough into a roll, 5 inches long and 2-1/2 inches in diameter. Wrap in plastic wrap and refrigerate about 1 hour 30 minutes or until very firm.

③ Heat oven to 375°F. Cut dough into 1/4-inch slices. On ungreased cookie sheet, place slices 2 inches apart. With 1-inch round cookie cutter or cleaned plastic bottle cap, cut out centers of cookies. Cut each cutout center part cookie in half. Place 2 halves at bottom of each wreath to shape bow.

④ Bake 6 to 11 minutes or until edges just begin to brown. Immediately remove from cookie sheet to wire rack. Cool completely, about 30 minutes.

⑤ Reserve 1/2 cup of the frosting in small microwavable bowl. Spread remaining frosting on cookies. Spoon 1/4 cup of reserved frosting into another small microwavable bowl. Microwave each bowl of frosting uncovered on High about 5 seconds or until warm; stir until pourable. Stir green food color into frosting in one bowl; stir red food color into frosting in other bowl.

⑥ Create a wreath pattern on frosted cookies by dipping one fingertip into warm green frosting and lightly pressing onto wreath part of cookies, repeating to resemble wreath. Create a bow by dipping another fingertip into warm red frosting and lightly coating bow part of cookies. Rewarm the frosting if it gets too stiff. Press 3 to 9 cinnamon candies onto wreath to look like berries.

High Altitude (3500-6500 ft): No change.

1 COOKIE: Calories 240; Total Fat 10g (Saturated Fat 5g, Trans Fat 0.5g); Cholesterol 20mg; Sodium 40mg; Total Carbohydrate 36g (Dietary Fiber 0g); Protein 2g. EXCHANGES: 1 Starch, 1-1/2 Other Carbohydrate, 1-1/2 Fat. CARBOHYDRATE CHOICES: 2-1/2.

chocolate-covered cherry diamonds

PREP TIME: 10 minutes • START TO FINISH: 1 hour 15 minutes • MAKES: 48 bars

1 jar (6 oz) maraschino cherries
1 cup powdered sugar
1 cup butter or margarine, softened
1/2 teaspoon almond extract
2-1/2 cups Gold Medal® all-purpose flour
1/2 teaspoon salt
1 bag (11.5 oz) milk chocolate chips (2 cups)
12 red candied cherries, cut into fourths, if desired

(1) Heat oven to 325°F (if using dark or nonstick pan, heat oven to 300°F). Drain and finely chop maraschino cherries, reserving liquid.

(2) In large bowl, beat powdered sugar, butter, cherry liquid and almond extract with electric mixer on low speed until well mixed. Beat in the flour and salt until well mixed. Stir in maraschino cherries. On bottom of ungreased 15x10x1-inch pan, spread dough. Bake 25 to 30 minutes or until edges are light golden brown.

(3) Immediately sprinkle with chocolate chips. Let stand about 5 minutes or until chocolate is softened; spread chocolate evenly over bars with spatula. Cool in pan on wire rack 30 minutes. For diamond shapes, cut bars diagonally into 8 rows by 6 rows. Garnish with candied cherries.

High Altitude (3500-6500 ft): Heat oven to 350°F (for dark or nonstick pan, 325°F). Bake 30 to 35 minutes.

1 BAR: Calories 110; Total Fat 6g (Saturated Fat 3g, Trans Fat 0g); Cholesterol 10mg; Sodium 55mg; Total Carbohydrate 13g (Dietary Fiber 0g); Protein 1g. EXCHANGES: 1 Starch, 1/2 Other Carbohydrate, 2 Fat. CARBOHYDRATE CHOICES: 1.

caramel-cashew bars

PREP TIME: 20 minutes • START TO FINISH: 1 hour 25 minutes • MAKES: 48 bars

1/2 cup shortening
1/2 cup butter or margarine, softened
3/4 cup granulated sugar
3/4 cup packed brown sugar
2 eggs
1 teaspoon vanilla
2-1/4 cups Gold Medal® all-purpose flour
1 teaspoon ground cinnamon
1 teaspoon baking soda
1-1/2 cups chopped salted cashews
1 bag (14 oz) caramels, unwrapped
1/4 cup milk

(1) Heat oven to 350°F (if using dark or nonstick pan, heat oven to 325°F). Spray 15x10x1-inch pan with cooking spray.

(2) In large bowl, beat shortening, butter, granulated sugar and brown sugar with electric mixer on medium speed until smooth. Beat in eggs and vanilla. Beat in flour, cinnamon and baking soda, scraping bowl occasionally, until well blended. Stir in 1 cup of the cashews. Spread dough in pan. Bake 20 to 25 minutes or until golden brown. Cool 10 minutes.

(3) Meanwhile, in 2-quart saucepan, heat caramels and milk over medium heat, stirring frequently, until caramels are melted; keep warm.

(4) Spread caramel over slightly cooled bars. Sprinkle remaining 1/2 cup cashews over caramel. Cool completely, about 30 minutes. For bars, cut into 8 rows by 6 rows. Store covered in refrigerator.

High Altitude (3500-6500 ft): Bake 25 to 30 minutes.

1 BAR: Calories 150; Total Fat 7g (Saturated Fat 2.5g, Trans Fat 0g); Cholesterol 15mg; Sodium 75mg; Total Carbohydrate 19g (Dietary Fiber 0g); Protein 2g. EXCHANGES: 1 Starch, 1-1/2 Fat. CARBOHYDRATE CHOICES: 1.

hazelnut lace cookies

PREP TIME: 30 minutes • **START TO FINISH:** 50 minutes • **MAKES:** about 2-1/2 dozen cookies

1/4 cup butter or margarine
1/3 cup packed brown sugar
3/4 teaspoon instant coffee crystals
1/4 cup light corn syrup
1/3 cup Gold Medal® all-purpose flour
  1 tablespoon baking cocoa
1/2 cup finely chopped hazelnuts (filberts)
  1 teaspoon vanilla
  1 cup white baking chips
  1 teaspoon vegetable oil

① Heat oven to 375°F (if using dark or nonstick cookie sheet, heat oven to 350°F). In 2-quart saucepan, melt butter over medium heat. Stir in brown sugar, coffee crystals and corn syrup. Heat to boiling over medium-high heat, stirring constantly, until sugar is dissolved. Remove from heat. Stir in flour, cocoa, hazelnuts and vanilla until blended.

② Heat ungreased cookie sheet in oven for 5 minutes. On warm cookie sheet, drop hazelnut mixture by teaspoonfuls 3 inches apart. Bake 5 to 7 minutes or until cookies spread thin and are deep brown. Cool 1 minute; working quickly with spatula, remove from cookie sheet to wire rack. Cool completely, about 15 minutes.

③ In small resealable plastic food-storage bag, place white baking chips and oil; seal bag. Microwave on High 1 minute. Gently squeeze bag until chips are smooth. Cut off tiny corner of bag. Squeeze bag to make snowflake design on cookies with glaze.

High Altitude (3500-6500 ft): No change.

1 COOKIE: Calories 100; Total Fat 5g (Saturated Fat 2.5g, Trans Fat 0g); Cholesterol 0mg; Sodium 25mg; Total Carbohydrate 11g (Dietary Fiber 0g); Protein 0g. EXCHANGES: 1 Other Carbohydrate, 1 Fat. CARBOHYDRATE CHOICES: 1.

tips&ideas

Keep these delicate sweet treats from crumbling by packing them in a rigid box or tin.

orange-pecan wafers

PREP TIME: 50 minutes • **START TO FINISH:** 3 hours 20 minutes • **MAKES:** about 4 dozen cookies

1-3/4 cups Gold Medal® all-purpose flour
3/4 cup butter or margarine, softened
1/2 cup powdered sugar
1 teaspoon grated orange peel
1/2 teaspoon vanilla
1/4 teaspoon baking powder
1 egg
1/4 cup finely chopped pecans
1 cup semisweet chocolate chips
1 teaspoon shortening

① In large bowl, beat all ingredients except pecans, chocolate chips and shortening with electric mixer on medium speed until well mixed. Stir in pecans.

② Place dough on 14-inch length of plastic wrap. Use wrap to shape dough into a roll, 12 inches long and 2 inches in diameter. Wrap in plastic and refrigerate about 2 hours or until firm.

③ Heat oven to 375°F (if using dark or nonstick cookie sheet, heat oven to 350°F). Cut dough into 1/4-inch slices with sharp knife. On ungreased cookie sheet, place slices 1 inch apart.

④ Bake 8 to 12 minutes or until edges begin to brown. Remove from cookie sheet to wire rack. Cool completely, about 30 minutes.

⑤ In small microwavable dish, microwave chocolate chips and shortening uncovered on High about 1 minute or until softened; stir until smooth. Dip half of each cookie into chocolate, allowing excess to drip back into dish. Place on waxed paper; let stand about 30 minutes or until chocolate is set.

High Altitude (3500-6500 ft): Bake 10 to 14 minutes.

1 COOKIE: Calories 70; Total Fat 4.5g (Saturated Fat 2g, Trans Fat 0g); Cholesterol 15mg; Sodium 25mg; Total Carbohydrate 7g (Dietary Fiber 0g); Protein 0g. EXCHANGES: 1/2 Starch, 1 Fat. CARBOHYDRATE CHOICES: 1/2.

fiesta fudge cookies

PREP TIME: 1 hour • **START TO FINISH:** 1 hour • **MAKES:** 5 dozen cookies

1/3 cup butter or margarine

6 oz unsweetened baking chocolate

1 can (14 oz) sweetened condensed milk (not evaporated)

1 pouch (1 lb 1.5 oz) Betty Crocker® sugar cookie mix

1 teaspoon ground cinnamon

60 white- and chocolate-striped candy drops or pieces, unwrapped

1 Heat oven to 350°F. In large microwavable bowl, microwave butter and chocolate uncovered on High 1 minute. Stir; microwave on High 1 minute longer or until butter is melted and chocolate can be stirred smooth.

2 Stir condensed milk into chocolate mixture. Stir in the cookie mix and cinnamon until well blended.

3 Using 1 level tablespoonful of dough for each cookie, shape into 60 balls. On ungreased cookie sheets, place balls 2 inches apart.

4 Bake 6 to 7 minutes or until edges lose their shiny look (do not overbake). Immediately press 1 chocolate candy into center of each cookie. Cool cookies on cookie sheets 5 minutes; remove from cookie sheets to cooling racks. To get candy to spread slightly on top of cookie, tap edge of each cookie lightly. Cool completely. Store covered at room temperature.

High Altitude (3500-6500 ft): Bake 8 to 9 minutes.

1 COOKIE: Calories 110; Total Fat 5g (Saturated Fat 2.5g, Trans Fat 0g); Cholesterol 5mg; Sodium 40mg; Total Carbohydrate 14g (Dietary Fiber 0g); Protein 2g. EXCHANGES: 1/2 Starch, 1/2 Other Carbohydrate, 1 Fat. CARBOHYDRATE CHOICES: 1.

chunky peppermint fudge dream cookies

PREP TIME: 50 minutes • START TO FINISH: 50 minutes • MAKES: about 20 large cookies

3/4 cup packed brown sugar

3/4 cup granulated sugar

1/2 cup butter or margarine, softened

1/2 cup shortening

1 teaspoon vanilla

2 eggs

2 oz unsweetened baking chocolate, melted, cooled

2-1/4 cups Gold Medal® all-purpose flour

1 teaspoon baking soda

2 packages (4.67 oz each) foil-wrapped rectangular creme de menthe thin chocolate mints, unwrapped, coarsely chopped

1-1/2 cups semisweet chocolate chunks

① Heat oven to 350°F. In large bowl, beat brown sugar, granulated sugar, butter, shortening, vanilla and eggs with electric mixer on medium speed until smooth. Beat in melted baking chocolate. On low speed, beat in flour and baking soda until well blended. Reserve 1 cup of the chopped mints. Stir remaining mints and the chocolate chunks into dough.

② On ungreased cookie sheets, drop dough by 1/4 cupfuls 2 inches apart.

③ Bake 11 to 15 minutes or until centers of cookies no longer look moist (do not overbake). Immediately sprinkle cookies with reserved mints. Cool 1 minute; remove from cookie sheets to cooling racks.

High Altitude (3500-6500 ft): Bake 12 to 16 minutes.

1 LARGE COOKIE: Calories 370; Total Fat 20g (Saturated Fat 9g, Trans Fat 1g); Cholesterol 35mg; Sodium 115mg; Total Carbohydrate 43g (Dietary Fiber 2g); Protein 4g. EXCHANGES: 1 Starch, 2 Other Carbohydrate, 4 Fat. CARBOHYDRATE CHOICES: 3.

tips&ideas

Wrap these fun, flavorful cookies singly or in pairs in a holiday print cellophane bag. Tie with a festive bow and give as a small gift to your co-workers.

chocolate-caramel turtle cookies

PREP TIME: 1 hour 40 minutes • **START TO FINISH:** 1 hour 40 minutes • **MAKES:** 4 dozen cookies

2-1/2 cups pecan halves
1/2 cup water
1/2 cup sugar
3/4 cup butter or margarine, softened
1 teaspoon vanilla
1 egg
1-1/2 cups Gold Medal® all-purpose flour
1/4 cup unsweetened baking cocoa
48 round milk chocolate-covered chewy caramels (from 13-oz bag), unwrapped

① Heat oven to 375°F (if using dark or nonstick cookie sheet, heat oven to 350°F). In medium bowl, soak pecans in water while making dough; drain well.

② In medium bowl, beat sugar, butter, vanilla and egg with electric mixer on medium speed until light and fluffy. On low speed, beat in flour and cocoa until dough forms.

③ On ungreased cookie sheets, for each cookie, arrange 5 pecans to look like head and legs of a turtle. Shape dough by rounded teaspoonfuls into 1-inch balls. Place 1 ball on top of each group of 5 pecans, pressing lightly into pecans with palm of hand.

④ Bake cookies 7 to 10 minutes or until set. Immediately press 1 caramel gently onto top of each cookie; let stand 5 minutes to soften caramel. Use small spatula to flatten candy slightly. Remove cookies from cookie sheets to cooling racks.

High Altitude (3500-6500 ft): Bake 9 to 12 minutes.

1 COOKIE: Calories 120; Total Fat 8g (Saturated Fat 2.5g, Trans Fat 0g); Cholesterol 15mg; Sodium 30mg; Total Carbohydrate 10g (Dietary Fiber 0g); Protein 1g. EXCHANGES: 1/2 Starch, 1-1/2 Fat. CARBOHYDRATE CHOICES: 1/2.

tips&ideas

Arrange these little snappers on a festive holiday plate, or place them inside a special holiday gift box.

baklava bars

PREP TIME: 25 minutes • START TO FINISH: 2 hours 50 minutes • MAKES: 24 bars

COOKIE BASE
1 pouch (1 lb 1.5 oz) Betty Crocker® sugar cookie mix
1/2 cup butter or margarine, softened
1/2 teaspoon grated lemon peel
1 egg

FILLING
1-1/2 cups chopped walnuts
1/3 cup granulated sugar
1/4 cup butter or margarine, softened
1 teaspoon ground cinnamon
1/8 teaspoon salt
8 frozen mini phyllo (filo) shells (from 2.1-oz package)

GLAZE
1/3 cup honey
2 tablespoons butter or margarine, softened
1 tablespoon packed brown sugar
1/2 teaspoon lemon juice
1/4 teaspoon ground cinnamon
1 teaspoon vanilla

GARNISH
5 tablespoons honey

① Heat oven to 350°F. Spray bottom only of 13x9-inch pan with cooking spray.

② In large bowl, stir cookie base ingredients until soft dough forms. Press dough in bottom of pan. Bake 15 minutes.

③ Meanwhile, in medium bowl, stir walnuts, granulated sugar, 1/4 cup butter, 1 teaspoon cinnamon and the salt with fork until mixture is well mixed and crumbly.

④ Sprinkle nut mixture evenly over partially baked base. With hands, crumble frozen fillo shells evenly over nut mixture. Bake 18 to 20 minutes longer or until golden brown.

⑤ Meanwhile, in small microwavable bowl, microwave 1/3 cup honey, 2 tablespoons butter, the brown sugar, lemon juice and 1/4 teaspoon cinnamon uncovered on High for about 1 minute or until bubbly. Stir in vanilla.

⑥ Drizzle glaze evenly over phyllo. Cool completely, about 2 hours.

⑦ For bars, cut into 6 rows by 4 rows. Before serving, drizzle about 1/2 teaspoon honey over each bar. Store covered at room temperature.

High Altitude (3500-6500 ft): In Step 2, bake crust 17 minutes.

1 BAR: Calories 250; Total Fat 14g (Saturated Fat 5g, Trans Fat 1g); Cholesterol 25mg; Sodium 115mg; Total Carbohydrate 29g (Dietary Fiber 0g); Protein 2g. EXCHANGES: 1/2 Starch, 1-1/2 Other Carbohydrate, 2-1/2 Fat. CARBOHYDRATE CHOICES: 2.

tips&ideas

This award-winning recipe offers the same flavor as classic Greek baklava but takes a lot less time to make!

chocolate-topped peanut-toffee bars

PREP TIME: 30 minutes • START TO FINISH: 3 hours 15 minutes • MAKES: 32 bars

COOKIE BASE
1 pouch (1 lb 1.5 oz) Betty Crocker®
   peanut butter cookie mix
3 tablespoons vegetable oil
1 tablespoon water
1 egg

FILLING
1 cup butter, cut into small pieces
1 cup packed brown sugar
1-1/2 cups lightly crushed potato chips
1 cup salted peanuts

TOPPING
2 cups semisweet chocolate chips (12 oz)

① Heat oven to 350°F. Spray bottom and sides of 13x9-inch pan with cooking spray. In large bowl, stir cookie base ingredients until soft dough forms. Press dough in bottom of pan. Bake 10 minutes or just until dough is set.

② Meanwhile, in 1-quart saucepan, melt butter over medium heat. Stir in brown sugar. Heat to boiling, stirring frequently. Boil 1 minute, stirring constantly.

③ Sprinkle potato chips and peanuts over partially baked base. Pour brown sugar mixture over chips and peanuts. Bake 15 minutes longer or until surface is bubbly.

④ Sprinkle chocolate chips evenly over chips and peanuts; return to oven for 2 minutes to soften chocolate. Spread chocolate over filling. Cool completely, about 2 hours. Refrigerate 30 minutes or until chocolate is set. For bars, cut into 8 rows by 4 rows. Store covered at room temperature.

High Altitude (3500-6500 ft): In Step 1, bake 12 minutes. In Step 4, return to oven for 3 minutes.

1 BAR: Calories 260; Total Fat 16g (Saturated Fat 7g, Trans Fat 0g); Cholesterol 20mg; Sodium 150mg; Total Carbohydrate 26g (Dietary Fiber 1g); Protein 3g. EXCHANGES: 1-1/2 Other Carbohydrate, 1/2 High-Fat Meat, 2-1/2 Fat. CARBOHYDRATE CHOICES: 2.

alfajores (dulce de leche sandwich crème cookies)

PREP TIME: 1 hour 20 minutes • **START TO FINISH:** 1 hour 20 minutes • **MAKES:** 24 sandwich cookies

1 pouch (1 lb 1.5 oz) Betty Crocker®
   sugar cookie mix
1 cup coconut
1/2 cup pecan halves, toasted, finely chopped
1/3 cup butter or margarine, melted
1 egg
1 can (13.4 oz) dulce de leche
   (caramelized sweetened condensed milk)
2 tablespoons powdered sugar

① Heat oven to 375°F. Line cookie sheets with parchment paper.

② In large bowl, stir cookie mix, 1/2 cup of the coconut, the pecans, melted butter and egg until stiff dough forms.

③ On floured surface, roll half of dough to 1/4-inch thickness. Cut with 2-inch round or fluted cookie cutter. Place 2 inches apart on cookie sheets. Repeat with remaining half of dough.

④ Bake 7 to 9 minutes or until set. Cool 2 minutes; remove from cookie sheets to cooling racks. Cool completely.

⑤ To make each sandwich cookie, spread about 2 teaspoons dulce de leche on bottom of 1 cookie. Top with second cookie, bottom side down; gently press cookies together so some of filling seeps out around edges. Roll edges in remaining 1/2 cup coconut. Place cookies on cooling rack.

⑥ Sprinkle tops of sandwich cookies with powdered sugar. Store between sheets of waxed paper in tightly covered container.

High Altitude (3500-6500 ft): No change.

1 SANDWICH COOKIE: Calories 190; Total Fat 8g (Saturated Fat 4g, Trans Fat 1g); Cholesterol 15mg; Sodium 95mg; Total Carbohydrate 28g (Dietary Fiber 0g); Protein 3g. EXCHANGES: 1/2 Starch, 1-1/2 Other Carbohydrate, 1-1/2 Fat. CARBOHYDRATE CHOICES: 2.

tips&ideas

Look for cans of dulce de leche in the Hispanic-foods section at the grocery store. Dulce de leche is like sweetened condensed milk, but it has been caramelized and is much thicker.

orange-spice drops

1 pouch (1 lb 1.5 oz) Betty Crocker®
   sugar cookie mix
1/3 cup mascarpone cheese or 1 package
   (3 oz) cream cheese
1/4 cup butter or margarine, softened
1 tablespoon grated orange peel
1 tablespoon fresh orange juice
1/4 teaspoon pumpkin pie spice
1 egg
1 cup finely chopped pecans
2 cups white candy melts, coating wafers or
   white vanilla baking chips (12 oz)
Edible orange glitter, if desired

① Heat oven to 375°F. In large bowl, beat cookie mix, mascarpone cheese and butter on low speed until well mixed. Add orange peel, orange juice, pumpkin pie spice and egg; beat until thoroughly mixed.

② Using small cookie scoop, shape dough into 1-inch balls. Roll balls in pecans. On ungreased cookie sheet, place balls 2 inches apart.

③ Bake 11 to 13 minutes or until edges are light golden brown. Cool 5 minutes. Remove from cookie sheet to cooling rack and cool completely.

④ In small microwavable bowl, microwave candy melts uncovered on High 1 to 2 minutes, stirring every 30 seconds, until melted and smooth. Dip each cookie halfway into melted candy, letting excess drip off. Place on waxed paper; let stand until almost set. Sprinkle dipped half of each cookie with edible glitter. Let cookies stand until candy coating is completely set, about 1 hour. Store cookies between sheets of waxed paper in tightly covered container.

High Altitude (3500-6500 ft): No change.

1 COOKIE: Calories 150; Total Fat 8g (Saturated Fat 3.5g, Trans Fat 0.5g); Cholesterol 10mg; Sodium 65mg; Total Carbohydrate 18g (Dietary Fiber 0g); Protein 2g. EXCHANGES: 1 Starch, 1-1/2 Fat. CARBOHYDRATE CHOICES: 1.

tips&ideas

Look for edible glitter in the baking section of craft stores or specialty kitchen stores.

glazed eggnog spritz

PREP TIME: 45 minutes • START TO FINISH: 45 minutes • MAKES: about 6 dozen cookies

COOKIES

3/4 cup granulated sugar
1 cup butter or margarine, softened
2 teaspoons vanilla
2 teaspoons rum flavor
1 egg
2-1/4 cups Gold Medal® all-purpose flour
1 teaspoon ground nutmeg

RUM DRIZZLE

2 tablespoons butter or margarine, melted
1 cup powdered sugar
1 teaspoon rum flavor
1 tablespoon water
1/2 teaspoon ground nutmeg, if desired

(1) Heat oven to 350°F (if using dark or nonstick cookie sheet, heat oven to 325°F). In large bowl, beat granulated sugar and 1 cup butter with electric mixer on medium speed until fluffy. Beat in the vanilla, 2 teaspoons rum flavor and the egg until smooth. Beat in the flour and 1 teaspoon nutmeg.

(2) Place 1/4 of the dough at a time in cookie press. On ungreased cookie sheet, form desired shapes with dough.

(3) Bake 6 to 10 minutes until edges are lightly browned. Cool 1 minute; remove from cookie sheet to wire rack.

(4) In small bowl, stir all glaze ingredients except nutmeg with spoon until smooth and thin enough to drizzle. Pour mixture into small resealable plastic food-storage bag; cut off tiny corner of bag. Squeeze bag to drizzle glaze on the cookies. Before the glaze is set, sprinkle 1/2 teaspoon nutmeg over cookies.

High Altitude (3500-6500 ft): No change.

1 COOKIE: Calories 60; Total Fat 3g (Saturated Fat 1.5g, Trans Fat 0g); Cholesterol 10mg; Sodium 20mg; Total Carbohydrate 7g (Dietary Fiber 0g); Protein 0g. EXCHANGES: 1/2 Starch, 1/2 Fat. CARBOHYDRATE CHOICES: 1/2.

cinnamon stars

PREP TIME: 1 hour 55 minutes • START TO FINISH: 3 hours 5 minutes • MAKES: about 8 dozen cookies

(1) In large bowl, beat 1-1/2 cups powdered sugar and the butter with electric mixer on medium speed until smooth. Beat in egg and vanilla until smooth. Beat in flour, baking soda, cream of tartar and cinnamon until well blended. Cover; refrigerate 1 hour or until firm.

(2) Heat oven to 375°F (if using dark or nonstick cookie sheet, heat oven to 350°F). Divide dough in half. On lightly floured surface, roll half of dough at a time 1/4 inch thick. Cut with 2-inch star-shaped cookie cutter. On ungreased cookie sheets, place stars 1 inch apart.

(3) Bake 7 to 8 minutes or until light golden. Cool 1 minute; remove from cookie sheets to cooling racks. Cool cookies completely, about 30 minutes.

(4) In 2-quart saucepan, heat candies and water to boiling over medium-high heat, stirring frequently. Reduce heat to medium-low; simmer uncovered 5 to 6 minutes, stirring frequently, until candies are melted. Remove from heat. With wire whisk, stir in 2-1/2 cups powdered sugar, 1/2 cup at a time, until smooth. Drizzle icing over cookies. (Icing sets up quickly; if necessary, add water, 1 teaspoon at a time, for drizzling consistency.)

High Altitude (3500-6500 ft): Bake 6 to 7 minutes.

1 COOKIE: Calories 50; Total Fat 2g (Saturated Fat 1g, Trans Fat 0g); Cholesterol 5mg; Sodium 25mg; Total Carbohydrate 9g (Dietary Fiber 0g); Protein 0g. EXCHANGES: 1/2 Other Carbohydrate, 1/2 Fat. CARBOHYDRATE CHOICES: 1/2.

COOKIES

1-1/2 cups powdered sugar
1 cup butter or margarine, softened
1 egg
1 teaspoon vanilla
2-1/2 cups Gold Medal® all-purpose flour
1 teaspoon baking soda
1 teaspoon cream of tartar
1 teaspoon ground cinnamon

CINNAMON ICING

1/2 cup red cinnamon candies
1/2 cup water
2-1/2 cups powdered sugar

tips&ideas

If you are in a hurry, skip making the icing from scratch and use decorating icing instead.

raspberry-frosted canes

PREP TIME: 30 minutes • **START TO FINISH:** 1 hour 5 minutes • **MAKES:** 3 dozen cookies

3/4 cup granulated sugar
1 cup butter or margarine, softened
2 teaspoons vanilla
1 egg
3 cups Gold Medal® all-purpose flour
2 cups powdered sugar
3 tablespoons butter or margarine, softened
3 tablespoons raspberry-flavored syrup
2 to 3 teaspoons milk
3 or 4 drops red food color
1 cup white baking chips
1 teaspoon vegetable oil

1 COOKIE: Calories 180; Total Fat 9g (Saturated Fat 4.5g, Trans Fat 0g); Cholesterol 20mg; Sodium 50mg; Total Carbohydrate 24g (Dietary Fiber 0g); Protein 2g. EXCHANGES: 1 Starch, 1/2 Other Carbohydrate, 1-1/2 Fat. CARBOHYDRATE CHOICES: 1-1/2.

tips&ideas

Hang these pastel candy canes on a small artificial tree for a tasty tabletop decoration.

(1) Heat oven to 350°F (if using dark or nonstick cookie sheet, heat oven to 325°F). In large bowl, beat granulated sugar, 1 cup butter, the vanilla and egg with electric mixer on medium speed until well blended. Beat in flour.

(2) Divide dough into 9 pieces. On floured surface, shape each piece of dough into a 16-inch rope, slightly less than 1/2 inch in diameter. Cut each rope into 4-inch lengths; place on ungreased cookie sheet. Bend 1 end of each cookie into candy cane shape.

(3) Bake 10 to 14 minutes or until bottoms are light golden brown. Immediately remove from cookie sheet to wire rack. Cool completely, about 20 minutes.

(4) In small bowl, stir together powdered sugar, 3 tablespoons butter, the syrup, milk and food color. Spread on top and sides of cookies; let stand until set before drizzling with melted white chips.

(5) In small resealable plastic food-storage bag, place white baking chips and oil; seal bag. Microwave on High 1 minute. Gently squeeze bag until chips are smooth. Cut off tiny corner of bag. Squeeze bag to make stripes on cookies to look like candy canes. Let stand until frosting is set before storing.

High Altitude (3500-6500 ft): Bake for 12 to 16 minutes.

christmas candy cane cookies

PREP TIME: 45 minutes • **START TO FINISH:** 45 minutes • **MAKES:** 4 dozen cookies

1 pouch (1 lb 1.5 oz) Betty Crocker®
   sugar cookie mix
1/3 cup butter or margarine, melted
1 egg
2 to 3 drops red food color

① Heat oven to 375°F. In large bowl, stir cookie mix, melted butter and egg until soft dough forms. Divide dough in half. Stir food color into 1 half; mix well.

② For each candy cane, shape 1 teaspoon dough from each half into 4-inch rope. On ungreased cookie sheets, place 1 red and 1 white rope side by side; press together lightly and twist. Curve top of cookie down to form handle of cane.

③ Bake 7 to 8 minutes or until set. Cool 1 minute; remove from cookie sheets to cooling racks.

High Altitude (3500-6500 ft): Decrease melted butter to 1/4 cup.

1 COOKIE: Calories 60; Total Fat 2.5g (Saturated Fat 1g, Trans Fat 0g); Cholesterol 10mg; Sodium 35mg; Total Carbohydrate 8g (Dietary Fiber 0g); Protein 0g. EXCHANGES: 1/2 Other Carbohydrate, 1/2 Fat. CARBOHYDRATE CHOICES: 1/2.

tips&ideas

Brush cookies with a thin vanilla glaze and then sprinkle with crushed peppermint candies. Or, try making some of these festive treats with green and white dough. It will enhance your cookie plate.

holiday white chocolate macaroon cookies

PREP TIME: 35 minutes • **START TO FINISH:** 1 hour 5 minutes • **MAKES:** about 3 dozen cookies

1 pouch (1 lb 1.5 oz) Betty Crocker® sugar cookie mix
1/2 cup butter or margarine, melted
1 egg
1 cup flaked coconut
1-2/3 cups white vanilla baking chips
1/2 teaspoon coconut extract
1 teaspoon shortening
Red and green sugars
Coarse white sparkling sugar

1 Heat oven to 375°F. In large bowl, stir cookie mix, melted butter, egg, coconut, 1 cup of the baking chips and the extract until soft dough forms. Drop dough by rounded teaspoonfuls 2 inches apart onto ungreased cookie sheet.

2 Bake 9 to 11 minutes or until cookies are golden brown around edges. Cool 1 minute before removing from cookie sheet; cool completely, about 20 minutes.

3 In small microwavable bowl, microwave remaining 2/3 cup baking chips and shortening uncovered on High 30 to 60 seconds or until mixture can be stirred smooth. Drizzle over cookies; sprinkle with sugars as desired.

High Altitude (3500-6500 ft): No change.

1 COOKIE: Calories 140; Total Fat 7g (Saturated Fat 4.5g, Trans Fat 0.5g); Cholesterol 15mg; Sodium 75mg; Total Carbohydrate 18g (Dietary Fiber 0g); Protein 1g. EXCHANGES: 1 Other Carbohydrate, 1-1/2 Fat. CARBOHYDRATE CHOICES: 1.

turtle bars

PREP TIME: 10 minutes • **START TO FINISH:** 1 hour • **MAKES:** 36 bars

1 cup Original Bisquick® mix
1 cup quick-cooking oats
3/4 cup packed brown sugar
1/4 cup butter or margarine, melted
1 jar (12.25 oz) caramel topping
1-1/2 cups pecan halves
1 cup swirled semisweet and white chocolate chips (6 oz)

① Heat oven to 350°F. Line 13x9-inch pan with foil; spray with cooking spray.

② In large bowl, stir Bisquick mix, oats, brown sugar and butter until well blended. Press in bottom of pan. Bake 15 to 18 minutes or until golden brown. Remove pan from oven.

③ Spread caramel topping over crust. Sprinkle with pecan halves and chocolate chips. Bake 20 to 30 minutes longer or until caramel is bubbly. For bars, cut into 6 by 6 rows.

High Altitude (3500-6500 ft): No change.

1 BAR: Calories 130; Total Fat 6g (Saturated Fat 2g, Trans Fat 0g); Cholesterol 0mg; Sodium 90mg; Total Carbohydrate 18g (Dietary Fiber 1g); Protein 1g. EXCHANGES: 1 Other Carbohydrate, 1-1/2 Fat. CARBOHYDRATE CHOICES: 1.

tips&ideas

Lining the pan with foil and spraying the foil makes removing and cutting the bars easier. It also makes cleanup a breeze!

linzer cookie tarts

PREP TIME: 1 hour 15 minutes • START TO FINISH: 2 hours • MAKES: about 32 cookies

1 pouch (1 lb 1.5 oz) Betty Crocker®
   sugar cookie mix
1/3 cup slivered almonds, toasted, finely chopped
1/3 cup butter or margarine, melted
1/2 teaspoon almond extract
  1 egg
2/3 cup seedless raspberry jam
1/3 cup dark or semisweet chocolate chips

1 COOKIE: Calories 120; Total Fat 4.5g (Saturated Fat 2g, Trans Fat 0.5g); Cholesterol 10mg; Sodium 55mg; Total Carbohydrate 18g (Dietary Fiber 0g); Protein 1g. EXCHANGES: 1/2 Starch, 1/2 Other Carbohydrate, 1 Fat. CARBOHYDRATE CHOICES: 1.

tips&ideas

Use whatever flavor of preserves or jam your family prefers. Or use several kinds in different colors for a party cookie tray.

① Heat oven to 375°F. In large bowl, stir together cookie mix and almonds. Stir in melted butter, almond extract and egg until stiff dough forms.

② On floured surface, roll half of dough to 1/4-inch thickness. Cut with 2-inch round, fluted or star cookie cutter. On ungreased cookie sheets, place cookies 2 inches apart.

③ Bake 7 to 9 minutes or until set. Cool 5 minutes; remove from cookie sheets to cooling racks. Cool completely.

④ Meanwhile, on floured surface, roll other half of dough to 1/4-inch thickness. Cut with linzer cutter with hole in center, or cut with same 2-inch round cookie cutter and use small 1-inch cutter to cut round hole out of center of each cookie. On ungreased cookie sheets, place cookies 2 inches apart.

⑤ Bake 7 to 9 minutes or until set. Cool 5 minutes; remove from cookie sheets to cooling racks. Cool completely.

⑥ Spread 1 teaspoon jam on bottom of each whole cookie; top each with cutout cookie to make sandwich cookie. In small microwavable bowl, microwave chocolate chips uncovered on High about 1 minute, stirring after 30 seconds, until melted and stirred smooth. Using tip of fork or knife, drizzle chocolate in lines over cookies. Let stand until chocolate is set, about 45 minutes. Or, sprinkle with powdered sugar instead of drizzling with chocolate. Store between sheets of waxed paper in tightly covered container.

High Altitude (3500-6500 ft): No change.

fudge-filled peanut butter cookies

PREP TIME: 50 minutes • **START TO FINISH:** 2 hours 20 minutes • **MAKES:** about 2 dozen sandwich cookies

① Heat oven to 375°F (if using dark or nonstick cookie sheet, heat oven to 350°F). In large bowl, beat 1/2 cup peanut butter, the shortening, granulated sugar and brown sugar with electric mixer on medium speed until fluffy. Beat in egg until smooth. Beat in flour, baking powder and baking soda.

② Shape dough into 48 one-inch balls. On ungreased cookie sheet, place balls 1 inch apart. Flatten balls to 1/4-inch thickness by pressing with a fork in a crisscross pattern.

③ Bake 4 to 8 minutes or until bottoms are golden brown. Remove from cookie sheet to wire rack. Cool completely, about 30 minutes.

④ In small microwavable bowl, microwave chocolate chips uncovered on High about 1 minute or until softened; stir until smooth. Stir 1/4 cup peanut butter into chocolate until smooth. Cool to room temperature or until thickened.

⑤ Sandwich pairs of cookies, bottoms together, with 1 teaspoon chocolate mixture. Let stand about 1 hour or until chocolate is firm.

High Altitude (3500-6500 ft): Bake 6 to 10 minutes.

1 COOKIE: Calories 190; Total Fat 11g (Saturated Fat 3g, Trans Fat 1g); Cholesterol 10mg; Sodium 90mg; Total Carbohydrate 20g (Dietary Fiber 1g); Protein 3g. EXCHANGES: 1 Starch, 1/2 Other Carbohydrate, 2 Fat. CARBOHYDRATE CHOICES: 1.

1/2 cup creamy peanut butter
1/2 cup shortening
1/2 cup granulated sugar
1/2 cup packed brown sugar
  1 egg
1-1/3 cups Gold Medal® all-purpose flour
  1 teaspoon baking powder
1/2 teaspoon baking soda
  1 cup semisweet chocolate chips
1/4 cup creamy peanut butter

tips&ideas

Chocolate and peanut butter come together in this delicious bite-size treat.

turtle shortbread cookies

PREP TIME: 1 hour 10 minutes • START TO FINISH: 1 hour 25 minutes • MAKES: 6 dozen cookies

1-1/2 cups butter or margarine, softened
1/2 cup sugar
1 teaspoon almond extract
4 cups Gold Medal® all-purpose flour
1/2 teaspoon salt
24 caramels, unwrapped
1 cup semisweet chocolate chips (6 oz)
2 teaspoons shortening
1 cup chopped pecans
72 pecan halves

High Altitude (3500-6500 ft): No change.

1 COOKIE: Calories 110; Total Fat 7g (Saturated Fat 3g, Trans Fat 0g); Cholesterol 10mg; Sodium 50mg; Total Carbohydrate 11g (Dietary Fiber 0g); Protein 1g. EXCHANGES: 1/2 Starch, 1-1/2 Fat. CARBOHYDRATE CHOICES: 1.

tips&ideas

Use vanilla for the almond extract for a slightly different flavor.

① Heat oven to 350°F. In large bowl, mix butter, sugar and almond extract. Stir in flour and salt. (If dough is crumbly, mix in 1 to 2 tablespoons additional softened butter or margarine.)

② Divide dough into 12 equal parts. Roll each part into 1/4-inch-thick round. (If dough is sticky, refrigerate about 15 minutes.) Cut each round into 6 wedges. On ungreased cookie sheets, place wedges 1 inch apart. Bake 8 to 10 minutes or until set. Immediately remove from cookie sheets to cooling racks. Cool completely, about 30 minutes.

③ Meanwhile, in 1-quart saucepan, heat caramels over medium heat about 10 minutes, stirring frequently, until melted. In small microwavable bowl, microwave chocolate chips and shortening uncovered on High about 1 to 3 minutes, stirring halfway through heating time, until melted and thin enough to drizzle.

④ Dip 2 straight edges of each cookie into melted caramel, then into chopped pecans. (If caramel thickens, add up to 1 teaspoon water and heat over low heat, stirring constantly, until caramel softens.)

⑤ Place dot of melted chocolate on top of each cookie; place pecan half on chocolate. Drizzle remaining chocolate on tops of cookies.

peppermint candy cookies

PREP TIME: 15 minutes • START TO FINISH: 1 hour 15 minutes • MAKES: 2-1/2 dozen cookies

1 pouch (1 lb 1.5 oz) Betty Crocker®
   sugar cookie mix
1/2 cup butter or margarine, melted
1 egg
1/4 cup Gold Medal® all-purpose flour
1 container (12 oz) Betty Crocker® Whipped
   fluffy white frosting
1 teaspoon peppermint extract
Betty Crocker® red sugar

① Heat oven to 375°F. In large bowl, stir cookie mix, melted butter, egg and flour until soft dough forms. Roll dough into 1-1/4-inch balls. On ungreased cookie sheets, place balls 2 inches apart. Flatten slightly with bottom of glass.

② Bake 8 to 10 minutes or until edges are light golden brown. Cool 1 minute; remove from cookie sheets to cooling racks. Cool completely, about 30 minutes.

③ In small bowl, mix frosting and extract. Spread each cookie with frosting. Spoon red sugar onto cookies in spiral design to look like peppermint candies.

High Altitude (3500-6500 ft): No change.

1 COOKIE: Calories 160; Total Fat 8g (Saturated Fat 2.5g, Trans Fat 0g); Cholesterol 15mg; Sodium 75mg; Total Carbohydrate 21g (Dietary Fiber 0g); Protein 0g. EXCHANGES: 1-1/2 Other Carbohydrate, 1-1/2 Fat. CARBOHYDRATE CHOICES: 1-1/2.

raspberry crumb bars

PREP TIME: 10 minutes • **START TO FINISH:** 1 hour 25 minutes • **MAKES:** 48 bars

2-1/2 cups Gold Medal® all-purpose flour
2-1/2 cups quick-cooking oats
1-1/2 cups packed brown sugar
   1/2 cup finely chopped hazelnuts (filberts) or pecans
   1/4 teaspoon baking soda
1-1/2 cups butter or margarine, melted
   1 can (21 oz) raspberry pie filling
   1 teaspoon ground cinnamon

① Heat oven to 350°F (if using dark or nonstick pan, heat oven to 325°F). In large bowl, mix flour, oats, brown sugar, hazelnuts and baking soda, using pastry blender (or pulling 2 table knives through ingredients in opposite directions). Stir in butter until well mixed.

② In small bowl, reserve 2 cups oat mixture for topping. On bottom of ungreased 15x10x1-inch pan, firmly press remaining oat mixture. Bake crust 15 to 18 minutes or until it just begins to brown.

③ Carefully spread pie filling over warm crust. Stir cinnamon into reserved oat mixture. Sprinkle oat mixture over filling; press lightly into filling.

④ Bake 20 to 25 minutes or until top is deep golden brown. Cool completely in pan on wire rack, about 30 minutes. For bars, cut into 8 rows by 6 rows.

High Altitude (3500-6500 ft): In Step 2, bake 18 to 21 minutes. In Step 4, bake 25 to 30 minutes.

1 BAR: Calories 140; Total Fat 7g (Saturated Fat 3g, Trans Fat 0g); Cholesterol 15mg; Sodium 50mg; Total Carbohydrate 18g (Dietary Fiber 0g); Protein 2g. EXCHANGES: 1 Starch, 1-1/2 Fat. CARBOHYDRATE CHOICES: 1.

tips&ideas

Enjoy these fruit and crumble bars with a comforting cup of hot chocolate.

holiday snickerdoodles (from scratch)

PREP TIME: 30 minutes • **START TO FINISH:** 1 hour 30 minutes • **MAKES:** 6 dozen cookies

2 tablespoons Betty Crocker® Decors red sugar
1 tablespoon ground cinnamon
2 tablespoons Betty Crocker® Decors green sugar
1-1/2 cups granulated sugar
1/2 cup shortening
1/2 cup butter or margarine, softened
2 eggs
2-3/4 cups Gold Medal® all-purpose flour
2 teaspoons cream of tartar
1 teaspoon baking soda
1/4 teaspoon salt

① Heat oven to 400°F. In small bowl, mix red sugar and 1-1/2 teaspoons of the cinnamon; set aside. In another small bowl, mix green sugar and remaining 1-1/2 teaspoons cinnamon; set aside.

② In large bowl, beat granulated sugar, shortening, butter and eggs with electric mixer on medium speed, or mix with spoon. Stir in flour, cream of tartar, baking soda and salt.

③ Shape dough into 3/4-inch balls. Roll in sugar-cinnamon mixtures. Place about 2 inches apart on ungreased cookie sheet.

④ Bake 8 to 10 minutes or until centers are almost set. Cool 1 minute; remove from cookie sheet to wire rack. Cool completely, about 30 minutes.

High Altitude (3500-6500 ft): Bake 7 to 9 minutes.

1 COOKIE: Calories 60; Total Fat 3g (Saturated Fat 1g, Trans Fat 0g); Cholesterol 10mg; Sodium 35mg; Total Carbohydrate 9g (Dietary Fiber 0g); Protein 0g. EXCHANGES: 1/2 Starch, 1/2 Fat. CARBOHYDRATE CHOICES: 1/2.

tips&ideas

Cookie dough can be covered and refrigerated for as long as 24 hours before baking. If it's too firm, let dough stand at room temperature for 30 minutes.

holiday snickerdoodles

PREP TIME: 30 minutes • START TO FINISH: 1 hour 30 minutes • MAKES: 3 dozen cookies

1 pouch (1 lb 1.5 oz) Betty Crocker®
  sugar cookie mix
1/3 cup butter or margarine, melted
2 tablespoons Gold Medal® all-purpose flour
1 egg
1/4 cup sugar
1 teaspoon ground cinnamon
Betty Crocker® red and green decorating icings
(from 4.25-oz tubes)

① Heat oven to 375°F. In large bowl, stir cookie mix, butter, flour and egg until soft dough forms.

② In small bowl, mix sugar and cinnamon. Shape dough into 1-inch balls; carefully roll in sugar-cinnamon mixture. On ungreased cookie sheets, place balls 2 inches apart.

③ Bake 11 to 12 minutes or until set. Cool 1 minute; remove from cookie sheets to cooling racks. If desired, roll tops of warm cookies in additional sugar-cinnamon mixture. Cool completely, about 20 minutes. Decorate as desired with icings.

High Altitude (3500-6500 ft): No change.

1 COOKIE: Calories 80; Total Fat 3g (Saturated Fat 1.5g, Trans Fat 0.5g); Cholesterol 10mg; Sodium 45mg; Total Carbohydrate 13g (Dietary Fiber 0g); Protein 0g. EXCHANGES: 1 Other Carbohydrate, 1/2 Fat. CARBOHYDRATE CHOICES: 1.

mexican hot chocolate cookies

PREP TIME: 1 hour • **START TO FINISH:** 1 hour • **MAKES:** 4 dozen cookies

1/4 cup sugar
1/4 teaspoon ground cinnamon
1/2 cup butter or margarine
1 tablet Mexican hot chocolate drink mix
   (from 19-oz package)
1 pouch (1 lb 1.5 oz) Betty Crocker® sugar cookie mix
1 egg
1 cup miniature semisweet chocolate chips (6 oz)

① Heat oven to 375°F. In small bowl, mix sugar and cinnamon; set aside. In 1-quart saucepan, melt butter and hot chocolate tablet over low heat, stirring constantly.

② Place cookie mix in large bowl. Stir in melted butter mixture and egg until soft dough forms. Stir in chocolate chips.

③ Shape dough into 1-inch balls; roll in cinnamon-sugar mixture. On ungreased cookie sheets, place balls 2 inches apart.

④ Bake 10 to 12 minutes or until set (do not overbake). Cool 3 minutes; remove from cookie sheets to cooling racks. Store covered at room temperature.

High Altitude (3500-6500 ft): No change.

1 COOKIE: Calories 90; Total Fat 4.5g (Saturated Fat 2g, Trans Fat 0g); Cholesterol 10mg; Sodium 40mg; Total Carbohydrate 13g (Dietary Fiber 0g); Protein 0g. EXCHANGES: 1 Other Carbohydrate, 1 Fat. CARBOHYDRATE CHOICES: 1.

raspberry-almond foldovers

PREP TIME: 40 minutes • **START TO FINISH:** 2 hours 15 minutes • **MAKES:** about 2-1/2 dozen cookies

1 cup Gold Medal® all-purpose flour
1/2 cup butter or margarine, softened
4 oz (half of 8-oz package) cream cheese, softened
1/2 teaspoon almond extract
1/4 cup seedless raspberry jam
1 egg white, beaten
2 tablespoons sliced almonds
2 teaspoons sugar

① In medium bowl, beat flour, butter, cream cheese and almond extract with electric mixer on medium speed until well blended and crumbly. Press dough into ball; flatten slightly, wrap in plastic wrap and refrigerate about 1 hour 30 minutes or until firm.

② Heat oven to 375°F (if using dark or nonstick cookie sheet, heat oven to 350°F). Divide dough in half (refrigerate half of dough until needed). On lightly floured surface, roll half of dough 1/4 inch thick. Cut into 2-1/2-inch rounds. On ungreased cookie sheet, place rounds 1/2 inch apart. Reroll any remaining dough.

③ Place 1/4 teaspoon of the jam off center on each cookie to within 1/4 inch of edge. Fold cookies in half over jam; press edges firmly with fingers. Seal edges with tines of fork. Brush the cookies with egg white. Sprinkle with almonds and sugar.

④ Bake 11 to 15 minutes or until edges are golden brown and tops are lightly browned. Immediately remove from cookie sheet to wire rack. Cool completely, about 15 minutes.

High Altitude (3500-6500 ft): Bake 13 to 17 minutes.

1 COOKIE: Calories 70; Total Fat 4.5g (Saturated Fat 2.5g, Trans Fat 0g); Cholesterol 10mg; Sodium 35mg; Total Carbohydrate 5g (Dietary Fiber 0g); Protein 0g. EXCHANGES: 1/2 Other Carbohydrate, 1 Fat. CARBOHYDRATE CHOICES: 1/2.

tips&ideas

Treat yourself to a nice, relaxing afternoon with these wonderful European bakery-style cookies and a cup of hot tea.

cranberry bars

PREP TIME: 15 minutes • START TO FINISH: 1 hour 25 minutes • MAKES: 48 bars

1 Heat oven to 350°F. Spray bottom and sides of 15x10x1-inch pan with cooking spray.

2 In large bowl, beat granulated sugar, 3/4 cup butter, 2 teaspoons vanilla and the eggs with electric mixer on medium speed, scraping bowl frequently, until well mixed. Beat in flour, baking soda and salt on low speed. Continue beating on low speed, scraping bowl frequently, until well mixed. Stir in cranberry-orange sauce. Spread in pan.

3 Bake 30 to 40 minutes or until edges are golden brown. Cool completely in pan on wire rack, about 30 minutes.

4 In small bowl, beat 1/3 cup butter, the cream cheese and 1 teaspoon vanilla on medium speed 1 to 2 minutes, scraping bowl frequently, until well mixed. Continue beating on low speed, gradually adding powdered sugar and enough milk until spreadable. Spread frosting over bars; sprinkle with walnuts. For bars, cut into 8 rows by 6 rows. Store covered in refrigerator.

High Altitude (3500-6500 ft): Not recommended.

1 BAR: Calories 130; Total Fat 6g (Saturated Fat 2.5g, Trans Fat 0g); Cholesterol 20mg; Sodium 75mg; Total Carbohydrate 19g (Dietary Fiber 0g); Protein 1g. EXCHANGES: 1/2 Starch, 1/2 Other Carbohydrate, 1-1/2 Fat. CARBOHYDRATE CHOICES: 1.

BARS

1-1/2 cups granulated sugar

3/4 cup butter or margarine, softened

2 teaspoons vanilla

2 eggs

2-1/4 cups Gold Medal® all-purpose flour

1 teaspoon baking soda

1/4 teaspoon salt

1 package (10 oz) frozen cranberry-orange sauce, thawed

CREAM CHEESE FROSTING

1/3 cup butter or margarine, softened

1 package (3 oz) cream cheese, softened

1 teaspoon vanilla

2 cups powdered sugar

About 1 tablespoon milk

1/2 cup chopped walnuts

tips&ideas

When making bars, be sure to use the specified pan size and baking time. You will get better results.

noir bars

PREP TIME: 40 minutes • START TO FINISH: 5 hours • MAKES: 36 bars

COOKIE BASE

- 1 pouch (1 lb 1.5 oz) Betty Crocker® double chocolate chunk cookie mix
- 1/4 cup vegetable oil
- 2 tablespoons water
- 1 egg

FILLING

- 8 tablespoons butter or unsalted butter
- 3/4 cup semisweet or bittersweet chocolate chips
- 2 packages (8 oz each) cream cheese, softened
- 1-1/2 cups powdered sugar
- 1 teaspoon ground cinnamon
- 1 teaspoon vanilla

TOPPING

- 1/2 cup whipping (heavy) cream
- 2 cups semisweet or bittersweet chocolate chips (12 oz)
- 1/4 cup butter or unsalted butter
- 2 tablespoons instant espresso powder

① Heat oven to 350°F. In large bowl, stir cookie base ingredients until soft dough forms. Spread in bottom of ungreased 13x9-inch pan. Bake 12 to 15 minutes or just until set. Cool completely, about 30 minutes.

② Meanwhile, in 1-quart saucepan, melt 2 tablespoons of the butter and 3/4 cup chocolate chips over medium-low heat, stirring constantly. Set aside to cool.

③ In large bowl, beat cream cheese and remaining 6 tablespoons butter with electric mixer on medium speed until smooth. On low speed, beat in powdered sugar, cinnamon and vanilla until blended. Beat in cooled chocolate on medium speed until well blended. Spread filling over cooled base. Cover; refrigerate until chilled, about 2 hours.

④ In 2-quart saucepan, heat cream, 2 cups chocolate chips, 1/4 cup butter and the espresso powder over medium-low heat, stirring constantly, until melted and smooth. Cool until lukewarm, about 10 minutes.

⑤ Pour chocolate topping over filling; spread to cover bars. Refrigerate uncovered until set, at least 2 hours or overnight. For bars, cut with wet knife into 9 rows by 4 rows. Store covered in refrigerator.

High Altitude (3500-6500 ft): In Step 1, bake crust 14 to 17 minutes.

1 BAR: Calories 250; Total Fat 16g (Saturated Fat 9g, Trans Fat 0g); Cholesterol 35mg; Sodium 120mg; Total Carbohydrate 24g (Dietary Fiber 0g); Protein 2g. EXCHANGES: 1-1/2 Other Carbohydrate, 1/2 High-Fat Meat, 2-1/2 Fat. CARBOHYDRATE CHOICES: 1-1/2.

jolly snowman cookies

PREP TIME: 30 minutes • **START TO FINISH:** 30 minutes • **MAKES:** 2 dozen cookies

1 pouch (1 lb 1.5 oz) Betty Crocker®
   sugar cookie mix
1/2 cup butter or margarine, melted
1 egg
1 container (12 oz) Betty Crocker® Whipped
   vanilla frosting
Black shoestring licorice
1/3 cup raisins
1/4 cup red cinnamon candies

① Heat oven to 375°F. In medium bowl, stir cookie mix, melted butter and egg until soft dough forms. On ungreased cookie sheets, drop dough by rounded tablespoonfuls 3 inches apart. Flatten drops of dough until 1/4 inch thick and 2 inches across.

② Bake 7 to 9 minutes or until edges are light golden brown. Cool 1 minute; remove from cookie sheets to cooling racks. Cool completely, about 30 minutes.

③ Frost and decorate one cookie at a time. Spread frosting on 1 cookie. Add licorice across top third of cookie for hat, 3 raisins for eyes and nose and 5 candies for mouth. Repeat with remaining cookies.

High Altitude (3500-6500 ft): Follow High Altitude cookie mix directions on pouch.

1 COOKIE: Calories 200; Total Fat 9g (Saturated Fat 4g, Trans Fat 2g); Cholesterol 20mg; Sodium 110mg; Total Carbohydrate 29g (Dietary Fiber 0g); Protein 1g. EXCHANGES: 1/2 Starch, 0 Fruit, 1-1/2 Fat. CARBOHYDRATE CHOICES: 2.

tips & ideas

When you have lots of cookies to bake and just 1 or 2 cookie sheets, pick up cooking parchment paper near the aluminum foil at your supermarket. Just tear off the length of paper you need to cover your cookie sheet and place it curled side down on the cookie sheet. When cookies have baked, just slide the baked cookies along with the parchment paper off the cookie sheet onto the cooling rack. In no time, you'll have a cooled cookie sheet ready for the next batch.

almond toffee bars

PREP TIME: 15 minutes • **START TO FINISH:** 1 hour 20 minutes • **MAKES:** 40 bars

3/4 cup butter or margarine, softened
1/3 cup granulated sugar
1 egg
2 cups Gold Medal® all-purpose flour
1 cup butter or margarine
2/3 cup packed brown sugar
1/4 cup light corn syrup
2-1/2 cups coarsely chopped slivered almonds
1 cup semisweet chocolate chips

① Heat oven to 375°F (if using dark or nonstick pan, heat oven to 350°F). Grease bottom and sides of 15x10x1-inch pan with shortening or spray with cooking spray.

② In large bowl, beat 3/4 cup butter and the granulated sugar with electric mixer on medium speed until light and fluffy. Beat in egg. Beat in flour on medium speed until dough starts to form. Press dough in pan. Bake 13 to 18 minutes or until edges are light golden brown.

③ Meanwhile, in 2-quart heavy saucepan, heat 1 cup butter, the brown sugar and corn syrup to boiling over medium heat, stirring frequently. Boil 2 minutes without stirring. Quickly stir in almonds; spread over baked layer. Bake 15 to 20 minutes or until dark golden brown and bubbling.

④ Immediately sprinkle chocolate chips evenly over hot bars. Let stand 5 minutes to soften; gently swirl chips over hot bars with spatula. Cool completely, about 30 minutes. For bars, cut into 8 rows by 5 rows. Store tightly covered at room temperature.

High Altitude (3500-6500 ft): No change.

1 BAR: Calories 150; Total Fat 8g (Saturated Fat 3g, Trans Fat 0g); Cholesterol 15mg; Sodium 30mg; Total Carbohydrate 16g (Dietary Fiber 1g); Protein 2g. EXCHANGES: 1 Starch, 1-1/2 Fat. CARBOHYDRATE CHOICES: 1.

tips&ideas

Pull out those pretty holiday tins and fill them up with these yummy candy-like treats.

chocolate chip-cherry bars

PREP TIME: 20 minutes • START TO FINISH: 1 hour 45 minutes • MAKES: 32 bars

BARS

- 1 jar (10 oz) maraschino cherries
- 1 cup powdered sugar
- 1 cup butter or margarine, softened
- 1 teaspoon vanilla
- 2 eggs
- 2 cups Gold Medal® all-purpose flour
- 1 teaspoon baking soda
- 1/2 teaspoon salt
- 1 cup semisweet chocolate chips (6 oz)

TOPPING

- 1 cup semisweet chocolate chips (6 oz)

DRIZZLE

- 1 cup powdered sugar
- 2 tablespoons butter or margarine, softened
- Reserved cherry juice

① Heat oven to 325°F. Grease bottom and sides of 13x9-inch pan with shortening or cooking spray. Drain maraschino cherries, reserving juice for drizzle; set juice aside. Finely chop cherries; pat dry with paper towel.

② In large bowl, beat 1 cup powdered sugar and 1 cup butter with electric mixer on medium speed until well mixed. Beat in vanilla and eggs. On low speed, beat in flour, baking soda and salt. Stir in 1 cup chocolate chips and the cherries. Spread in pan.

③ Bake 30 to 35 minutes or until top is golden brown. Immediately sprinkle with 1 cup chocolate chips. Let stand 5 minutes or until chocolate is softened. Spread the chocolate evenly over crust.

④ In small bowl, mix 1 cup powdered sugar, 2 tablespoons butter and 2 to 3 tablespoons reserved cherry juice until smooth and thin enough to drizzle. Drizzle over chocolate. Cool completely, about 45 minutes. For bars, cut into 8 rows by 4 rows.

High Altitude (3500-6500 ft): No change.

1 BAR: Calories 190; Total Fat 10g (Saturated Fat 6g, Trans Fat 0g); Cholesterol 30mg; Sodium 130mg; Total Carbohydrate 24g (Dietary Fiber 1g); Protein 2g. EXCHANGES: 1/2 Starch, 1 Other Carbohydrate, 2 Fat. CARBOHYDRATE CHOICES: 1-1/2.

tips&ideas

Fill a resealable plastic food-storage bag with the cherry drizzle, and cut off a tiny bottom corner of the bag to easily drizzle the contents over the chocolate.

black & white cookies

PREP TIME: 45 minutes • START TO FINISH: 1 hour 20 minutes • MAKES: 2 dozen large cookies

COOKIE

- 1 pouch (1 lb 1.5 oz) Betty Crocker® sugar cookie mix
- 1/2 cup buttermilk
- 1/4 cup butter or margarine, melted
- 1 teaspoon grated lemon peel
- 2 eggs

ICING

- 3 cups powdered sugar
- 1/4 cup whipping (heavy) cream
- 2 tablespoons butter or margarine
- 1/2 teaspoon vanilla
- 1/3 cup dark chocolate chips (2 oz)
- 1 tablespoon whipping cream

(1) Heat oven to 350°F. In large bowl, stir cookie ingredients until soft batter-like dough forms.

(2) With medium cookie scoop or heaping tablespoon, scoop dough 3 inches apart onto ungreased cookie sheets.

(3) Bake 12 to 15 minutes or until edges are light golden brown. Cool 5 minutes; remove from cookie sheets to cooling racks. Cool completely.

(4) Place powdered sugar in large bowl; set aside. In small microwavable bowl, microwave 1/4 cup cream and 2 tablespoons butter uncovered on High about 1 minute; stir until butter is melted. Add butter mixture and vanilla to powdered sugar; stir until mixture is smooth.

(5) In medium microwavable bowl, microwave chocolate chips and 1 tablespoon cream uncovered on High 1 minute or until melted. Stir half of vanilla icing into melted chocolate mixture until smooth and well blended. If necessary, add additional cream to thin both vanilla and chocolate icings.

(6) For each cookie, turn cookie flat side up; spread chocolate icing in thin layer on half of cookie. Spread other half with white icing. Store covered at room temperature.

High Altitude (3500-6500 ft): Bake 14 to 17 minutes.

1 LARGE COOKIE: Calories 200; Total Fat 7g (Saturated Fat 3.5g, Trans Fat 1g); Cholesterol 30mg; Sodium 80mg; Total Carbohydrate 33g (Dietary Fiber 0g); Protein 2g. EXCHANGES: 2 Other Carbohydrate, 1/2 Medium-Fat Meat, 1 Fat. CARBOHYDRATE CHOICES: 2.

tips&ideas

Use a #67 or medium-sized spring-loaded ice cream scoop to make quick work of dropping the cookie dough. Using a scoop also ensures cookies will be the same size and will bake the same length of time.

p. 295

p. 308

memorable desserts

When you want the finale of your holiday meal to be as special as the occasion itself, turn to these divine recipes.

grasshopper dessert squares

PREP TIME: 15 minutes • START TO FINISH: 5 hours 10 minutes • MAKES: 16 servings

1-1/2 cups chocolate cookie crumbs
  (from 15-oz package)
  1/4 cup sugar
  6 tablespoons butter or margarine, melted
  2 packages (8 oz each) cream cheese,
   cubed and softened
  1/3 cup green crème de menthe liqueur*
  1/4 cup white crème de cacao liqueur*
1-1/2 jars (7 oz each) marshmallow creme
1-1/2 cups whipping (heavy) cream

① Line 13x9-inch pan with foil so edges of foil extend over sides of pan; spray with cooking spray. Mix cookie crumbs, sugar and butter in pan. Press evenly in bottom of pan.

② Beat cream cheese, crème de menthe and crème de cacao in large bowl with electric mixer on medium speed until smooth. Add the marshmallow creme; beat until smooth. Refrigerate about 45 minutes or until mixture mounds when dropped from a spoon.

③ Beat whipping cream in chilled large bowl on high speed until stiff peaks form. Fold whipped cream into marshmallow mixture until blended. Pour over crust. Freeze about 4 hours or until firm.

④ Remove dessert from pan, using foil to lift. Let stand at room temperature 10 minutes before cutting. Freeze any remaining dessert tightly covered.

*EDITOR'S NOTE: To substitute for the two liqueurs, use 2/3 cup creme de menthe syrup instead.

High Altitude (3500-6500 ft): No change.

1 SERVING: Calories 355; Total Fat 26g (Saturated Fat 16g, Trans Fat nc); Cholesterol 75mg; Sodium 190mg; Total Carbohydrate 26g (Dietary Fiber 0g); Protein 4g. EXCHANGES: 1 Starch, 1 Other Carbohydrate, 5 Fat. CARBOHYDRATE CHOICES: 2.

creamy key lime pie

PREP TIME: 30 minutes • START TO FINISH: 3 hours 30 minutes • MAKES: 8 servings

CRUST
2 cups Fiber One® cereal
1/4 cup butter or margarine, melted
1 tablespoon corn syrup
1 teaspoon vanilla

FILLING AND TOPPING
2 tablespoons cold water
1 tablespoon fresh lime juice
1-1/2 teaspoons unflavored gelatin
4 oz (half of 8-oz package) 1/3-less-fat cream cheese (Neufchâtel), softened
3 containers (6 oz each) Yoplait® Light Thick & Creamy Key lime pie yogurt
1/2 cup frozen (thawed) reduced-fat whipped topping
2 teaspoon grated lime peel

① Heat oven to 350°F. Place cereal in resealable food-storage plastic bag; seal bag and finely crush with rolling pin or meat mallet until cereal looks like graham cracker crumbs (or finely crush in food processor).

② In medium bowl, mix crust ingredients until blended. Press crust mixture evenly and firmly in bottom and up side of ungreased 9-inch glass pie plate. Bake 10 to 12 minutes or until firm. Cool completely, about 1 hour.

③ In 1-quart saucepan, mix water and lime juice. Sprinkle gelatin on lime juice mixture; let stand 1 minute. Heat over low heat, stirring constantly, until gelatin is dissolved. Cool slightly, about 2 minutes.

④ In medium bowl, beat cream cheese with electric mixer on medium speed until smooth. Add yogurt and lime juice mixture; beat on low speed until well blended. Fold in whipped topping and lime peel. Spoon into crust. Refrigerate until set, about 2 hours.

High Altitude (3500-6500 ft): No change.

1 SERVING: Calories 210; Total Fat 10g (Saturated Fat 6g, Trans Fat 0g); Cholesterol 25mg; Sodium 190mg; Total Carbohydrate 24g (Dietary Fiber 7g); Protein 5g. EXCHANGES: 1-1/2 Starch, 2 Fat. CARBOHYDRATE CHOICES: 1-1/2.

tips&ideas

A refreshing pie gets the benefit of high fiber when the crust is made with Fiber One® original bran cereal. It's delicious!

raspberry-laced vanilla cake

PREP TIME: 25 minutes • START TO FINISH: 2 hours 5 minutes • MAKES: 16 servings

CAKE

2-2/3 cups Gold Medal® all-purpose flour

3 teaspoons baking powder

1/2 teaspoon salt

1/4 teaspoon baking soda

1-1/2 cups butter or margarine, softened

1-1/4 cups granulated sugar

2/3 cup milk

1-1/2 teaspoons vanilla

4 eggs

1 cup seedless raspberry jam

FROSTING

1 cup butter or margarine, softened

3 cups powdered sugar

1/2 cup raspberry-flavored liqueur or raspberry syrup for pancakes

1/2 teaspoon vanilla

Fresh raspberries and white chocolate curls, if desired

① Heat oven to 350°F. Grease bottoms and sides of 3 (9-inch) round cake pans with shortening; lightly flour. In small bowl, mix flour, baking powder, salt and baking soda; set aside.

② In large bowl, beat 1-1/2 cups butter and the granulated sugar with electric mixer on high speed, scraping bowl occasionally, until fluffy. On medium speed, beat in flour mixture, milk, 1-1/2 teaspoons vanilla and the eggs until blended. Beat 2 minutes longer. Pour evenly into pans.

③ Bake 25 to 30 minutes or until toothpick inserted in center comes out clean. Cool 10 minutes; remove from pans to cooling racks. Cool completely, about 1 hour.

④ In medium bowl, beat 1 cup butter and the powdered sugar on medium speed until smooth. Gradually beat in liqueur and 1/2 teaspoon vanilla until smooth and spreadable.

⑤ Cut each cake horizontally to make 2 layers. (Mark side of cake with toothpicks and cut with long, thin serrated knife.) Place 1 layer, cut side up, on serving plate; spread with 1/3 cup raspberry jam to within 1/4 inch of edge. Top with another layer, cut side down; spread with 1/3 cup frosting. Repeat with remaining layers.

⑥ Frost side and top of cake with remaining frosting. Pipe frosting on top of cake if desired. Garnish with raspberries and white chocolate curls. Store loosely covered.

High Altitude (3500-6500 ft): Decrease baking powder to 2 teaspoons. Bake 28 to 33 minutes.

1 SERVING: Calories 590 (Calories from Fat 270), Total Fat 31g, (Saturated Fat 19g, Trans Fat 1g), Cholesterol 130mg; Sodium 420mg; Total Carbohydrate 71g, (Dietary Fiber 0g, Sugars 50g), Protein 4g. EXCHANGES: 1 Starch; 4 Other Carbohydrate; 6 Fat. CARBOHYDRATE CHOICES: 5.

danish apple-almond cake

PREP TIME: 20 minutes • START TO FINISH: 1 hour • MAKES: 8 servings

1/2 cup butter or margarine, softened
1/2 cup granulated sugar
 3 eggs
 1 teaspoon almond extract
1-1/2 cups Original Bisquick® mix
 3 medium baking apples, peeled, cut into eighths
 1 teaspoon powdered sugar
1/4 cup sliced almonds, toasted if desired

① Heat oven to 325°F. Spray bottom of 9-inch springform pan with cooking spray.

② In large bowl, beat butter and 1/2 cup granulated sugar with electric mixer on high speed 1 minute. Beat in eggs and almond extract on medium speed about 10 seconds. Add Bisquick mix; beat on medium speed about 30 seconds until combined.

③ Spread batter in bottom of pan. Press apple pieces, cut sides down, into batter. Bake 1 hour to 1 hour 10 minutes or until apples are tender and cake is golden brown.

④ Cool 30 minutes at room temperature. Remove side of pan. Sift or sprinkle powdered sugar over top of cake; sprinkle with almonds. Serve warm.

High Altitude (3500-6500 ft): No change.

1 SERVING: Calories 320; Total Fat 18g (Saturated Fat 9g, Trans Fat 1g); Cholesterol 110mg; Sodium 420mg; Total Carbohydrate 33g (Dietary Fiber 1g); Protein 5g. EXCHANGES: 1-1/2 Starch, 1/2 Other Carbohydrate, 3-1/2 Fat. CARBOHYDRATE CHOICES: 2.

tips&ideas

To toast the almonds, bake in an ungreased shallow pan at 350°F for 6 to 10 minutes, stirring nuts occasionally, until they're fragrant and light brown.

profiteroles

PREP TIME: 50 minutes • START TO FINISH: 2 hours • MAKES: 12 servings (3 profiteroles and 1 tablespoon topping each)

① Heat oven to 400°F. In 2-1/2-quart saucepan, heat water and 1/2 cup butter to rolling boil. Stir in flour. Reduce heat to low; stir vigorously over low heat about 1 minute or until mixture forms a ball. Remove from heat.

② Beat in eggs, all at once, with spoon. Continue beating until smooth. Drop dough by level tablespoonfuls about 1-1/2 inches apart on ungreased cookie sheets to make 36 profiteroles.

③ Bake 20 to 25 minutes or until puffed and golden. Cool away from draft, about 30 minutes.

④ Meanwhile, in 2-quart saucepan, mix granulated sugar, cornstarch and salt. Gradually stir in half-and-half. Cook over medium heat, stirring constantly, until mixture thickens and boils. Boil and stir 1 minute. Gradually stir at least half of the hot mixture into egg yolks, then stir back into hot mixture in saucepan. Boil and stir 1 minute. Remove from heat. Stir in 2 tablespoons butter and the vanilla.

⑤ Pour filling into bowl. Press plastic wrap on filling to prevent a tough layer from forming on top. Refrigerate at least 1 hour or until cool.

⑥ Cut puffs horizontally in half. Fill puffs with filling; replace tops. Sift powdered sugar over tops. Cover; refrigerate until serving. Serve drizzled with chocolate topping. Store any remaining profiteroles covered in refrigerator.

High Altitude (3500-6500 ft): No change.

1 SERVING: Calories 260; Total Fat 17g (Saturated Fat 10g, Trans Fat 0.5g); Cholesterol 145mg; Sodium 135mg; Total Carbohydrate 22g (Dietary Fiber 0g); Protein 5g. EXCHANGES: 1 Starch, 1/2 Other Carbohydrate, 3-1/2 Fat. CARBOHYDRATE CHOICES: 1-1/2.

PUFFS

- 1 cup water
- 1/2 cup butter or stick margarine
- 1 cup Gold Medal® all-purpose flour
- 4 whole eggs

FILLING

- 1/3 cup granulated sugar
- 2 tablespoons cornstarch
- 1/8 teaspoon salt
- 2 cups half-and-half
- 2 egg yolks, slightly beaten
- 2 tablespoons butter or margarine, softened
- 2 teaspoons vanilla

GARNISH

- 1 tablespoon powdered sugar
- 1/4 cup chocolate topping

orange marmalade crème brûlée

PREP TIME: 20 minutes • **START TO FINISH:** 7 hours • **MAKES:** 4 servings

1/4 cup orange marmalade
6 egg yolks
2 cups whipping (heavy) cream
1/3 cup sugar
1 teaspoon vanilla
Boiling water
8 teaspoons sugar

① Heat oven to 350°F. Spoon 1 tablespoon marmalade into bottom of each of 4 (6-ounce) ceramic ramekins.*

② In small bowl, slightly beat egg yolks with wire whisk. In large bowl, stir whipping cream, 1/3 cup sugar and the vanilla until well mixed. Add egg yolks to cream mixture; beat with wire whisk until evenly colored and well blended.

③ In 13x9-inch pan, place ramekins. Pour cream mixture evenly into ramekins. Carefully place pan with ramekins in oven. Pour enough boiling water into pan, being careful not to splash water into ramekins, until water covers 2/3 of the height of the ramekins.

④ Bake 30 to 40 minutes or until tops are light golden brown and sides are set (centers will be jiggly).

⑤ Carefully transfer ramekins to cooling rack, using tongs or grasping tops of ramekins with pot holder. Cool 2 hours or until room temperature. Cover tightly with plastic wrap; refrigerate until chilled, at least 4 hours but no longer than 2 days.

⑥ Uncover ramekins; gently blot any condensation on custards with paper towel. Sprinkle 2 teaspoons sugar over each custard. Holding kitchen torch 3 to 4 inches from custard, caramelize sugar on each custard by heating with torch about 2 minutes, moving flame continuously over sugar in circular motion, until sugar is melted and light golden brown. Serve immediately, or refrigerate up to 8 hours before serving.

*EDITOR'S NOTE: Do not use glass custard cups or glass pie plates; they cannot withstand the heat from the kitchen torch and may break.

High Altitude (3500-6500 ft): Bake 35 to 45 minutes.

1 SERVING: Calories 590; Total Fat 44g (Saturated Fat 25g, Trans Fat 1.5g); Cholesterol 440mg; Sodium 60mg; Total Carbohydrate 43g (Dietary Fiber 0g); Protein 7g. EXCHANGES: 3 Other Carbohydrate, 1 High-Fat Meat, 7 Fat. CARBOHYDRATE CHOICES: 3.

caramel cappuccino cheesecake

PREP TIME: 30 minutes • START TO FINISH: 8 hours 50 minutes • MAKES: 16 servings

CRUST
1-1/4 cups chocolate cookie crumbs (from 15-oz box)
   1/4 cup butter or margarine, melted

FILLING
   2 tablespoons instant espresso coffee granules
   2 teaspoons vanilla
   4 packages (8 oz each) cream cheese, softened
1-1/2 cups granulated sugar
   4 eggs
   1 teaspoon ground cinnamon
1/4 cup caramel topping

TOPPING
   1 cup whipping (heavy) cream
   2 tablespoons powdered or granulated sugar
   1/4 cup caramel topping

① Heat oven to 300°F. Wrap outside of 10-inch springform pan with foil. In small bowl, mix cookie crumbs and melted butter with fork. Press mixture evenly over bottom of pan. Refrigerate crust while preparing filling.

② In small bowl, stir coffee granules and vanilla until coffee is dissolved; set aside.

③ In large bowl, beat cream cheese with electric mixer on medium speed until smooth.

Gradually add 1-1/2 cups sugar, beating until light and fluffy. Add eggs, one at a time, beating well after each addition. Add espresso mixture, cinnamon and 1/4 cup caramel topping; beat about 30 seconds or until mixture is well blended. Pour over crust in pan.

④ Bake 1 hour 10 minutes to 1 hour 20 minutes or until cheesecake is set 1-1/2 inches from edge and center is slightly jiggly. Turn oven off; open oven door at least 4 inches. Let cheesecake remain in oven 30 minutes. Remove cheesecake from oven. Run knife around edge of pan to loosen; cool 30 minutes at room temperature. Cover; refrigerate 6 hours or overnight.

⑤ Remove side of pan. In chilled medium bowl, beat 1 cup whipping cream and 2 tablespoons sugar on high speed until soft peaks form. Spread whipped cream over top of cheesecake; drizzle 1/4 cup of caramel topping over the whipped cream.

High Altitude (3500-6500 ft): Heat oven to 325°F. Bake cheesecake in a water bath as directed below in "Tips & Ideas."

1 SERVING: Calories 440; Total Fat 30g (Saturated Fat 18g, Trans Fat 1g); Cholesterol 140mg; Sodium 300mg; Total Carbohydrate 35g (Dietary Fiber 0g); Protein 7g. EXCHANGES: 1/2 Starch, 2 Other Carbohydrate, 1 High-Fat Meat, 4 Fat. CARBOHYDRATE CHOICES: 2.

tips&ideas

For a perfect cheesecake without cracks, try baking the cake in a water bath. Place a filled foil-wrapped springform pan in a large roasting pan and pour enough boiling water into roasting pan to come halfway up the sides of springform pan. Bake as directed.

dark chocolate-hazelnut truffles

PREP TIME: 30 minutes • **START TO FINISH:** 2 hours 40 minutes • **MAKES:** 3 dozen truffles

4 oz bittersweet baking chocolate, chopped
4 oz semisweet baking chocolate, chopped
1/4 cup whipping (heavy) cream
5 tablespoons cold butter, cut into pieces
2 tablespoons hazelnut liqueur
4 oz (about 1 cup) hazelnuts (filberts)

1 In 1-quart heavy saucepan, heat both chocolates and whipping cream over low heat, stirring constantly, until chocolate is melted and smooth. Remove from heat. Stir in butter, a few pieces at a time. Stir in liqueur. Place plastic wrap over surface of chocolate. Refrigerate about 2 hours, stirring once, until firm enough to hold its shape.

2 Meanwhile, heat oven to 350°F. Place hazelnuts in ungreased shallow pan. Bake 6 to 10 minutes, stirring occasionally, until light brown. Rub with towel to remove skins. Cool 10 minutes. Place nuts in food processor. Cover; process with on-and-off pulses 20 to 30 seconds or until finely ground. Place on sheet of waxed paper.

3 Scoop rounded teaspoonfuls of chocolate mixture onto nuts. Roll lightly to coat and shape into 1-inch balls (truffles do not need to be smooth; they should be a little rough). Place on plate; cover loosely. Store loosely covered in refrigerator. Let stand at room temperature 15 minutes before serving.

High Altitude (3500-6500 ft): No change.

1 TRUFFLE: Calories 80; Total Fat 7g (Saturated Fat 3g, Trans Fat 0g); Cholesterol 5mg; Sodium 15mg; Total Carbohydrate 4g (Dietary Fiber 1g); Protein 1g.
EXCHANGES: 1-1/2 Fat. CARBOHYDRATE CHOICES: 0.

mint-chocolate ice cream cake

PREP TIME: 25 minutes • START TO FINISH: 5 hours 50 minutes • MAKES: 16 servings

CAKE
1 box Betty Crocker® SuperMoist® butter recipe chocolate cake mix
Water, butter and eggs called for on cake mix box

FILLING
6 cups green mint-flavored ice cream with chocolate chips or chocolate swirl, slightly softened

FROSTING
1-1/2 cups whipping (heavy) cream
2 tablespoons powdered sugar
4 drops green food color

① Heat oven to 350°F (or 325°F for dark or nonstick pans). Grease bottoms only of 2 (9-inch) round cake pans; line bottoms with waxed paper. Make cake mix as directed on box, using water, butter and eggs. Spoon evenly into pans.

② Bake as directed on box for 9-inch pans or until toothpick inserted in center comes out clean. Cool in pans 10 minutes. Remove from pans to cooling racks. Remove waxed paper. Cool completely, about 30 minutes.

③ Line 9-inch round cake pan with foil. Spoon and spread ice cream evenly in pan. Cover with foil; freeze until completely frozen, about 2 hours.

④ On serving plate, place 1 cake layer with rounded side down. Remove ice cream from pan; peel off foil. Place on top of cake. Top with remaining cake layer, rounded side up.

⑤ In medium bowl, beat whipping cream, powdered sugar and food color on high speed until stiff peaks form. Frost side and top of cake with whipped cream. Freeze about 2 hours or until firm. Let stand at room temperature 10 minutes before serving.

High Altitude (3500-6500 ft): No change.

1 SERVING: Calories 380; Total Fat 22g (Saturated Fat 13g, Trans Fat 1g); Cholesterol 105mg; Sodium 360mg; Total Carbohydrate 41g (Dietary Fiber 1g); Protein 5g.
EXCHANGES: 1 Starch, 1-1/2 Other Carbohydrate, 4-1/2 Fat.
CARBOHYDRATE CHOICES: 3.

french silk tarts

PREP TIME: 20 minutes • **START TO FINISH:** 2 hours 50 minutes • **MAKES:** 16 tarts

1 box Pillsbury® refrigerated pie crusts,
   softened as directed on box
3 oz unsweetened baking chocolate,
   cut into pieces
1 cup butter, softened (do not use margarine)
1 cup sugar
1/2 teaspoon vanilla
4 pasteurized eggs* or 1 cup fat-free egg product

① Heat oven to 425°F. Remove crusts from pouches; unroll on work surface. Pat or roll each crust into 11-1/2-inch circle. With 3-1/2-inch round cutter, cut 8 rounds from each crust; discard scraps. Fit rounds into 16 ungreased regular-size muffin cups, pressing in gently; prick sides and bottom with fork.

② Bake 7 to 9 minutes or until edges are golden brown. Cool 1 minute; remove from muffin cups to wire rack. Cool completely, about 15 minutes.

③ Meanwhile, in 1-quart saucepan, melt chocolate over low heat; cool. In small bowl, beat butter with electric mixer on medium speed until fluffy. Gradually beat in sugar until light and fluffy. Beat in cooled chocolate and vanilla until well blended. Add eggs, one at a time, beating on high speed 2 minutes after each addition; beat until mixture is smooth and fluffy.

④ Fill tart shells with chocolate mixture. Refrigerate at least 2 hours before serving. Store in refrigerator.

*EDITOR'S NOTE: Because the eggs in this recipe are not cooked, pasteurized eggs must be used. Pasteurization eliminates Salmonella and other bacteria; using regular eggs in this recipe would not be food safe.

High Altitude (3500-6500 ft): No change.

1 TART: Calories 280; Total Fat 20g (Saturated Fat 11g, Trans Fat 0.5g); Cholesterol 85mg; Sodium 170mg; Total Carbohydrate 22g (Dietary Fiber 0g); Protein 2g. EXCHANGES: 1/2 Starch, 1 Other Carbohydrate, 4 Fat. CARBOHYDRATE CHOICES: 1-1/2.

tips&ideas

You can skip the pie crust and make 8 quick dessert parfaits by layering chocolate filling, whipped cream and chocolate-covered toffee bits in clear 6-ounce plastic cups.

chocolate chip-toffee cheesecake

PREP TIME: 30 minutes • START TO FINISH: 5 hours 45 minutes • MAKES: 12 servings

CRUST

1-1/4 cups finely crushed chocolate graham crackers (18 squares)

2 tablespoons sugar

1/4 cup butter or margarine, melted

FILLING

2 packages (8 oz each) cream cheese, softened

1/2 cup sugar

1 teaspoon vanilla

2 eggs

2 cups chocolate-coated toffee bits (from two 8-oz bags)

TOPPING

1/2 cup semisweet chocolate chips

2 tablespoons whipping (heavy) cream

① Heat oven to 300°F. In medium bowl, mix cracker crumbs, 2 tablespoons sugar and the butter. In ungreased 9-inch springform pan, press crumb mixture in bottom and 1 to 1-1/2 inches up side.

② In large bowl, beat cream cheese, 1/2 cup sugar and the vanilla with electric mixer on medium speed until smooth. Add eggs, one at a time, beating until smooth after each addition. Reserve 2 tablespoons of the toffee bits for garnish; gently stir remaining toffee bits into cream cheese mixture. Pour mixture into crust.

③ Bake 50 to 60 minutes or until set. Turn off oven; leave door open 4 inches. Cool cheesecake in oven 30 minutes.

④ Remove cheesecake from oven; place on cooling rack. Without releasing or removing side of pan, run metal spatula carefully along side of cheesecake to loosen. Cool 30 minutes. Run metal spatula along side of cheesecake to loosen again. Refrigerate uncovered until thoroughly chilled, at least 3 hours.

⑤ In small microwavable bowl, microwave chocolate chips and whipping cream uncovered on High 20 to 30 seconds or until chips are melted and can be stirred smooth. Cool 5 minutes. Spread topping evenly over top of cheesecake. Sprinkle reserved 2 tablespoons toffee bits around outer edge. Refrigerate until topping is set, about 15 minutes. Remove side of pan before serving.

High Altitude (3500-6500 ft): Heat oven to 325°F.

1 SERVING: Calories 480; Total Fat 33g (Saturated Fat 20g, Trans Fat 1g); Cholesterol 100mg; Sodium 290mg; Total Carbohydrate 41g (Dietary Fiber 1g); Protein 6g. EXCHANGES: 1/2 Starch, 2 Other Carbohydrate, 1/2 High-Fat Meat, 6 Fat. CARBOHYDRATE CHOICES: 3.

tips&ideas

You can use mini chocolate chips instead of chocolate-coated toffee bits.

almond-amaretto tarts

PREP TIME: 40 minutes • **START TO FINISH:** 2 hours 15 minutes • **MAKES:** 48 mini tarts

PASTRY

1 cup butter or margarine, softened
1/2 cup granulated sugar
1 egg
1 teaspoon almond extract
2-1/2 cups Gold Medal® all-purpose flour

FILLING

2-1/4 cups blanched whole almonds
3 eggs
3/4 cup granulated sugar
3 tablespoons amaretto (or 2 teaspoons almond
   extract plus 2 tablespoons water)
2 tablespoons whipping (heavy) cream

GARNISH, IF DESIRED

1/2 cup whipping (heavy) cream
1 tablespoon powdered or granulated sugar
48 fresh raspberries (about 1 cup)

① In large bowl, beat butter, 1/2 cup sugar,
1 egg and 1 teaspoon almond extract with
electric mixer on medium speed 1 minute.
Gradually add flour, beating 1 to 2 minutes just
until blended. Cover and refrigerate at least
1 hour until thoroughly chilled.

② Heat oven to 350°F. Divide pastry into
48 pieces. Gently press pastry onto bottoms
and sides of 48 ungreased mini muffin cups.

③ Place almonds in food processor or blender;
cover and process until almonds are finely
ground. In medium bowl, mix almonds and
remaining filling ingredients with spoon. Spoon
about 2 heaping tablespoons filling into each
tart crust. Bake 20 to 25 minutes or until golden
brown and centers spring back when touched
lightly. Cool 5 minutes; gently remove tarts
from pan to wire rack. Cool 30 minutes.

④ In chilled small bowl, beat 1/2 cup whipping
cream and 1 tablespoon sugar on high speed
until soft peaks form.

⑤ Just before serving, place 1 teaspoon
whipped cream and 1 raspberry on each tart.

*High Altitude (3500-6500 ft): Bake 25 to 30
minutes.*

1 MINI TART: Calories 130; Total Fat 8g (Saturated Fat
3g, Trans Fat 0g); Cholesterol 30mg; Sodium 35mg;
Total Carbohydrate 12g (Dietary Fiber 1g); Protein 3g.
EXCHANGES: 1 Starch, 1-1/2 Fat. CARBOHYDRATE
CHOICES: 1.

tips&ideas

*These tarts freeze well and can be
stored in the freezer for up to one
month. Thaw at room temperature
before serving.*

raspberry-topped eggnog cheesecake

PREP TIME: 35 minutes • START TO FINISH: 8 hours 35 minutes • MAKES: 16 servings

CHEESECAKE

1-1/4 cups crushed shortbread cookies (21 cookies)
1/4 cup butter or margarine, melted
3 packages (8 oz each) cream cheese, softened
1 cup sugar
3 eggs
1/2 cup eggnog
1/2 teaspoon rum extract
1/4 teaspoon ground nutmeg

RASPBERRY SAUCE

1 package (10 oz) frozen raspberries in syrup, thawed, undrained
2 tablespoons sugar
2 teaspoons cornstarch
1-1/2 cups fresh raspberries

① Heat oven to 350°F. In small bowl, mix crushed cookies and butter. In ungreased 9-inch springform pan, press cookie mixture over bottom. Wrap foil around outside of pan to prevent drips. Bake crust about 10 minutes or until set.

② Reduce oven temperature to 325°F. In large bowl, beat cream cheese with electric mixer on medium speed until creamy. Gradually beat in 1 cup sugar until well blended. Beat in eggs, one at a time, on low speed until combined. Beat in eggnog, rum extract and nutmeg just until blended (do not overmix). Pour over crust.

③ Bake 50 to 60 minutes or until set but center still jiggles slightly when moved. Cool for 15 minutes; run knife around edge of pan to loosen cheesecake. Cool in pan on wire rack 1 hour. Refrigerate at least 6 hours or overnight.

④ In food processor, place raspberries. Cover; process until smooth. If desired, strain to remove seeds. In 1-quart saucepan, mix pureed raspberries, 2 tablespoons sugar and the cornstarch. Heat to boiling over medium heat, stirring constantly. Refrigerate sauce 30 minutes to cool. Stir fresh raspberries into sauce. Before cutting cheesecake, carefully remove side of pan. Serve sauce over wedges of cheesecake. Store cheesecake covered in refrigerator.

High Altitude (3500-6500 ft): Decrease butter to 2 tablespoons. Before heating oven, place small baking pan filled with 1 to 2 cups water on oven rack below cheesecake to help prevent cheesecake from cracking. In Step 3, bake 1 hour to 1 hour 10 minutes. In Step 4 after heating sauce ingredients to boiling, boil and stir 3 to 4 minutes.

1 SERVING: Calories 330; Total Fat 22g (Saturated Fat 12g, Trans Fat 1g); Cholesterol 100mg; Sodium 200mg; Total Carbohydrate 29g (Dietary Fiber 2g); Protein 6g. EXCHANGES: 2 Starch, 4 Fat. CARBOHYDRATE CHOICES: 2.

triple strawberry dessert

PREP TIME: 30 minutes • **START TO FINISH:** 2 hours 15 minutes • **MAKES:** 9 servings

1 cup boiling water

1 box (4-serving size) wild strawberry-flavored gelatin

1 container (6 oz) Yoplait® Original 99% Fat Free strawberry or French vanilla yogurt

3 cups Kix® cereal

1/4 cup butter or margarine, melted

1-1/2 cups fresh sliced strawberries

9 fresh strawberries, sliced into fans

① In medium bowl, pour boiling water on gelatin; stir until gelatin is dissolved. Stir in yogurt until melted and smooth. Cover; refrigerate until thickened but not set, about 1 hour 30 minutes.

② Meanwhile, heat oven to 350°F. Place cereal in resealable food-storage plastic bag; seal bag and crush with rolling pin or meat mallet to make 1 cup. In small bowl, stir crushed cereal and butter until well mixed. Press mixture firmly in bottom of ungreased 8-inch square pan. Bake about 10 minutes or until crust is light golden brown. Set aside to cool.

③ Beat gelatin mixture with electric mixer on high speed 7 to 8 minutes or until doubled in volume. Fold in sliced strawberries; pour over crust. Cover; refrigerate about 1 hour or until firm.

④ To serve, cut dessert into squares. Garnish each serving with strawberry fan.

High Altitude (3500-6500 ft): Bake crust about 13 minutes.

1 SERVING: Calories 150; Total Fat 6g (Saturated Fat 3.5g, Trans Fat 0g); Cholesterol 15mg; Sodium 150mg; Total Carbohydrate 22g (Dietary Fiber 1g); Protein 2g.
EXCHANGES: 1/2 Starch, 1 Other Carbohydrate, 1 Fat.
CARBOHYDRATE CHOICES: 1-1/2.

plum and walnut crisp

PREP TIME: 15 minutes • **START TO FINISH:** 1 hour 10 minutes • **MAKES:** 6 servings

6 medium red or purple plums, sliced
(about 5 cups)
3/4 cup sugar
3 tablespoons cornstarch
1/2 cup crushed gingersnap cookies
(about 15 cookies)
1/2 cup chopped walnuts
1/2 cup Original Bisquick® mix
1/4 cup butter or margarine, softened

① Heat oven to 350°F. Spray 8-inch square (2-quart) glass baking dish with cooking spray.

② In large bowl, stir sliced plums, 1/2 cup of the sugar and the cornstarch until combined. Spread in baking dish.

③ In medium bowl, mix crushed cookies, walnuts, Bisquick mix, butter and remaining 1/4 cup sugar with fork until crumbly. Sprinkle over plum mixture.

④ Bake 45 to 55 minutes or until mixture is hot and bubbly and topping is lightly browned. Serve warm.

High Altitude (3500-6500 ft): No change.

1 SERVING: Calories 410; Total Fat 17g (Saturated Fat 6g, Trans Fat 1g); Cholesterol 20mg; Sodium 260mg; Total Carbohydrate 60g (Dietary Fiber 3g); Protein 4g. EXCHANGES: 1 Starch, 1 Fruit, 2 Other Carbohydrate, 3-1/2 Fat. CARBOHYDRATE CHOICES: 4.

dark chocolate fondue

PREP TIME: 25 minutes • **START TO FINISH:** 25 minutes
MAKES: 20 servings (2-1/2 tablespoons fondue, 1 cake piece, 2 strawberries and 2 apple slices each)

8 oz bittersweet baking chocolate, chopped
8 oz semisweet baking chocolate, chopped
1 pint (2 cups) whipping (heavy) cream
1 tablespoon vanilla
1 package (10.75 oz) frozen pound cake,
cut into 1-inch cubes
40 small fresh strawberries
40 apple slices
Kiwifruit, cut up, if desired

① In 2-quart heavy saucepan, heat both chocolates and the whipping cream over low heat, stirring frequently, until cream is hot and chocolate is melted. Stir with wire whisk until smooth. Stir in vanilla. Pour into fondue pot. Keep warm with fuel canister on low heat.

② Arrange cake and fruit dippers on platter. Set fondue pot in center of platter.

High Altitude (3500-6500 ft): No change.

1 SERVING: Calories 290; Total Fat 21g (Saturated Fat 12g, Trans Fat 0.5g); Cholesterol 45mg; Sodium 25mg; Total Carbohydrate 22g (Dietary Fiber 3g); Protein 4g. EXCHANGES: 1 Starch, 1/2 Other Carbohydrate, 4 Fat. CARBOHYDRATE CHOICES: 1-1/2.

tips&ideas

Other tasty dippers could include banana chunks, orange or tangerine segments, marshmallows or coconut macaroon cookies.

white silk raspberry tart

PREP TIME: 30 minutes • **START TO FINISH:** 4 hours 30 minutes • **MAKES:** 12 servings

20 creme-filled chocolate sandwich cookies, crushed (2 cups)

1/4 cup butter or margarine, melted

1 package (6 oz) white chocolate baking bars, chopped

2 cups whipping (heavy) cream

1 teaspoon vanilla

1 package (8 oz) cream cheese, softened

1 package (10 oz) frozen raspberries in syrup, thawed

2 teaspoons cornstarch

1 cup fresh raspberries

① Heat oven to 375°F. In medium bowl, mix crushed cookies and butter. Press in bottom and 1 inch up side of ungreased 9- or 10-inch springform pan. Bake 7 to 9 minutes or until set. Cool completely, about 30 minutes.

② Meanwhile, in 1-quart heavy saucepan, heat white baking bars and 1/2 cup of the whipping cream over low heat, stirring frequently, until chocolate is melted. Stir in vanilla. Cool to room temperature, about 15 minutes.

③ In large bowl, beat cream cheese with electric mixer on medium speed until smooth. Add white chocolate mixture; beat on medium speed until creamy. Set aside.

④ In chilled large bowl, beat remaining 1-1/2 cups whipping cream on high speed until stiff peaks form. Using rubber spatula, fold half of the whipped cream into the cream cheese mixture until blended. Fold in remaining whipped cream. Spoon into crust. Refrigerate 3 to 4 hours or until set.

⑤ Place small strainer over 1-quart saucepan. Pour package of raspberries into strainer. With back of spoon, press raspberries through strainer to remove seeds; discard seeds. Stir cornstarch into raspberry puree. Heat to boiling over medium heat. Cool completely, about 20 minutes.

⑥ To serve, spoon fresh raspberries around top edge of tart. Remove side of pan. Cut tart into wedges; place on individual dessert plates. Drizzle raspberry sauce over individual servings.

High Altitude (3500-6500 ft): No change.

1 SERVING: Calories 420; Total Fat 31g (Saturated Fat 18g, Trans Fat 1.5g); Cholesterol 75mg; Sodium 220mg; Total Carbohydrate 30g (Dietary Fiber 3g); Protein 4g. EXCHANGES: 1 Starch, 1 Other Carbohydrate, 6 Fat. CARBOHYDRATE CHOICES: 2.

ginger-almond pears

PREP TIME: 50 minutes • **START TO FINISH:** 3 hours 25 minutes • **MAKES:** 8 servings

1-1/2 cups sugar

1-1/2 cups water

1/3 cup chopped crystallized ginger

2 tablespoons lemon juice

1/8 teaspoon almond extract

4 Anjou pears, peeled, cut in half lengthwise and cored

1/4 cup sliced almonds

4 teaspoons sugar

1 cup vanilla frozen yogurt

① In 4-quart Dutch oven, mix 1-1/2 cups sugar, the water, ginger and lemon juice. Heat to boiling over medium-high heat. Boil 2 minutes, stirring occasionally, until sugar is melted. Stir in almond extract. Add pear halves; cover and return to boiling. Reduce heat; simmer covered 8 to 10 minutes or until pears are tender when pierced with tip of knife. Remove pears from liquid, using slotted spoon, to bowl; cover and refrigerate until serving.

② Boil remaining pear liquid over high heat 8 to 10 minutes, stirring occasionally, until slightly thickened and syrupy. Cool 30 to 40 minutes or until warm. Refrigerate 2 hours or until serving.

③ Meanwhile, in 10-inch nonstick skillet, cook almonds over medium heat 4 to 6 minutes, stirring constantly, until just beginning to brown. Sprinkle 4 teaspoons sugar over almonds. Continue cooking and stirring 2 to 3 minutes longer or until sugar is melted and almonds are coated. Spread almond mixture on sheet of foil sprayed with cooking spray. Cool 2 to 3 minutes; break apart.

④ Place pear halves, cut sides up, in individual dessert bowls. (If desired, cut thin slice from rounded side of each pear half so that it won't roll around in bowl.)

⑤ Place small scoop (about 2 tablespoons) frozen yogurt in center of each pear half. Spoon syrup over top. Sprinkle with almonds.

High Altitude (3500-6500 ft): No change.

1 SERVING: Calories 280; Total Fat 2g (Saturated Fat 0g, Trans Fat 0g); Cholesterol 0mg; Sodium 20mg; Total Carbohydrate 62g (Dietary Fiber 3g); Protein 2g. EXCHANGES: 1/2 Starch, 1/2 Fruit, 3 Other Carbohydrate, 1/2 Fat. CARBOHYDRATE CHOICES: 4.

tips & ideas

Crystallized ginger can be found in the produce section of supermarkets in small plastic bags. It can also be found in jars in the spice section, but buying it this way is often more expensive.

caramel-coffee fondue

PREP TIME: 20 minutes • START TO FINISH: 20 minutes
MAKES: 8 servings (1/4 cup dip, 4 apple slices, 3 pineapple chunks and 1/2 cup cake cubes each)

1/4 cup water
  1 tablespoon instant coffee crystals
  1 can (14 oz) sweetened condensed milk
  1 bag (14 oz) caramels, unwrapped
1/2 cup coarsely chopped pecans
  2 apples (1 Braeburn, 1 Granny Smith),
    cut into 1/2-inch slices
  2 cups fresh pineapple chunks
1/2 package (16-oz size) pound cake,
    cut into 1-inch cubes (about 4 cups)

1 In 2-quart nonstick saucepan, heat water over high heat until hot. Dissolve coffee crystals in water.

2 Add milk, caramels and pecans to coffee. Heat over medium-low heat, stirring frequently, until caramels are melted and mixture is hot. Pour mixture into fondue pot and keep warm.

3 Arrange apples, pineapple and cake on serving plate. Use skewers or fondue forks to dip into fondue.

High Altitude (3500-6500 ft): No change.

1 SERVING: Calories 590; Total Fat 21g (Saturated Fat 10g, Trans Fat 1g); Cholesterol 55mg; Sodium 210mg; Total Carbohydrate 90g (Dietary Fiber 3g); Protein 9g. EXCHANGES: 3 Starch, 3 Other Carbohydrate, 4 Fat. CARBOHYDRATE CHOICES: 6.

cranberry mousse torte

PREP TIME: 35 minutes • START TO FINISH: 6 hours 40 minutes • MAKES: 16 servings

BROWNIE BASE

1 box (1 lb 2.3 oz) Betty Crocker® fudge
   brownie mix
1/4 cup water
2/3 cup vegetable oil
2 eggs
1/2 cup miniature semisweet chocolate chips

FILLING

2 tablespoons water
1 envelope (2-1/2 teaspoons) unflavored gelatin
1 can (16 oz) jellied cranberry sauce
1/2 cup sugar
1 teaspoon grated orange peel
1-1/2 cups whipping (heavy) cream
3 drops red food color, if desired

CRANBERRY SAUCE

1/2 cup sugar
4 teaspoons cornstarch
1 can (11.5 oz) frozen cranberry juice cocktail
   concentrate, thawed

① Heat oven to 350°F. Wrap foil around outside of bottom and side of 10-inch springform pan to catch drips. Spray bottom only of pan with cooking spray. In large bowl, beat all base ingredients except chocolate chips with spoon for 50 strokes; fold in chocolate chips. Spread in pan. Bake 35 to 40 minutes or until base pulls away from side of pan; do not overbake. Cool completely, about 1 hour 30 minutes.

② Meanwhile, place 2 tablespoons water in 2-quart saucepan; sprinkle gelatin over water. Let stand 1 minute to soften. Spoon cranberry sauce and 1/2 cup sugar over gelatin. Heat to rolling boil over medium-high heat. Cook over medium-high heat, stirring frequently, until gelatin is completely dissolved. Stir in orange peel. Cool at room temperature 20 minutes. Cover; refrigerate 1 hour 30 minutes to 2 hours, stirring every 30 minutes, until mixture is slightly thickened.

③ In medium bowl, beat whipping cream with electric mixer on high speed until stiff peaks form. Fold into cranberry mixture. Fold in food color. Spoon mixture over cooled brownie base. Cover; refrigerate about 2 hours or until set.

④ Meanwhile, in 1-1/2-quart saucepan, mix 1/2 cup sugar and the cornstarch. Stir in cranberry juice concentrate. Heat to boiling over high heat, stirring constantly. Boil 4 to 5 minutes, stirring constantly, until slightly thickened. Cool for 20 minutes at room temperature. Pour sauce into small resealable container. Refrigerate about 1 hour 30 minutes or until chilled.

⑤ To serve, spoon sauce over each serving of torte.

High Altitude (3500-6500 ft): Follow High Altitude brownie directions for base batter.

1 SERVING: Calories 460; Total Fat 20g (Saturated Fat 7g, Trans Fat 0g); Cholesterol 50mg; Sodium 140mg; Total Carbohydrate 69g (Dietary Fiber 2g); Protein 3g. EXCHANGES: 1/2 Starch, 4 Other Carbohydrate, 4 Fat. CARBOHYDRATE CHOICES: 4-1/2.

creamy rice pudding with brandied cherry sauce

PREP TIME: 15 minutes • **START TO FINISH:** 4 hours 20 minutes • **MAKES:** 8 servings

RICE PUDDING

- 4 cups milk
- 3/4 cup uncooked regular long-grain rice
- 1/3 cup sugar
- 1/4 teaspoon salt
- 2 eggs, beaten
- 1 cup whipping (heavy) cream
- 1 teaspoon vanilla

BRANDIED CHERRY SAUCE

- 1/2 cup sugar
- 1 tablespoon cornstarch
- 1/4 cup orange juice
- 1-1/2 cups frozen unsweetened tart red cherries (from 1-lb bag)
- 2 tablespoons brandy or orange juice

1 SERVING: Calories 350; Total Fat 13g (Saturated Fat 7g, Trans Fat 0g); Cholesterol 95mg; Sodium 160mg; Total Carbohydrate 49g (Dietary Fiber 0g); Protein 8g. EXCHANGES: 1 Starch, 1-1/2 Other Carbohydrate, 1 Milk, 2 Fat. CARBOHYDRATE CHOICES: 3.

tips & ideas

The rice should just barely bubble as it cooks. The milk may evaporate during cooking, so you may have to stir in a little hot water to keep the sauce-like consistency.

① In 2-quart saucepan, heat milk, rice, 1/3 cup sugar and the salt to boiling over medium-high heat. Reduce heat to medium-low. Simmer uncovered 40 to 45 minutes, stirring frequently, until rice is tender and mixture is thickened.

② Stir a small amount of the hot rice mixture into eggs, then stir eggs back into mixture in saucepan. Continue cooking over medium heat about 3 minutes, stirring constantly, until heated through. Cool 45 minutes, stirring occasionally.

③ In chilled large serving bowl, beat whipping cream and vanilla with electric mixer on high speed until thickened. Fold in cooled rice mixture. Cover and refrigerate at least 3 hours until well chilled.

④ In 1-quart saucepan, mix 1/2 cup sugar and the cornstarch. Stir in orange juice and frozen cherries. Heat over medium-high heat, stirring frequently, until mixture boils and thickens slightly. Stir in brandy. Serve sauce warm or chilled with pudding.

High Altitude (3500-6500 ft): No change.

tiramisu tart

PREP TIME: 35 minutes • START TO FINISH: 3 hours 5 minutes • MAKES: 12 servings

① Heat oven to 350°F. In food processor, place crust ingredients. Cover; process until soft dough forms. Spread dough evenly with fingers on bottom and up side of ungreased 9- or 10-inch tart pan. Bake 12 to 15 minutes or until edge begins to brown. Cool 5 minutes.

② In small bowl, reserve 3 tablespoonfuls of the chopped chocolate. In 1-cup glass measuring cup, microwave remaining chocolate uncovered on High about 45 seconds; stir until chocolate is melted. Stir in oil. Spread mixture over baked crust. Place in freezer to cool chocolate.

③ Meanwhile, in medium bowl, mix granulated sugar and 2 tablespoons flour; set aside. In 2-cup liquid measuring cup, beat 1 cup whipping cream, the coffee granules, egg and vanilla with wire whisk until well blended. Beat cream mixture into sugar mixture until well blended. Pour over chocolate in pan.

④ Bake 35 to 40 minutes or until the edge is golden brown and the center is set. Cool completely in pan on cooling rack, about 1 hour 30 minutes.

⑤ In medium bowl, beat topping ingredients with electric mixer on medium speed about 2 minutes or until fluffy. Spread over top of cooled tart in pan. Sprinkle with reserved chopped chocolate. Remove side of pan before serving. Store covered in refrigerator.

High Altitude (3500-6500 ft): In Step 4, bake 45 to 50 minutes.

1 SERVING: Calories 410; Total Fat 30g (Saturated Fat 18g, Trans Fat 1g); Cholesterol 90mg; Sodium 130mg; Total Carbohydrate 29g (Dietary Fiber 2g); Protein 5g. EXCHANGES: 1/2 Starch, 1-1/2 Other Carbohydrate, 1/2 High-Fat Meat, 5 Fat. CARBOHYDRATE CHOICES: 2.

CRUST
1 cup Gold Medal® all-purpose flour
1/2 cup cold butter or margarine, cut into 1/8-inch slices
1/4 cup powdered sugar

CHOCOLATE LAYER
1 bar (4 oz) bittersweet baking chocolate, coarsely chopped
2 teaspoons vegetable oil

FILLING
1/2 cup granulated sugar
2 tablespoons Gold Medal® all-purpose flour
1 cup whipping (heavy) cream
1 tablespoon instant espresso coffee granules
1 egg
1/2 teaspoon vanilla

TOPPING
1 package (8 oz) cream cheese, softened
1/2 cup whipping (heavy) cream
1/2 cup powdered sugar

bourbon pecan pie with pecan crust

PREP TIME: 30 minutes • **START TO FINISH:** 4 hours • **MAKES:** 8 servings

CRUST

- 1/3 cup finely chopped pecans
- 2 tablespoons Gold Medal® all-purpose flour
- 1 Pillsbury® refrigerated pie crust, softened as directed on box

FILLING

- 3 eggs
- 3/4 cup packed brown sugar
- 3 tablespoons Gold Medal® all-purpose flour
- 1 cup dark corn syrup
- 2 tablespoons butter or margarine, melted
- 2 tablespoons bourbon
- 1-1/2 cups pecan halves

TOPPING

- 3/4 cup whipping (heavy) cream
- 2 tablespoons packed brown sugar
- 1 teaspoon vanilla

① Heat oven to 325°F. In bottom of ungreased 9-inch glass pie plate, mix 1/3 cup chopped pecans and 2 tablespoons flour. Place pie crust over pecan mixture in pie plate as directed on box for One-Crust Filled Pie.

② In large bowl, beat eggs slightly with hand beater or wire whisk. Beat in 3/4 cup brown sugar, 3 tablespoons flour, the corn syrup, butter and bourbon until smooth. Stir in pecan halves. Pour into crust-lined pie plate.

③ Bake 15 minutes. Cover top of crust with foil to prevent excessive browning; bake 40 to 45 minutes longer or until filling is set and center of pie is puffed and golden brown. Cool completely on cooling rack, about 2 hours 30 minutes.

④ In chilled medium bowl, beat topping ingredients with electric mixer on high speed until soft peaks form. Serve pie topped with whipped cream.

High Altitude (3500-6500 ft): Heat oven to 375°F. In Step 3, bake 20 minutes uncovered. Cover crust and bake 30 to 35 minutes.

1 SERVING: Calories 640; Total Fat 35g (Saturated Fat 11g, Trans Fat 0g); Cholesterol 115mg; Sodium 210mg; Total Carbohydrate 76g (Dietary Fiber 2g); Protein 6g. EXCHANGES: 2-1/2 Starch, 2-1/2 Other Carbohydrate, 6-1/2 Fat. CARBOHYDRATE CHOICES: 5.

double-chocolate cherry torte

PREP TIME: 30 minutes • **START TO FINISH:** 6 hours 35 minutes • **MAKES:** 12 servings

① Heat oven to 400°F. Spray 9-inch springform pan with cooking spray. In 3-quart saucepan, melt semisweet chocolate and butter over medium-low heat, stirring constantly, until smooth. Cool 30 minutes.

② In medium bowl, beat eggs with electric mixer on high speed about 5 minutes or until about triple in volume. Using rubber spatula, fold eggs into cooled chocolate mixture. Pour into springform pan.

③ Bake 15 to 20 minutes or until edge is set but center is still soft and jiggles slightly when moved. Cool completely in pan, about 1 hour 30 minutes. Then cover and refrigerate 1 hour 30 minutes.

④ In medium microwavable bowl, place white chocolate and 2 tablespoons of the whipping cream. Microwave uncovered on High 20 to 40 seconds, stirring after 20 seconds, until chocolate is melted. Stir until well blended; set aside. In medium bowl, beat cream cheese on medium speed until smooth. Gradually beat in white chocolate mixture until smooth. Add 1 cup of the pie filling; beat on medium speed until well blended and cherries are broken up.

⑤ In chilled medium bowl, beat remaining whipping cream and almond extract on high speed until stiff peaks form. Fold in cherry-chocolate mixture until well blended. Spread over semisweet chocolate layer. Refrigerate at least 2 hours but no longer than 48 hours.

⑥ In small bowl, stir remaining pie filling and liqueur until well blended. Remove side of pan. Cut torte into wedges; place on individual dessert plates. Top individual servings with cherry sauce.

High Altitude (3500-6500 ft): No change.

2 packages (8 oz each) semisweet baking chocolate, coarsely chopped
1 cup butter or margarine
6 eggs
8 oz white chocolate baking bars, coarsely chopped (about 1-1/2 cups)
1-1/2 cups whipping (heavy) cream
4 oz cream cheese (from 8-oz package), softened
1 can (21 oz) cherry pie filling
1/4 teaspoon almond extract
2 tablespoons amaretto liqueur

1 SERVING: Calories 660; Total Fat 48g (Saturated Fat 29g, Trans Fat 1.5g); Cholesterol 190mg; Sodium 200mg; Total Carbohydrate 49g (Dietary Fiber 3g); Protein 8g. EXCHANGES: 3 Other Carbohydrate, 1 High-Fat Meat, 8 Fat. CARBOHYDRATE CHOICES: 3.

decadent chocolate tart

PREP TIME: 40 minutes • START TO FINISH: 2 hours 50 minutes • MAKES: 12 servings

CRUST
1/3 cup butter or margarine, softened
1/4 cup powdered sugar
1/2 cup Gold Medal® all-purpose flour
2 tablespoons unsweetened baking cocoa

FILLING
1/4 cup butter or margarine
4 oz semisweet baking chocolate
1/4 cup granulated sugar
2 eggs
1/4 cup sour cream
2 tablespoons Gold Medal® all-purpose flour

TOPPING
2 oz semisweet baking chocolate
1 tablespoon butter or margarine
1 tablespoon honey
2 kiwifruit, cut up
1 can (11 oz) mandarin orange segments, drained

(1) Heat oven to 350°F. Grease 9-inch tart pan with removable bottom with shortening or cooking spray. In medium bowl, beat 1/3 cup butter and the powdered sugar with electric mixer on medium speed until blended. Beat in 1/2 cup flour and the cocoa until coarse crumbs form. With floured fingers, press in bottom of tart pan.

(2) Bake 5 to 7 minutes or until set. Meanwhile, in 1-quart saucepan, heat 1/4 cup butter and 4 oz chocolate over low heat 2 to 3 minutes, stirring constantly, until melted and smooth. Set aside to cool.

(3) In large bowl, beat granulated sugar and eggs with electric mixer on high speed 3 to 4 minutes, scraping bowl frequently, or until foamy and light in color. Add sour cream, 2 tablespoons flour and the chocolate mixture; continue beating 1 to 2 minutes, scraping bowl frequently, until well blended. Spread filling over crust.

(4) Bake 20 to 25 minutes or until firm to the touch. Cool 15 minutes. Remove side of pan. Cool completely, about 30 minutes.

(5) In 1-quart saucepan, heat 2 ounces chocolate, 1 tablespoon butter and the honey over low heat 2 to 3 minutes, stirring constantly, until melted and smooth. Spread chocolate mixture over tart. Lightly press fruit around outer edge of tart. Refrigerate until firm, about 1 hour. Let stand at room temperature about 20 minutes before serving.

High Altitude (3500-6500 ft): No change.

1 SERVING: Calories 260; Total Fat 16g (Saturated Fat 10g, Trans Fat 0g); Cholesterol 65mg; Sodium 85mg; Total Carbohydrate 26g (Dietary Fiber 2g); Protein 3g. EXCHANGES: 1-1/2 Other Carbohydrate, 1/2 High-Fat Meat, 2-1/2 Fat. CARBOHYDRATE CHOICES: 2.

eggnog pots de crème

PREP TIME: 15 minutes • START TO FINISH: 8 hours 15 minutes • MAKES: 4 servings

1-1/2 cups dairy eggnog
1/2 cup half-and-half
3 egg yolks
2 teaspoons cornstarch
1/2 teaspoon rum extract
Ground nutmeg

① In 2-quart saucepan, heat eggnog and half-and-half over medium-low heat, stirring occasionally, until hot.

② In medium bowl, beat egg yolks, cornstarch and rum extract with wire whisk. Stir a small amount of the hot eggnog mixture into egg mixture, then gradually stir egg mixture back into eggnog mixture in saucepan. Continue cooking over medium-low heat, stirring constantly, until mixture just begins to boil and thicken. Immediately remove from heat.

③ Pour into 4 (4.5-ounce) serving dishes. Sprinkle with nutmeg. Refrigerate at least 8 hours until well chilled and set.

High Altitude (3500-6500 ft): No change.

1 SERVING: Calories 220; Total Fat 14g (Saturated Fat 8g, Trans Fat 0g); Cholesterol 220mg; Sodium 70mg; Total Carbohydrate 16g (Dietary Fiber 0g); Protein 7g. EXCHANGES: 1 Other Carbohydrate, 1 Medium-Fat Meat, 2 Fat. CARBOHYDRATE CHOICES: 1.

tips&ideas

You can make this dessert up to 24 hours ahead of time. Just cover each dish tightly with plastic wrap and refrigerate.

white chocolate-raspberry cheesecake

PREP TIME: 35 minutes • **START TO FINISH:** 5 hours 45 minutes • **MAKES:** 16 servings

CRUST
1-1/2 cups crushed thin chocolate wafer cookies
    (about 24 cookies)
  1/4 cup butter or margarine, melted

FILLING
    1 bag (12 oz) white vanilla baking chips
    3 packages (8 oz each) cream cheese, softened
  1/2 cup sugar
  1/2 cup whipping (heavy) cream
    3 eggs

GLAZE AND GARNISH
    1 pint (2 cups) fresh raspberries
    3 tablespoons raspberry jelly

① Heat oven to 325°F. Lightly grease 9-inch springform pan with shortening or cooking spray. In medium bowl, mix cookie crumbs and melted butter. Press evenly in bottom and 1 inch up side of pan.

② In small microwavable bowl, microwave vanilla baking chips on High 1 minute or until melted; stir until smooth. In large bowl, beat cream cheese with electric mixer on medium speed about 1 minute or until smooth. Beat in sugar until well blended. Beat in melted baking chips until well blended. Beat in whipping cream and eggs until well blended and smooth. Pour over crust in pan.

③ Bake 1 hour to 1 hour 10 minutes or until edge is set but center of cheesecake still jiggles slightly when moved.

④ Turn oven off; open oven door at least 4 inches. Let cheesecake remain in oven 30 minutes. Remove cheesecake from oven; cool on cooling rack at room temperature 30 minutes.

⑤ Without releasing side of pan, carefully run knife around edge of pan to loosen cheesecake. Refrigerate uncovered about 3 hours or until chilled.

⑥ Arrange raspberries on top of chilled cheesecake. In small microwavable bowl, microwave jelly uncovered on High 20 to 30 seconds or until melted; stir until smooth. Brush or spoon over raspberries. Store cheesecake covered in refrigerator.

High Altitude (3500-6500 ft): Place rectangular pan containing hot water on bottom oven rack; place cheesecake on rack above pan of water.

1 SERVING: Calories 410; Total Fat 28g (Saturated Fat 18g, Trans Fat 1g); Cholesterol 105mg; Sodium 270mg; Total Carbohydrate 33g (Dietary Fiber 1g); Protein 7g. EXCHANGES: 1/2 Starch, 1-1/2 Other Carbohydrate, 1 High-Fat Meat, 4 Fat. CARBOHYDRATE CHOICES: 2.

apple, pear and cranberry pie

PREP TIME: 30 minutes • START TO FINISH: 1 hour 40 minutes • MAKES: 8 servings

CRUST

1 box Pillsbury® refrigerated pie crusts, softened as directed on box

FILLING

3/4 cup granulated sugar
2 tablespoons cornstarch
1 teaspoon ground cinnamon
1/2 teaspoon ground nutmeg
3 cups thinly sliced, peeled tart apples
3 cups thinly sliced, peeled ripe pears
1/2 cup sweetened dried cranberries

TOPPING

1/2 cup Gold Medal® all-purpose flour
1/4 cup packed brown sugar
1/4 cup cold butter
1/2 cup coarsely chopped walnuts

① Heat oven to 400°F. Place pie crust in 9-inch glass pie plate as directed on box for One-Crust Filled Pie.

② In large bowl, mix granulated sugar, cornstarch, cinnamon and nutmeg. Gently stir in apples, pears and dried cranberries. Pour filling into crust-lined pie plate.

③ In small bowl, mix topping ingredients until crumbly; sprinkle over filling.

④ Line 15x10-inch pan with foil; place on oven rack below the rack where pie will be baked to catch any drips. Loosely cover pie with sheet of foil; bake 1 hour. Remove foil; bake 10 minutes longer or until apples are tender and topping is golden brown. Cool completely, about 1 hour, before serving.

High Altitude (3500-6500 ft): No change.

1 SERVING: Calories 440; Total Fat 18g (Saturated Fat 7g, Trans Fat 0g); Cholesterol 20mg; Sodium 150mg; Total Carbohydrate 69g (Dietary Fiber 4g); Protein 2g. EXCHANGES: 1 Starch, 1/2 Fruit, 3 Other Carbohydrate, 3-1/2 Fat. CARBOHYDRATE CHOICES: 4-1/2.

tips&ideas

Purchase ripe Anjou or Bosc pears for great results. At the market, choose fruit that is fragrant and slightly soft to the touch.

chocolate silk pecan pie

PREP TIME: 25 minutes • **START TO FINISH:** 3 hours 40 minutes • **MAKES:** 10 servings

1 Pillsbury® refrigerated pie crust, softened as directed on box
1/3 cup granulated sugar
1/2 cup dark corn syrup
3 tablespoons butter or margarine, melted
1/8 teaspoon salt, if desired
2 eggs
1/2 cup chopped pecans
1 cup hot milk
1/4 teaspoon vanilla
1-1/3 cups semisweet chocolate chips
1 cup whipping (heavy) cream
2 tablespoons powdered sugar
1/4 teaspoon vanilla
Chocolate curls, if desired

tips&ideas

For quick chocolate curls, pull a vegetable peeler along a chunky bar of milk chocolate. The milk variety of chocolate is softer than semisweet or bittersweet. Lift the curls onto the pie with a toothpick.

① Prepare pie crust as directed on package for one-crust filled pie using 9-inch pie plate. Heat oven to 350°F. Beat granulated sugar, corn syrup, butter, salt and eggs in small bowl with electric mixer on medium speed 1 minute. Stir in pecans. Pour into pie crust in pie plate. Bake 35 to 45 minutes or until center of pie is puffed and golden brown. Cool 1 hour.

② While filled crust is cooling, place hot milk, 1/4 teaspoon vanilla and the chocolate chips in blender or food processor; cover and blend on medium speed about 1 minute or until smooth. Refrigerate about 1 hour 30 minutes or until mixture is slightly thickened but not set. Gently stir; pour over cooled filling in pie crust. Refrigerate about 1 hour or until firm.

③ Beat whipping cream, powdered sugar and 1/4 teaspoon vanilla in chilled small bowl on high speed until stiff peaks form. Spoon or pipe over filling. Garnish with chocolate curls. Store in refrigerator.

High Altitude (3500-6500 ft): No change.

1 SERVING: Calories 445; Total Fat 28g (Saturated Fat 13g, Trans Fat nc); Cholesterol 80mg; Sodium 160mg; Total Carbohydrate 44g (Dietary Fiber 2g); Protein 5g.
EXCHANGES: 2 Starch, 1 Other Carbohydrate, 5 Fat.
CARBOHYDRATE CHOICES: 3.

white chocolate-berry bread pudding

PREP TIME: 30 minutes • START TO FINISH: 10 hours 10 minutes • MAKES: 12 servings

PUDDING
4-1/2 cups Original Bisquick® mix
1-1/3 cups milk
3/4 cup grated white chocolate baking bars
2/3 cup sugar
3-1/2 cups milk
1-1/2 cups whipping (heavy) cream
2 tablespoons butter or margarine, melted
1 tablespoon vanilla
4 eggs
1 cup frozen unsweetened raspberries (do not thaw)
1 cup frozen unsweetened blueberries (do not thaw)

BERRY SAUCE AND GARNISH
1/3 cup sugar
2 tablespoons Original Bisquick® mix
1 cup frozen unsweetened raspberries (do not thaw)
1 cup frozen unsweetened blueberries (do not thaw)
1/2 cup water
Fresh berries, if desired

① Heat oven to 450°F. Butter bottom and sides of 13x9-inch (3-quart) glass baking dish. In large bowl, stir 4-1/2 cups Bisquick mix and 1-1/3 cups milk until soft dough forms. On ungreased large cookie sheet, drop dough by heaping tablespoonfuls.

② Bake 8 to 10 minutes or until golden. Cool on cooling rack, about 30 minutes.

③ Break up biscuits into random-sized pieces; spread in baking dish. Sprinkle with grated baking bars. In large bowl, beat 2/3 cup sugar, the milk, whipping cream, butter, vanilla and eggs with electric mixer on low speed until blended. Pour over biscuits in baking dish. Cover; refrigerate at least 8 hours but no longer than 24 hours.

④ Heat oven to 350°F. Stir 1 cup frozen raspberries and 1 cup frozen blueberries into biscuit mixture. Bake uncovered about 1 hour or until top is golden brown and toothpick inserted in center comes out clean.

⑤ In 1-quart saucepan, place 1/3 cup sugar and 2 tablespoons Bisquick mix. Stir in 1 cup frozen raspberries, 1 cup frozen blueberries and the water. Cook over medium heat, stirring constantly, until mixture thickens and boils. Boil and stir 1 minute; remove from heat. Serve pudding warm topped with sauce. Garnish with fresh berries. Store in refrigerator.

High Altitude (3500-6500 ft): Bake bread pudding about 1 hour 10 minutes.

1 SERVING: Calories 530; Total Fat 24g (Saturated Fat 12g, Trans Fat 2g); Cholesterol 120mg; Sodium 660mg; Total Carbohydrate 67g (Dietary Fiber 5g); Protein 11g. EXCHANGES: 3 Starch, 1-1/2 Other Carbohydrate, 4-1/2 Fat. CARBOHYDRATE CHOICES: 4-1/2.

hot buttered rum cheesecake with brown sugar-rum sauce

PREP TIME: 45 minutes • **START TO FINISH:** 15 hours 20 minutes • **MAKES:** 16 servings

CRUST
1-1/4 cups graham cracker crumbs
1/4 cup butter or margarine, melted

FILLING
5 packages (8 oz each) cream cheese, softened
1-1/4 cups granulated sugar
1/3 cup whipping (heavy) cream
2 tablespoons rum
1/4 teaspoon ground cinnamon
1/8 teaspoon ground cloves
1/8 teaspoon ground nutmeg
3 eggs

SAUCE
1/2 cup packed brown sugar
1/4 cup butter or margarine
1/3 cup whipping (heavy) cream
1/4 cup rum
1/4 cup golden raisins, if desired

① Heat oven to 350°F. In small bowl, mix crust ingredients. Press firmly in bottom of ungreased 9-inch springform pan. Bake 10 minutes. Cool completely. Reduce oven temperature to 325°F.

② While crust is cooling, in large bowl, beat all filling ingredients except eggs with electric mixer on medium speed about 1 minute or until smooth. On low speed, beat in eggs until well blended. Pour over crust; smooth top.

③ Bake 1 hour 15 minutes to 1 hour 25 minutes or until edge is set and center is still soft. Turn off oven; leave oven door open about 4 inches. Leave cheesecake in oven 30 minutes. Remove from oven; cool in pan on cooling rack away from drafts for 30 minutes.

④ Without releasing or removing side of pan, run metal spatula carefully along side of cheesecake to loosen. Refrigerate uncovered about 3 hours or until chilled. Cover; continue refrigerating at least 9 hours but no longer than 48 hours.

⑤ In 1-1/2 quart saucepan, mix sauce ingredients. Heat to boiling over medium heat, stirring constantly. Boil 3 to 4 minutes, stirring constantly, until slightly thickened.

⑥ To serve, run metal spatula along side of cheesecake to loosen again; remove side of pan. Serve with warm sauce. Store cheesecake and sauce covered in refrigerator.

High Altitude (3500-6500 ft): Before heating oven, place small baking pan filled with 1 to 2 cups water on oven rack below cheesecake to help prevent cheesecake from cracking.

1 SERVING: Calories 470; Total Fat 35g (Saturated Fat 22g, Trans Fat 1.5g); Cholesterol 145mg; Sodium 300mg; Total Carbohydrate 30g (Dietary Fiber 0g); Protein 7g. EXCHANGES: 2 Other Carbohydrate, 1 High-Fat Meat, 5-1/2 Fat. CARBOHYDRATE CHOICES: 2.

raspberry bread pudding

PREP TIME: 25 minutes • START TO FINISH: 55 minutes • MAKES: 8 servings (1/2 cup pudding and 3 tablespoons sauce each)

BREAD PUDDING

6 cups cubed (1 inch) day-old French bread

1 cup fresh raspberries

2 tablespoons miniature semisweet chocolate chips

2 cups fat-free (skim) milk

1/2 cup fat-free egg product

1/4 cup packed brown sugar

1 teaspoon vanilla

SAUCE

1/2 cup granulated sugar

2 tablespoons cornstarch

3/4 cup water

1 bag (12 oz) frozen unsweetened raspberries, thawed, undrained

① Heat oven to 350°F. Spray bottom and sides of 8-inch square (2-quart) glass baking dish with cooking spray. In large bowl, place bread, 1 cup raspberries and chocolate chips.

② In medium bowl, mix milk, egg product, brown sugar and vanilla with wire whisk or fork until blended. Pour egg mixture over bread mixture; stir gently until bread is coated. Spread in baking dish.

③ Bake 40 to 50 minutes or until golden brown and set.

④ Meanwhile, in 2-quart saucepan, mix granulated sugar and cornstarch. Stir in water and thawed raspberries. Heat to boiling over medium heat, stirring constantly and pressing raspberries to release juice. Boil about 1 minute or until thick. Place small strainer over small bowl. Pour mixture through strainer to remove seeds; discard seeds. Serve sauce with warm bread pudding.

High Altitude (3500-6500 ft): Bake 45 to 55 minutes. In Step 4, boil 2 to 3 minutes.

1 SERVING: Calories 230; Total Fat 2g (Saturated Fat 1g, Trans Fat 0g); Cholesterol 0mg; Sodium 210mg; Total Carbohydrate 46g (Dietary Fiber 5g); Protein 7g. EXCHANGES: 1-1/2 Starch, 1-1/2 Other Carbohydrate, 1/2 Fat. CARBOHYDRATE CHOICES: 3.

bananas foster with ice cream

PREP TIME: 10 minutes • START TO FINISH: 10 minutes • MAKES: 4 servings (1/2 cup ice cream and 1/2 cup banana mixture each)

1/2 cup fat-free caramel topping

2 teaspoons dark rum or 1 teaspoon rum extract

2 bananas, cut into chunks

2 cups vanilla low-fat ice cream

① In small microwavable bowl, mix caramel topping and rum. Microwave uncovered on High 30 seconds or until very warm. Stir in bananas.

② Scoop ice cream into dessert dishes; top with banana mixture.

High Altitude (3500-6500 ft): No change.

1 SERVING: Calories 290; Total Fat 3g (Saturated Fat 2g, Trans Fat 0g); Cholesterol 20mg; Sodium 200mg; Total Carbohydrate 60g (Dietary Fiber 2g); Protein 5g. EXCHANGES: 1 Fruit, 2-1/2 Other Carbohydrate, 1/2 Low-Fat Milk, 1/2 Fat. CARBOHYDRATE CHOICES: 4.

tips&ideas

For the best texture and flavor, use medium-ripe bananas.

tiramisu cheesecake dessert

PREP TIME: 20 minutes • **START TO FINISH:** 2 hours 25 minutes • **MAKES:** 24 servings

2 cups crushed vanilla wafer cookies
  (about 60 cookies)
1/3 cup butter or margarine, melted
2 tablespoons whipping (heavy) cream
2 tablespoons instant espresso coffee granules
3 packages (8 oz each) cream cheese, softened
3/4 cup sugar
3 eggs
1 oz bittersweet baking chocolate, grated
Chocolate-covered espresso beans, if desired

① Heat oven to 350°F. Line 13x9-inch pan with foil; spray with cooking spray. In small bowl, mix crushed cookies and melted butter with fork. Carefully press mixture in bottom of pan. Refrigerate while continuing with recipe.

② In small bowl, mix whipping cream and coffee granules with fork until coffee is dissolved; set aside.

③ In large bowl, beat cream cheese with electric mixer on medium speed 2 to 3 minutes, scraping bowl occasionally, until smooth and creamy. On low speed, beat in sugar, eggs and coffee mixture, about 30 seconds. Beat on medium speed about 2 minutes longer or until ingredients are well blended. Using rubber spatula, spread cream cheese filling over crust. Bake 25 to 35 minutes or until center is set.

④ Cool 30 minutes. Sprinkle with grated chocolate, and top with espresso beans if desired. Refrigerate about 1 hour or until completely chilled. For servings, cut into 6 rows by 4 rows, using sharp knife dipped in water.

High Altitude (3500-6500 ft): No change.

1 SERVING: Calories 200; Total Fat 15g (Saturated Fat 9g, Trans Fat 0.5g); Cholesterol 65mg; Sodium 140mg; Total Carbohydrate 12g (Dietary Fiber 0g); Protein 4g. EXCHANGES: 1/2 Starch, 1/2 Other Carbohydrate, 1/2 High-Fat Meat, 2 Fat. CARBOHYDRATE CHOICES: 1.

tips&ideas

Dress up these rich-tasting dessert bars by serving them in colorful paper baking cups.

general recipe index

APPETIZERS & SNACKS

COLD APPETIZERS
Amaretto Cheese-Filled Apricots, 39
Beef and Swiss Roll-Ups, 32
Cheese and Fruit Kabobs with Cranberry Dip, 12
Dilled Salmon, 15
Holiday Shrimp Wreath with Cocktail Dip, 9
Mini Crab Points, 29
Salmon-Pimiento Appetizers, 47
Sesame Toast-Vegetable Bites, 37
Shrimp Cocktail Platter, 21
Shrimp with Bourbon Cocktail Sauce, 13
Smoked Salmon with Dill Spread, 20
Stuffed Eggs with Smoked Salmon and Herb Cheese, 11

DIPS
Bacon-Tomato Dip, 35
Bloody Mary Dip, 33
Raspberry-Mint-Marshmallow Creme Dip, 36
Seven-Layer Bean Dip, 38
Zesty Beef and Bean Dip, 46
Zippy Dill Vegetable Dip, 43

HOT APPETIZERS
Apricot Baked Brie, 34
Artichoke Triangles, 45
Brie with Cranberry Chutney, 41
Crab Bites, 42
Crab Fondue, 40
Creamy Buffalo-Style Cocktail Wieners, 48
Creamy Roasted Garlic and Onion Meatballs, 23
Hot Crab Crostini, 19
Meatballs with Roasted Red Pepper Sauce, 26
Pesto-Cheese Cups, 22
Potato Bites, 31
Smoky Cranberry Chicken Wings, 49
Southwest Chicken Nachos, 27
Warm Cheddar and Olive Dip, 10
Warm Chicken Spread, 14

SNACKS
Chili and Garlic Snack Mix, 215
Chocolate-Covered Caramel Corn, 218
Crunchy Cranberry-Almond Snack, 224
Curried Snack Mix, 219
Easy Butterscotch-Almond Pralines, 221
Holiday Spiced Snack Mix, 16
Reindeer Feed, 216
Sugar 'n Spice Snack, 227
White Candy Fantasy Clusters, 214

SPREADS
Cranberry-Topped Three-Cheese Spread, 16
Curried Cheese Ball with Fruit, 30
Fruit-Cheese Log, 8
Garlic-Herb Cheese Spread, 44
Layered Shrimp Spread, 28

Nutty Cheese Spread with Fruit Chutney, 18
Pepper Jack Cheese Ball, 25
Sun-Dried Tomato Spread, 224

APPLES
Apple-Gorgonzola Salad with Red Wine Vinaigrette, 103
Apple, Pear and Cranberry Pie, 306
Apple Streusel Cheesecake Bars, 243
Cranberry-Apple-Nut Bread, 226
Creamy Fruit Salad, 182
Curried Cheese Ball with Fruit, 30
Danish Apple-Almond Cake, 283
French Toast with Gingered Applesauce, 205
Mixed Greens with Cranberry Vinaigrette, 74
Sausage 'n Apple Cheddar Biscuit Bake, 209
Winter Fruit Waldorf Salad, 80

APRICOTS
Amaretto Cheese-Filled Apricots, 39
Apricot Baked Brie, 34
Apricot-Bourbon Glazed Ham, 138
Apricot-Glazed Carrots, 106
Cranberry-Apricot Bars, 240
Pork Loin with Apricot-Rosemary Glaze, 113

ARTICHOKES
Artichoke Triangles, 45
Cheesy Chicken and Artichoke Pizza, 181

ASPARAGUS
Quinoa Pilaf with Salmon and Asparagus, 140
Roasted Parmesan Asparagus, 86

BACON
Bacon-Cheddar Muffins, 63
Bacon-Tomato Dip, 35
Country French Beef Stew, 129
Egg-Topped Biscuits Florentine, 193
Mashed Sweet Potatoes with Bacon, 75
Scrambled Egg Biscuit Cups, 207
Shrimp Alfredo Primavera, 133

BANANAS
Banana-Chocolate Bread, 222
Banana Cream Waffles, 203
Bananas Foster with Ice Cream, 310
Upside-Down Banana-Walnut French Toast, 196

BARS
Almond Toffee Bars, 275
Apple Streusel Cheesecake Bars, 243
Baklava Bars, 253
Caramel-Cashew Bars, 246
Chocolate Chip-Cherry Bars, 276
Chocolate-Covered Cherry Diamonds, 246

Chocolate-Topped Peanut-Toffee Bars, 254
Cranberry-Apricot Bars, 240
Cranberry Bars, 272
Elegant Almond Bars, 232
Irish Cream-Coffee Bars, 239
Lemon Linzer Bars, 230
Noir Bars, 273
Raspberry Crumb Bars, 267
Salty Sweet Peanutty Treat, 212
Turtle Bars, 262

BEANS

APPETIZERS AND SNACKS
Seven-Layer Bean Dip, 38
Zesty Beef and Bean Dip, 46

MAIN DISH
French Pork and Bean Casserole, 118

SIDE DISHES
Balsamic Green Beans and Fennel, 96
Green Beans with Garlic Butter and Walnuts, 82
Green Beans with Glazed Shallots in Lemon-Dill Butter, 99
Green Beans with Lemon-Herb Butter, 102
Green Beans with Pickled Onions, 84

SOUP
Smoked Sausage and Bean Soup, 185

BEEF *(also see Ground Beef)*

APPETIZER
Beef and Swiss Roll-Ups, 32

MAIN DISHES
Bavarian-Style Beef Roast and Sauerkraut, 136
Beef Tenderloin with Red Wine Sauce, 124
Country French Beef Stew, 129
Garlic and Mushroom Beef Roast, 147
Ginger Beef Roast, 148
Herbed Beef Stroganoff, 137
Italian Beef Short Ribs, 138
Latin-Style Flank Steak with Spicy Parsley Pesto, 178
Peppered Beef Tenderloin with Mushroom Sauce, 111

SANDWICH
Philly Cheese Steak Sandwiches, 171

BEVERAGES
Cosmo Slush, 24
Frosty Mocha, 48
Sangria, 36
Spiced Dessert Coffee, 44

BISCOTTI *(see Cookies)*

BISCUITS & SCONES
Egg-Topped Biscuits Florentine, 193
Orange Scone Wedges with Cream Cheese Filling, 61

alphabetical recipe index